CARRYING ALL BEFORE HER

PERFORMING CELEBRITY

Performing Celebrity publishes single-authored monographs and essay collections that explore the dynamics of fame, infamy, and technologies of image-making from the early modern period to the present day. This series of books seeks to add to exciting recent developments in the emerging field of celebrity studies by publishing outstanding works that explore mechanisms of self-fashioning, stardom, and notoriety operating across genres and media in a broad range of historical and national contexts. It focuses on interdisciplinary projects that employ current research and a wide variety of theoretical approaches to performance and celebrity in relation to literature, history, art history, media, fashion, theater, gender(s), sexuality, race, ethnicity, disability, material culture, etc.

Series Titles

Celebrity across the Channel, 1750–1850, edited by Anaïs Pédron and Clare Siviter

CARRYING ALL BEFORE HER

CELEBRITY PREGNANCY AND THE LONDON STAGE, 1689–1800

Chelsea Phillips

UNIVERSITY OF DELAWARE | UNIVERSITY OF DELAWARE PRESS

Newark

Library of Congress Cataloging-in-Publication Data

Names: Phillips, Chelsea, author.
Title: Carrying all before her : celebrity pregnancy and the London stage, 1689-1800 / by Chelsea Phillips.
Description: Newark : University of Delaware Press, 2022. | Series: Performing celebrity | Includes bibliographical references and index.
Identifiers: LCCN 2021019121 | ISBN 9781644532485 (paperback) | ISBN 9781644532492 (cloth) | ISBN 9781644532508 (epub) | ISBN 9781644532515 (pdf)
Subjects: LCSH: Pregnant women in the theater—England—History—18th century. | Theater—England—London—History—18th century. | Actresses—England—London—History—18th century. | Theater and society—England—London—History—18th century. | London (England)—Social life and customs—18th century.
Classification: LCC PN2592.13.P74 P45 2022 | DDC 792.09421/09033—dc23
LC record available at https://lccn.loc.gov/2021019121

A British Cataloging-in-Publication record for this book is available from the British Library.

∞ The paper used in this publication meets the requirements of the American National Standard for Information Sciences—Permanence of Paper for Printed Library Materials, ANSI Z39.48-1992.

udpress.udel.edu

Distributed worldwide by Rutgers University Press

Manufactured in the United States of America

To Andy

CONTENTS

FIGURES

ACKNOWLEDGMENTS

This project has had a long gestation and therefore benefited from the generosity of many midwives. My thanks to my dissertation committee: Lesley Ferris, who guided the process with confidence in its potential and has remained a steadfast supporter; to Jennifer Schlueter for her wit and incisive feedback; to Stratos Constantinidis for generous reading; and to David Brewer for his enthusiasm, expertise, and encouragement. There from the early days as well were Alan Stewart, Carole Levin, and the 2012–13 dissertation seminar at the Folger Shakespeare Library, who provided useful feedback and good fellowship as the project took shape. I also benefitted from the Renaissance Reading Group at Ohio State University—Richard Dutton, Jennifer Higginbotham, and Chris Highley in particular—who kindly stretched the bounds of their time period to take in and read early drafts of material about the eighteenth century. To the many mentors-turned-friends in eighteenth-century and theatre studies I relied on along the way, including Emily Friedman, Elaine McGirr, and Fiona Ritchie, my thanks for providing advice, encouragement, and honest perspective. In this vein, I offer my redoubled thanks to David Brewer, who has continued to be an invaluable source of wisdom, balance, and assurance in the intervening years as I moved this manuscript toward its final form.

In the course of this work, I received generous funding from the Folger Shakespeare Library and the American Society for

Eighteenth-Century Studies (FI-ASECS Fellowship); the Houghton Library at Harvard University (Maryette Charlton Fellowship in the Performing Arts); Yale University's Lewis Walpole Library (2016 Travel Grant); The Ohio State University (Presidential Fellowship, Graduate Student Research Award, and Coca-Cola Critical Difference for Women grant); and Villanova University (University Summer Grant Program, pre-tenure sabbatical), without which necessary travel and archival research would not have been possible. My gratitude to all those who served on committees, as readers, and as administrators in these processes, including Adele Lindenmeyr (Dean of the College of Liberal Arts and Sciences, Villanova University) and Barry Selinsky (Associate Dean for Research, Villanova University).

There was no roadmap for this work when I began. That one was built at all is thanks in large part to the many archivists and administrators whose knowledge of their collections was vital in enabling my research. My thanks to the whole staff at the Folger Shakespeare Library and Folger Institute, who have been a constant over nearly ten years of work, including Kathleen Lynch, Owen Williams, and Amanda Herbert. In particular, my thanks to Abbie Weinberg for her perpetual enthusiasm and near-magical ability to find things, and to the reading room staff for their care, support, and supply of blankets; to Matthew Wittmann, Dale Stinchcomb, and Anne-Marie Eze at the Harvard Theatre Collection; Nicole Bouché, Cynthia Roman, and the team at the Lewis Walpole Library; Gayle Richardson and Molly Gipson (Huntington Library, California); Marcus Risdell (Garrick Club Library, London); Anne Buchanan (Bath Central Library); Heather Romaine (Kathleen Barker Collection, University of Bristol); the staff of the British Library, Wellcome Library, and National Archives (London); Maggie Reilly (Hunterian Museum, Glasgow); the reading room staff at the National Library of Scotland (Edinburgh); and Julie Crocker and Thomas Gray (Royal Archives, Windsor, UK).

To the last, I add my thanks to Her Majesty Queen Elizabeth II for permission to use material from the Royal Archives and from the Royal Collection Trust in this document. I also extend my thanks to the editors at Rowman and Littlefield Publishing Group and *Women's History* for permission to republish material in chapters 3 and 4, and to the archives and repositories who gave permission for the images in this book.

Copious thanks are due to my editors. Julia Oestreich has deftly and generously guided this project to fruition with insightful perspective and attention. Laura Engel has championed the book from its early days with boundless energy and great wisdom. I offer my thanks as well to the anonymous readers who reviewed the manuscript with sagacity and provided detailed feedback that strengthened it. My thanks as well to Sherry Gerstein, Brice Hammack, Alissa Zarro, and the staffs at Delaware University Press, Rutgers University Press, and Westchester Publishing for their work shepherding the book through production. Thank you to Diane Ersepke for her copyediting work, and to Scott Sheldon for indexing.

Writing can be a lonely activity, but I was bolstered by an active and generous community of fellow scholars. My gratitude is due to my prolific writing group. Jane Wessel, Leah Benedict, and Mattie Burkert brought tireless close reading, evocative questions, and consistency throughout these crucial last two years. Tita Chico and Chloe Wigston Smith offered timely advice about making space to finish the book. Both Tita and Carrie Shanafelt took it upon themselves to create online community spaces that have been a source of much-needed support and cross-disciplinary exchange. I have also found inspiration in the ASECS Women's Caucus, who have made and continue to make a vibrant and stalwart community that has transformed the field, and in the work of the Theatre and Performance Studies Caucus.

More locally, my thanks to my students, whose enthusiasm and capacity for wonder energize and inspire me. I also owe much appreciation to my exceptionally ambitious and supportive staff and faculty colleagues at Villanova, who have never met an idea or project they won't "yes, and." I have at various points benefitted from graduate student research hours: my thanks to Zach Apony, Cristy Chory, Zandra Espinoza, Jaried Kimberley, Ethan Mitchell, and Shawneen Rowe for research and writing support. Villanova is enriched by several faculty writing programs which have benefitted me greatly: thank you to Emily Carson, Amanda Grannas, and Mary Beth Simmons for these. To Emily Carson I owe a particular debt for her assistance in preparing important grant and fellowship applications.

My gratitude to many, many friends, among them Madelynn von Baeyer and Shauna MacDonald for their warmth and timely advice.

And to James Ijames, Michael Hollinger, Edward Sobel, and Peter Hilliard, whose support and cheerful confidence are much appreciated. To Bess Rowen and Sarah Wingo for ever-joyful encouragement, smart reading, and many laughs. And my especial and eternal gratitude to Valerie Joyce for her friendship, her kindness, and her wisdom in all things.

To my exceptionally patient, generous, and loving husband, Andrew Blasenak, who has been an unflagging advocate for me, and champion of my work, for over a decade. To my darling parents, Jack and Charlotte, and to my grandparents, Betty and Sandy, who I wish were here to see this project completed. To my family, near and far.

And last but far from least to the precious, precocious, and perspicacious Colleen Kennedy, who read many, many drafts and improved them all. Your friendship and intelligence have been a boon since the moment we met: I can no other answer make than thanks, and thanks, and ever thanks.

INTRODUCTION

Women's bodies are the stuff of history.
—Mary Fissell, *Vernacular Bodies: The Politics of Reproduction in Early Modern England*

Happy was the actress who had no history.
—John Harold Wilson, *All the King's Ladies: Actresses of the Restoration*

In May 2016, six-time Tony Award winner Audra McDonald, then starring in George C. Wolfe's original musical *Shuffle Along: Or the Making of the Musical Sensation of 1921 and All That Followed* on Broadway tweeted, "Who knew that tap dancing during perimenopause could lead 2 pregnancy?"[1] McDonald's announcement came in conjunction with a statement from producers about plans for accommodating her maternity leave. McDonald would remain in the tap-heavy role of Lottie Gee (with her doctor's blessing) until July 24, the end of her second trimester. Once she stepped down, Grammy Award–winning artist Rhiannon Giddens would take McDonald's role, and celebrity choreographer Savion Glover would join the cast. With its award-winning chorus and the star power and dynamism of the rest of the veteran ensemble (including now-megastar Billy Porter), these accommodations aimed to keep the show—which had received ten Tony nominations and was making about a million dollars a week—afloat until McDonald returned that winter.

Celebrity is a mechanism for imagining, magnifying, and scrutinizing human experience. Consequently, McDonald's tweet drew attention to the experiences of many. Those unfamiliar with the potential for increased fertility during perimenopause, for example, might learn of this phenomenon not from a doctor but from social media, where disbelief from some about McDonald was met with personal confirmation from others. McDonald also demonstrated her capacity for economic labor, working in a physically demanding profession for the first six months of her pregnancy; she thus signaled the capacity for pregnant people to remain viable economic agents despite their condition. The planned maternity leave was a rarity for a new Broadway musical, possibly opening an important conversation for the American professional theater that would have implications for thousands of other performers. Ultimately, however, producer Scott Rudin announced the show would close after McDonald's final performance on July 24, citing a belief that her absence would result in greater losses "than the show can responsibly absorb."[2] The decision left nearly two hundred people out of work with one month's notice.

Producers faced additional criticism when they then demanded payment from their insurance company, Lloyd's of London, of fourteen million dollars under clauses for McDonald's "Death, Accident or Illness" ($2 million) and the producer's "Abandonment" of the production ($12 million). Producers maintained that any unexpected medical event depriving them of McDonald's presence qualified under the first clause, emphasizing McDonald's age (forty-five) as reason to consider the pregnancy an "accident." In labeling her pregnancy an accident, producers emphasized lack of intent on the part of McDonald and her husband but also drew on long-standing associations with female bodies as unruly and excessive. Her body was positioned as having autonomously acted, disrupting and destroying the commercial viability of an artistic project, which played into contentious questions about the relationship between women's reproductive and commercial labor in recent decades. Lloyd's denied that a pregnancy should fall under the accident or illness clause; rather, pregnancy was proof of a healthy, normally functioning body. To the second claim, Lloyd's countered that closing the show was a choice, not an inevitability, and that claiming McDonald's pregnancy made the action unavoidable was an obvious attempt to secure a multimillion-dollar payout. After four years, in October 2020, the parties agreed to drop the case.[3]

This is a book about an earlier history of pregnant celebrity performers in the English-speaking world. For celebrity pregnancy is a phenomenon that predates both Demi Moore on the cover of *Vanity Fair* in 1991 and Lucille Ball in *I Love Lucy* in 1952, commencing with the first generations of female stage celebrities in the eighteenth century. This prior history mirrors features of McDonald's story, including a sharing of intimate details in public that unites celebrity and fans; celebrity pregnancy's impact on box office, repertory, and hiring in a commercial setting; and the way pregnancy is seen to engage with pre-existing beliefs about or associations with a celebrity.[4] Pregnant celebrities are both ordinary and extraordinary, simultaneously "just like us" and the embodiment of often unattainable ideals. This essential nature of celebrity has changed little in the past three hundred years, but both the commercial and the cultural contexts of past and present celebrities' experiences are markedly different. Here, I center six women's stories to better understand how pregnancy, celebrity, and theatrical practice intersected in the eighteenth century as women claimed new ground in the public and professional world, and I shed light on a theatrical culture that regularly accommodated pregnancy and childbearing without presuming a fundamental conflict between reproductive and economic labor.

Dorothy Jordan (1761–1816) was the most beloved comic actress of her age. Before rising to stardom in London, she acted in Dublin, traveled to England, and entered Tate Wilkinson's Yorkshire company in the summer of 1782. There, she performed a wide variety of roles in comedy, tragedy, farce, and opera with an enchanting and seemingly natural performance style. Wilkinson recalled in his memoirs that Jordan's success earned the jealousy of other performers, including the pregnant actress Henrietta Smith, who gave birth on or around October 2 of that year. The normal practice in such cases was for the absence of one actress to be covered by others in the company. Accordingly, the plan was that Jordan would undertake a number of Smith's roles when she withdrew to give birth and recover, just as Rhiannon Giddens would have taken over for Audra McDonald. For Wilkinson, this kind of planning was commonplace as the company included several married couples with children. Smith, however, feared Jordan's popularity might cause Wilkinson to permanently reassign some of her roles to the younger performer. Her concern was valid, for Wilkinson had already given Jordan at least one role belonging to another company member: the travesty part of Signor Arionelli, a castrato, in *The Son-in-Law*.[5] The more popular the parts one played, the more exposure and more opportunity to build celebrity capital with audiences. The more popular a performer was with audiences, the more lucrative the perks they received, like benefit nights (when an actor kept the night's box office minus house charges), became. If Smith lost parts to Jordan, it would affect both her standing in the company and her earning potential just as her family and financial obligations were growing.

Jordan's biographer James Boaden, desiring to cast his heroine as triumphant in the face of pointless and pompous opposition, described the situation as follows: "Mrs. Smith . . . expected, at the end of September, an increase to her family, and the great object of her thoughts was to make the periods before and after her confinement, as short as possible, that her rival might not appear, or, at least, not be seen often in any of the characters that she considered her own. . . . She, therefore, rendered the virgin purity of some of them rather questionable to the eye."[6] Boaden's critique of Smith centers on the blatant contradiction between her pregnant body as the actress and the virginal bodies of her characters. His criticism, recorded decades after the event, has been taken as evidence that audiences objected to seeing pregnant actresses perform, suggesting it was a practice that displayed poor taste and was avoided whenever possible.[7] There is only one problem with Boaden's assessment: Jordan was pregnant too.

Jordan made her last appearance on November 1, just a month after Smith's, and her daughter Fanny was born later that month. Until that point, Jordan had been playing virginal roles in both comedy and tragedy for several months while her condition was obvious.[8] She even played Signor Arionelli in breeches a mere two weeks before she left the stage to give birth. Boaden was fully aware of

Jordan's condition, mentioning it barely a page later in the memoir, yet he says nothing about the impropriety or oddness of the many parts Jordan played as she neared her own confinement. In its full context, Boaden's objection makes little sense when applied broadly because he is not making a general statement about pregnancy and performance; he is attacking a specific performer on the basis of poor taste and vanity in order to champion another. To take Boaden's assessment of Smith as indicative of a general attitude toward pregnant performers is thus problematic. At best, Boaden is implicitly endowing Jordan with the power to overcome her bodily condition in ways that Smith was unable to do; at worst, he is erasing Jordan's body when it becomes inconvenient for his larger purpose. In short, Boaden is selective about the meaning and impact of pregnancy so he can create the story he wishes to tell. In uncritically repeating his comment, scholars since have inadvertently perpetuated ahistorical claims about pregnancy on stage.[9]

Tate Wilkinson—the manager putting pregnant women in virginal roles—also wrote an account of this event in his history of Yorkshire theater, *The Wandering Patentee* (1795). In contrast to Boaden, Wilkinson displays no concerns for verisimilitude as he recounts the tale. Instead, he focuses on Smith's actions as unnecessarily detrimental to her health and expresses his admiration at Jordan's unbounded energy and ability to quickly memorize all the necessary new parts.[10] Both Wilkinson and Boaden rely on memory or imagination to guide their meditations on past events and on the significance these pregnancies had for both audience reception and managerial labor, but only one of them was actually there. Because later historians have privileged Boaden's account over Wilkinson's, however, perhaps feeling it would be more objective because he was writing after Jordan's death, Boaden's comments about Smith have been allowed to stand as a representative response to the pregnant body on stage, and Jordan's pregnancy has been obscured. This book takes up the tension between these two accounts, mapping a broader history of pregnancy in the eighteenth-century theater and expanding, in the process, our understanding of celebrity, repertory, and women's history.

Two forms of women's labor collided in the eighteenth-century British theater: the childbearing and childrearing that affected fertile, sexually active women of all classes, and the theatrical labor of professional actresses. In the course of the century, birth rates rose significantly, particularly within marriage or other long-term partnerships. Aristocratic women doubled their average birth rate from four children to eight, and married middle-class women were not far behind, averaging seven births by the end of the century.[11] Not all actresses attained the economic resources equivalent to those living in the middle and upper classes, but the six women in this study did. Not all actresses had children, but many did, and those in this study had them at rates similar to their nontheatrical counterparts.[12] In the same century, as recent scholarship has shown, women in the professional theater were helping to shape and example new forms of public womanhood, capitalizing on a burgeoning culture of female celebrity, and, in some cases, wielding exceptional economic and artistic power. At no time during the century, moreover, does it appear to have been a policy of London theatrical managers to dismiss salaried pregnant actresses or force them to enter temporary retirement to disguise their condition.[13] This means actresses' pregnancies—so very visible at the time but so easily invisible today—were a common circumstance that performers and managers negotiated and audiences witnessed. Despite this, while Ellen Donkin called the study of pregnancy on stage a potential "gold mine of cultural investigation" in 2007, eight years later Helen E.M. Brooks could still rightly claim that it remained a topic "almost entirely overlooked" in studies of eighteenth-century performers.[14]

Carrying All before Her is the first full-length study to address pregnancy as a specific and significant phenomenon in its own right. My aims are simple: to offer evidence of the consistent presence of celebrity pregnancy on the eighteenth-century stage, and to demonstrate the myriad ways in which these embodied experiences mattered in and beyond the theater. I use the histories of six celebrity performers—Susanna Mountfort Verbruggen (1666–1703), Anne Oldfield (1783–1730), Susannah Cibber (1714–1766), George Anne Bellamy (c.1731–1788), Sarah Siddons (1755–1831), and Dorothy Jordan (1761–1816)—to bring reproductive bodies back into the historical record, radically altering our understandings of eighteenth-century London theater and women's place within it. Throughout the book, I argue that pregnancy affected celebrity identity, impacted audience reception and interpretation of performance, changed company repertory and altered company hierarchy, influenced the development and performance of new work, and had substantial economic consequences both for women and for the companies for which they worked. In short, this study is interested in how pregnancy mattered to theatrical celebrity, and how celebrity pregnancy mattered to theater.

Historical performing bodies are always elusive, glimpsed only imperfectly. Compounding this problem is the ephemerality and, in the eighteenth century, ubiquity of pregnancy. The existence of few reliable forms of birth control and rising birth rates made pregnant bodies far from rare. Audiences might therefore have observed pregnant performers, even discussed them, but felt no need to comment on them in written sources. Celebrity performers, because of the focused attention they inspired, help to make these bodies visible. Even their stories, however, are subject to inflation, omission, and simply bad information, all of which challenge our ability to see pregnancy and its influence clearly. For example, eighteenth-century biographers attributed both George Anne Bellamy and Susannah Cibber's extended absences in 1749–50 to actresses' proverbial unprofessionalism and caprice. Later writers drawing on those histories repeated their assessments, and so the true reasons for the actresses' actions—pregnancy and childbirth—were obscured, despite the fact that in Bellamy's case the tale of her eleven-day labor was available in her memoir.[15]

Scholars of the body and bodily decorum among female performers, meanwhile, are often aware that the pregnant body existed on the professional stage, though analyses are at times still dominated by moments when an audience member or manager grumbled about pregnancy's impact on verisimilitude.[16] Such evidence is frequently cited, especially when it comes from men like Wilkinson, Boaden, or David Garrick, whom we have been trained to look to as our windows into the century's theater. As I will continue to show, however, their commentary on the subject is neither the totality of responses available to us nor an accurate reflection of managerial behavior. This leaves us with a quandary of seemingly clear and authoritative examples of negative responses to actresses' pregnancies set against a dearth of positive or neutral responses. Throughout this book, I bring to light a far wider spectrum of reactions to the pregnant celebrity body and situate them within individualized contexts.

Childbearing and professional work were and are simultaneous rather than siloed activities. One major aim in writing this book is to demonstrate why an awareness of this simultaneity matters. For example, important biographical sources for actresses' lives, such as Philip H. Highfill, Kalman A. Burnim, and Edward A. Langhan's *Biographical Dictionary of Actors* (*BDA*), and the *Oxford Dictionary of National Biography* (*DNB*), often include information on performers' families, though the level of detail offered varies widely. When information on actresses' reproductive lives is present, however, the structure of the entries often bifurcates the professional and personal, with children usually recorded at the end of an entry in the context of wills or other legal documentation. This creates a false division between public and private that requires the reader to collate the personal information with the earlier analysis of professional work, while tacitly suggesting that the two forms of labor are, in fact, entirely separate. Information from wills and legal documents also often fails to grasp the full experience of a woman's reproductive life: miscarriages and stillbirths, for example, might leave no parish records to uncover, even if they leave marks on the woman, her family, and the repertory calendar. This book follows in the footsteps of those who have brought celebrity studies to bear on their examinations of professional theater, breaking down these divisions between the professional and the personal. This honors the full reality of women's multifaceted lives. Bringing their historical experiences to light also allows them to productively speak to our own time where, as the closing of *Shuffle Along* demonstrates, ambivalence exists around accommodating the reproductive lives of performers in the context of a commercial system.

In addition to these historiographical challenges, this work addresses common assumptions about pregnancy and performance that have, perhaps, discouraged more pointed attention to the topic before now. First, as Ellen Donkin has claimed, there is "very little" evidence beyond parish records from which to build a study of pregnancy on stage.[17] Parish records are a vital starting place, but my work shows that there are many other markers a reproductive life leaves on the archives. Writing this book was in part learning to "listen for echoes" within these pregnant pauses.[18] Secondly, I offer significant evidence to counter the belief that those pregnant women who did remain on stage without criticism did so only by concealing their pregnancies. In fact, audiences were regularly aware of women's reproductive lives. Finally, I disrupt the presumption that pregnancy had a predominantly detrimental effect on women's lives and careers, economically or otherwise. When pregnant actresses appeared on stage, audience response was neither uniform nor consistent; it lay at the intersection of public and private, the social and the individual, and stage fiction and offstage celebrity, and it changed with the woman and situation in question.

Before going further, it is important to explain the breadth and limits of the experience signaled by the term "pregnancy" in this book. In principle, my analysis is predicated on a biological experience that is temporally bound and that has changed little in the intervening two to three hundred years, even if understandings and sociocultural experiences of pregnancy have altered radically. Pregnancy points to a specific kind of body, a distinctive shape that is culturally legible across time and that changes the childbearer's orientation to themselves and the world, blurring the lines between self and other, public and private; what Imogen Tyler calls a "transitional form of subjectivity."[19] Pregnancy also indicates a set of potential physical experiences integral to the stories told here, such as fatigue, pain, swelling, nausea, faintness, weight gain, heartburn, constipation, frequent urination, and others. The embodied experience of pregnancy is highly individual and begins long before bodily change becomes obvious to an outside observer. As we will see, however, even the public-facing nature of pregnancy could begin before the body changed visibly, as when papers announced Sarah Siddons's pregnancy six months before she gave birth in 1785.

While pregnancy can often be temporally complex—easily seen predominantly as the outcome of past activity or the predecessor of future birth and parenthood—it is also important as a liminal yet progressive, persistently present state. Our bodies are always working (digesting, breathing, fighting potential infection), but pregnancy makes this a conscious experience. In addition to the symptoms already noted, the gurgles, kicks, hiccups, stretches, and flutters of a growing child provide constant physical reminders of their presence from within the body. Pregnant performers experience these now, as they did then, before and after their bodies become legible to others, while traveling, meeting with managers and playwrights, negotiating contracts, performing, rehearsing, being fitted for costumes, caring for other children and family members, and socializing with patrons. The presentness of pregnancy is important to this study because not every pregnancy ends in birth, and not all births produce living children: these losses do not erase the experience of pregnancy before the loss, nor do they efface the knowledge of that experience and loss in the minds of those around the subject. Further, as instances in Dorothy Jordan's life will show, the very fact that her body had the potential to be pregnant shaped public reception of her as a woman and a theater artist. This is not dissimilar to the way those today seen to be "of childbearing age" have their daily experiences weighed and shaped by their perceived reproductive potential—from questioning about and testing for pregnancy from medical professionals to the reading of the body and social behavior as a clue to their gravid state. The term "pregnancy," therefore, can encode a range of experiences and expectations.

To understand the specific context in which performers and their pregnancies existed necessitates hard limits on the book's scope. The first is chronological. The long eighteenth century was a time period of sweeping changes in the perception of gender, women, and childbirth, and is therefore a productive site of inquiry for a project intrinsically tied to women's sexuality and stage celebrity.[20] The records for the earliest decades of women's participation on the professional London stage, however, are limited. This includes both our knowledge of repertory (which approaches completion only after 1705) and biographical information about actresses. I therefore begin with the earliest actress I can identify who had a recognizable brand of celebrity and most certainly performed into the late stages of at least two pregnancies: Susanna Percival Mountfort Verbruggen (1666–1703). I end with Dorothy Jordan's 1790s pregnancies, the last during which she consistently appeared on the London stage.

The second major restriction is geographical: I focus on London, specifically the patent theaters of Drury Lane and Covent Garden and their antecedent organizations for which we have a large number of surviving records.[21] This restriction leaves out hundreds, perhaps thousands, of women with careers outside the capital's patent theaters, whether in other London houses, or in provincial theatrical centers, such as Dublin, Edinburgh, or Bath, or on touring circuits. The third restriction is my focus on a select group of "celebrity" performers who earned high salaries, became widely recognized and discussed figures, and held identifiable public personas. Such a label inevitably leaves out many other women who faced the struggle of maintaining a career during and after pregnancy without the benefits and burdens that came with celebrity power, or whose celebrity we have yet to acknowledge. There will be occasional glimpses of such women as they orbit around those on whom this book centers, but the sample offered here is selected to demonstrate a range of ways women wielded celebrity power around reproductive issues. This project is an explicit call for future and further study that will move beyond the patent houses, London, and celebrity performers, and transcend this limited time frame.

Some years ago, Ellen Donkin provided a series of provocations and musings that set this project in motion. While adding an epilogue to her chapter on Sarah Siddons in the revised edition of *Critical Theory and Performance*, Donkin confessed that there was an important circumstance she had initially missed in unpacking the night in October of 1784 when Siddons confronted a hostile audience.[22] The missed circumstance was a pregnancy, and Donkin mused on whether or not this contributed to Siddons's anger, or to her willingness to "look back" at her audience as subject rather than object. Donkin remarked, "I am struck by how difficult it is, short of working deductively from birth records, to discover which among the actresses of the period was performing onstage gravid, and who was not."[23] She went on to lay out the basic methodology one would need to use to write about pregnancy in theater history: "Work begins with . . . the birth dates of children and a simple act of subtraction."[24] That is where I have begun. She also suggested that economics would play an important factor in women's decisions about when and how to work. Finally, she mused on the erotic implications of visibly pregnant female bodies: "The fact of public pregnancy being socially acceptable begs the larger question of whether or not pregnancy itself functioned in the public imagination as a source of erotic pleasure;" at what point, she asked, did "the erotic become the grotesque"?[25] While I will not always be considering the erotic potential of pregnant bodies, the question of how audiences read pregnancy—in relation to celebrity identity, in relation to stage character—is at the core of my work. In important ways, Donkin suggested the framework and methods of this book, and provided the initial impetus to investigate.

My methodology, then, involves identifying the birth dates for actresses' children, establishing from this the timing of their pregnancies, and executing close readings and comparisons of repertory records and primary source material to determine how, if at all, pregnancy and childbirth impacted women's careers, earning potential, and public reputation, as well as the theatrical organizations for which they worked. Of course, to understand and value change, it is also crucial to study surrounding seasons for control data. Whenever possible, I have drawn on women's own writings and rely on a vast range of primary sources to understand and contextualize women's lives and careers: biography, memoir, autobiography, correspondence, private journals, receipt and commonplace books, public advertisements, reviews, bon mots, social commentary, medical texts, parish records, theatrical documents (contracts, promptbooks, financial records, play texts), anecdotes, and visual representations (portraits, engravings, satirical cartoons). I also draw on a wealth of secondary writings on theater history, celebrity, and eighteenth-century culture to ask how these women's bodies matter to disciplinary conversations and excavate historiographical tendencies that have rendered those bodies invisible. Together, these sources and approaches place pregnancy at the center of our awareness, where we can see and understand its impact on women and systems in the eighteenth century, as well as the consequences of its exclusion from our scholarship.

In recovering women's stories, articulating the importance of their experiences in shifting our understanding of larger systems and cultures, and speaking back to existing narratives, this is a specifically feminist history.[26] In many cases, parish records and/or newspaper sources documenting birth or baptismal dates for actresses' children offer ways of accessing essential data, but a history of women's embodied experiences must always live between objectivity and subjectivity, between archival and speculative histories. As Thomas Postlewait contends in his study of Shakespearean anecdotes, a choice between "objective" data or "scientific" methods and subjective and imaginative sources is predicated on a false binary: "The choice is not really between fact and fiction—objectivity and subjectivity—in the handling of evidence. The two traditions are our heritage, and our abiding struggle."[27] Susan Bennett and Tracy C. Davis point to the specific challenge women's experiences can pose to historiographical approaches that depend on such binaries, and Bennett calls historiography "both a road block and a means of reinvigorating theatre history."[28] She locates the writing of women's history in theater in a state of tension between creating something new (new approaches, new methodologies), and using familiar methods, which "inevitably pulls our history—even our alternative histories—back into the trajectory of what has always already been known."[29] From opening up the possible landscape of pregnancy's impact on individual women to better understanding the consequences of pregnancy for the repertory system, this project expands what is known by finding pregnancy's place in existing narratives of prominent women's lives, and using it to ask bigger questions about eighteenth-century theater and social history.

To connect women to the world at large, my methodologies also draw from social and cultural histories. In focusing on a particular set of women, I follow Amanda Vickery's assertion that critiques of large-scale historical narratives, such as the rise of domesticity, women's exclusion from the labor market, and gendered Habermasian "separate spheres" are best grounded in deep, specific examples.[30] I apply rigorous standards of evidence, but do not limit interpretation and well-informed speculation where doing so enables the articulation of questions and theories that can stimulate future work. Peter Burke offers a useful approach when grappling with a definition of cultural history and what it can legitimately accomplish: "an approach to the past which asks present-minded questions but refuses to give present-minded answers, which concerns itself with traditions but allows for their continual reinterpretation; and which notes the importance of unintended consequences in the history of historical writing as well as the history of political events."[31] Burke's "present-minded questions"—coupled with celebrity studies' exploration of the "deep" eighteenth century—inform much of the range and scope of this project, which is interested in how the intersection of pregnancy, celebrity, and professional work remains a fraught and relevant topic.[32]

Pregnancy and Celebrity Identity

In recent decades, a major focus in the study of eighteenth-century British theater has been the power and significance of celebrity actresses. Works from Elizabeth Howe's *The First Actresses* (1992) to Felicity Nussbaum's *Rival Queens* (2010), Laura Engel's *Fashioning Celebrity* (2011), and Helen Brooks's *Actresses, Gender, and the Eighteenth Century Stage* (2015) have decisively shifted our attention to women as a driving force of the repertory system and redefined the so-called age of the actor as "the age of the *actress*."[33] Scholars of celebrity studies and what Engel has termed "actress studies" have explored the ways these women leveraged celebrity into lucrative careers, using a combination of performing self and performing character to craft personal brands that drove audience demand for their persons and performances.[34] Such demand granted celebrity actresses economic power and varying degrees of agency to advance their professional careers. The demand also meant that individual strengths in, for example, she-tragedy or cross-dressing roles could shape repertory planning and have wide-ranging consequences for the theatrical system. Attention to women's personal brands and self-advocacy challenge a long tradition of representing the professional actress as passive or powerless, or solely within the "actress/whore" conflation.[35]

Instead, scholars have explored the means by which actresses could reinforce, challenge, or create new conceptions of womanhood. Laura Engel and Elaine McGirr's *Stage Mothers: Women, Work, and the Theatre 1660–1830* (2014) takes up the topic of working motherhood's impact on celebrity actresses, for, as they rightly charge, the "combination of 'public display and personal revelation,' which has been the nexus of many discussions of eighteenth-century actresses, becomes more complex when considering the realities and representations of maternity on stage and off."[36] The work in this volume offers crucial insights into women's lives and careers and asks rigorous questions of our assumptions about maternity and sexuality. Even so, pregnancy itself remains elusive in conversations of the time period. The material import of pregnancy—the way it marks the body, shapes a woman's place in the world, and alters the behavior of both the woman and those around her—is a largely untapped history.

Pregnancy on stage in the eighteenth century married sex and sensibility within a public body. Pregnancy was and is overdetermined: one person's body might read as transgressive, excessive, and grotesque while another might signal contained, desirable respectability. The primary focus of this project is the impact of pregnancy on six women's celebrity identities and individual repertoires, asking how the changing body challenged, modified, or supported performances of celebrity self and of fictional stage characters. My contention is that these women—thanks to a growing celebrity culture whose technologies facilitated self-fashioning—had tools at their disposal to help them shape the impact and meaning of their changing bodies.

Women's repertoires and performance styles, as well as private circumstances, such as marriage or other sexual relationships, informed their public personas. In his 2007 study of celebrity, *It*, Joseph Roach identifies components that work together to create the genius of "it," a quality vital to celebrity. These components are "public intimacy," which confers an illusion of availability and knowability upon the subject and drives a desire for "synthetic experiences" of the celebrity (stage performances, but also the viewing and purchasing of images and play texts); together, these contribute to the rise of the "It-Effect" or "personality-driven mass attraction" to the subject.[37] Roach's criteria are useful not only for determining who qualifies as a celebrity, but also for understanding where the labor of celebrity creation took place: not just on stage, but in periodicals, portrait studios, print shops, and other venues in which private information (real or not) about and images of celebrity women circulated.[38] Leslie Ritchie's study of David Garrick's creation and manipulation of his own celebrity image through the media, meanwhile, offers crucial context to this conversation and uncovers networks of influence vital to understanding what she calls the "cultural construction of celebrity."[39] These and other scholars have shown that the creation and maintenance of celebrity identity were complex and multimodal. Understanding how the changing physical body displayed onstage intersected with this wider self-fashioning labor is crucial to this study.

When theorizing the historical body in performance, particularly when the body is that of a celebrity, we quickly realize that we have an important question on our hands: just how many bodies did celebrity performers possess, and what was the relationship between them? Roach suggests that, like royalty, celebrities possess two bodies: the body natural, which decays and is mortal, and the body cinematic (what I will call the celebrity body), which is idealized and endures through the continued circulation of iconic images, performances, and information.[40] In performance, these two bodies are joined by the body of the character the actor is meant to represent. Celebrity actresses, then, have three potential perceptual bodies: the body natural of the actor, the body of the character they perform, and the celebrity body that reflects and represents the accumulation of fame and reputation. In analyzing these layered presences, some have focused on the intersection of the performer's body natural and the character's body; others have considered the impact of the celebrity body on that of the character.[41] Still other scholars raise questions about the relationship between the celebrity body and the body natural, particularly as the latter ages. Marvin Carlson, for example, has suggested that a celebrity's reputation and audience familiarity with a role can "ghost" performances, effacing differences as the actor's body natural ages.[42] More recently, Lisa Freeman has suggested that repeated exposure to an actor in a role over time has a more palimpsestic effect, not eliding difference but bringing attention to it.[43] These concepts can also be applied to the more temporary changes of pregnancy, prompting us to ask when these changes to the body natural are elided or effaced with character or celebrity, and when these temporary changes have a lingering effect as the memory of pregnant performance becomes a palimpsest.

When an actress grew increasingly pregnant, it changed her body natural in visible and identifiable ways that often conflicted with that of the character she played, as when Jordan played a castrato role in breeches about six weeks before giving birth. Her evolving body natural stood as distinct from her celebrity body, which remained unchanging. Even so, for many actresses such changes made little difference to the kinds of roles they played on stage. One common theme of this book is a reassessment of the importance of verisimilitude to audience reception of the performing pregnant body, for modifications to women's repertoire during pregnancy can be overwhelmingly traced instead to concerns for safety. Nevertheless, pregnancy did matter, both to a woman's celebrity identity and to the reception of roles she played, especially as it clearly signaled sexual activity. In 1782, for example, Jordan's pregnancy did not hamper her ability to perform in her company or gain popularity with audiences, whatever disconnect between her real and imagined bodies might have existed. It was not until after her daughter Fanny's birth that a challenge to her popularity arose, when rumors revealed that the child was illegitimate.

Jordan's first performance after the birth took place in Hull on December 26, 1782. She acted Calista in Nicholas Rowe's *The Fair Penitent*, an unrepentant adulteress whose sexual guilt is the downfall of her family. Though Calista does regret her behavior in the final scene, for most of the play she willfully deceives those around her and rails against the impossible position of women whose lives are controlled by men. Of the many "she-tragedy" heroines popular in the long eighteenth century, Calista is far from an innocent victim.[44] Wilkinson described the audience reception of Jordan that December as "cool" and noted that "her song of the 'Greenwood Laddie,' which she sung whimsically and excellently, *was hissed!*"[45] Both the play and this song openly addressed sexual transgression. In the context of new information about Jordan's private life, the relationship between her body natural and her character became dangerously conflated. Though no longer pregnant, the specter of Jordan's previously pregnant body and the new life it created became the symbol and proof of her transgression. Wilkinson praised Jordan for eventually overcoming the negative rumors about her behavior by consistently displaying her "merit" on stage and off—by leveraging a convincing and consistent performance of self that adhered to wider norms of acceptable femininity and effectively countered rumor and scandal.[46]

When Jordan moved to London, one paper preemptively described her young daughter as the result of her marriage to "a sea-faring man who left her the next morning," perhaps to forestall the kind of response she received in Hull.[47] That explanation was necessary speaks to Kristina Straub's argument that professional actresses could become caught "in crosscurrents that defined their sexuality as public by profession and private by gender."[48] There was no clearer illustration of this dichotomy than the performing pregnant body. Critiques of pregnant performers, for example, could bolster negative claims about a celebrity's professional taste or private character. In other cases, however, the pregnant body could testify to a woman's good character or professional dedication. Pregnancy was a flexible signifier, and celebrity actresses in the long eighteenth century found ways of using their changing physical condition to their advantage; in Roach's terms, to make pregnancy a "charismatic" force (or asset) when it has often been considered a "stigmatic" one (or detriment).[49] In manipulating the pregnant body as signifier, perhaps in collaboration with managers and supporters, actresses could garner audience sympathy and support, periodically (and perhaps paradoxically) expunge accusations of licentiousness or wrongdoing, and further their lucrative stage careers. Recovering the reproductive body as a context for a professional career helps us better understand the relationship between public and private in the eighteenth-century world and facilitates valuable connections between working pregnant women in the long eighteenth century and working pregnant women today.

Pregnancy and Theatrical Management

Actresses' professional experiences with pregnancy in the long eighteenth century were intimately connected to the workings of the repertory system, making the wide array of primary and secondary sources related to repertory and company management vital to understanding how women and managers approached accommodation. After 1705, when the major theaters began advertising each day's performances in the daily papers, it is possible to read, with relative accuracy, how the repertory of the major London houses unfolded day by day and week by week. This information is collected alongside data from playbills and other sources in the five-part, eleven-volume reference resource *The London Stage, 1660–1800* and subsequent emendations.[50] Newspapers, pamphlets, and play texts survive, as do account books, pay lists, diaries, contracts, correspondence, and other artifacts of managerial practice, and have been insightfully studied by the compendium's editors, historians Judith Milhous and Robert D. Hume, and others. While imperfect and far from complete, the archival material available to scholars of this time period is, in terms of quantity and potential for access, far beyond that available for the time periods that immediately precede it and, to some degree, those that follow it.[51] We therefore have many tools with which to reintegrate the reproductive experiences of professional actresses into the history of the commercial theater once we recognize the importance of doing so.

For individuals, the successful balancing of maternal and theatrical labor could be vital to a career and therefore to their family's survival, as we have seen with both Jordan and Smith. When pregnant, not only did women have to consider what their changing bodies might mean for their public personas and popularity, but also how and for how long they might safely perform, issues complicated by the vagaries in predicting when a birth might take place. While Sandra Richards is correct (as we have seen with Henrietta Smith) that absences for pregnancy and childbirth could risk allowing "upstarts" to advance their careers, theaters sometimes chose to simply suspend performances of certain plays until celebrity performers returned from lying-in.[52] For example, actresses substituted for Anne Oldfield (1720) and Dorothy Jordan (1780–90s) in many roles during their pregnancies, but no woman ever undertook Lady Betty Modish in *The Careless Husband* for Oldfield, and only twice in the course of eight pregnancies did another performer substitute as Viola in *Twelfth Night* for Jordan. When and where theaters used substitute performers, therefore, can tell us something about where the popularity of a piece lay—with the absent actress, or elsewhere. The relationship between performers and fans could also influence accommodations, for eighteenth-century audiences sometimes functioned as monitors of appropriate behavior among actors and managers. When Isabella Mattocks performed late in a pregnancy in 1773 a reporter for the *Morning Chronicle* noted her apparent discomfort and called for the management to "let her rest, and allow a substitute to represent her characters till she has got up from lying in!"[53] Four days later, Mattocks left the stage to await the birth; she returned two months later.

From a managerial perspective, the balance between allowing or requiring pregnant performers to continue working into late pregnancy and ensuring their long-term health and safety was critical for the theatrical companies that relied on their labor. This was not only because behavior toward pregnant performers might result in censure of theatrical management, but also because of the nature of the repertory system, which was dynamic, fiercely competitive, and complicated, relying on the labor of hundreds of people. The repertory system had to be both well organized and highly flexible, able to respond to audience tastes and desires fleetly, and to soldier on in the face of company members' absences, illnesses, and deaths. The default state was competition, both between Drury Lane and Covent Garden, and between the patent theaters and other entertainment venues.[54] The complexities of the system, and especially the celebrity capital women at the top of their profession accrued, meant that one could not simply dismiss a pregnant actress and hire a new one; longevity and stability of careers were a benefit to all. There were therefore a variety of arrangements aimed at keeping these women on stage safely for as long as possible. These included temporarily retiring plays with particularly strenuous parts, swapping genres (most often tragedy to comedy but sometimes the reverse), and not scheduling leading comedic actresses—who might normally appear in both the evening's mainpiece and the shorter afterpiece—for two performances in a single night from about the end of the fourth month of their pregnancy forward.[55] When Wilkinson critiqued Smith, it was not the spectacle of her body that troubled him, but that her behavior endangered her health unnecessarily and resulted in a longer postpartum recovery period, in turn making casting and performing plays more challenging. There were also economic consequences, but not the consequences historians have often assumed.

Explaining the challenges Smith and Jordan's pregnancies created, Wilkinson writes, "my ladies breed oftener than suits my inclination, as my pocket feels the effects of ladies when they are *in the straw*, adding to the live-stock of his majesty and liberty."[56] He is referring to the potential box office hit the company might take in the absence of two popular performers, but he is also referencing an important fact: Smith and Jordan were still being paid even though they were not actively contributing to the nightly takings. While touring troupe models differed from the patent theaters in many ways, an extensive review of surviving account records at the Folger Shakespeare Library and British Library shows both patent theaters had a consistent policy of providing paid leave during absences for pregnancy and childbirth from at least the late 1760s onward. Isabella Mattocks, for example, received her weekly salary throughout her two-month absence in 1773.[57] The eighteenth-century commercial theater provided economic as well as repertory accommodations that facilitated women's continued careers, countering assumptions that time off during pregnancy or after childbirth was unpaid, forcing women to work up to their due dates and return days after birth.[58]

The business of theater adjusted to social and medical norms around pregnancy and childbirth. These norms advocated a lessening of physical exertion in a woman's last weeks of pregnancy, as well as a cessation of professional work about a month before giving birth. After a birth, British women who could afford to do so would participate in a lying-in, a four- to six-week period of rest and recovery. Across the century, it is indeed common to find actresses taking absences of one to two months around the births of their children. This does not mean that coercion did not exist or that managers were not abusive of the power differential between themselves and their performers. Nor am I suggesting that four or even six weeks of paid leave was a generous length of time to recover from birth. But this seemingly standardized paid leave is a form of accommodation hitherto unrecognized that alters our understanding of the systems and practices that structured women's experiences. That these practices mirrored wider social expectations means that the commercial theater served to both reflect and reinforce such norms.

Pregnancy and Social Expectations

As Britain went to war repeatedly and built an empire that spanned the globe, changes were underway in the medical field that would permanently affect the experience of pregnancy and childbirth for Western women. The eighteenth century saw the establishment of obstetrics as a distinct medical field, the proliferation of men-midwives, and the founding of specialized schools and hospitals to serve the population's reproductive needs. In this context, Lisa Forman Cody argues, reproduction became a public concern, and "late eighteenth-century British culture valued motherhood and treated the successfully reproductive body as an aesthetic, cultural, and political ideal."[59] Cody locates these changes in the latter part of the century, coinciding with what Linda Colley has called the "cult of prolific maternity."[60] Toni Bowers's work, however, shows that the ideal of the full-time domestic mother was already widely present in Augustan England (broadly construed as 1682–1762), where one of its major purposes was to prop up patriarchal power by subduing and circumscribing maternal authority in a period of various monarchial and succession-related crises.[61] Bowers locates imagined and idealized motherhood as trapped in binaries (good-bad, silence-authority, public-private), but never addresses public figures such as performers whose lives challenged such binaries. Working actresses, as Nussbaum and Brooks have ably demonstrated, participated in a commercial economy, visibly asserting the value of their bodies and their physical capabilities in ways inconsistent with supposedly private ideals of femininity, including motherhood. As the meaning, significance, and understanding of their bodies changed over the course of the century, performing women navigated not only stage celebrity but also social norms and expectations to justify and continue their work.

The final context within which the book situates pregnant celebrity performers is the wider world in which they lived. It brings together scholarship on marriage and the history of maternity—which is construed as increasingly of "public" interest over the century, even as the experience of maternity was increasingly idealized as "private"—with the experiences of actresses living unequivocally public lives. In the chapters, this encourages us to attend to moments when women's experiences were shaped by the gaze of audiences who could compare actresses' bodies with their own or with their personal experiences, with their growing understanding of the nationalistic importance of reproduction, and with evolving interpretations of medical and biological processes. Performing women did not exist in a vacuum. Just as Straub and others argue that notions of women's sexuality as private and domestic are important in the conflation of acting and public display with sex work, so cultural norms and ideals surrounding marriage, pregnancy, birth, and motherhood influenced how actresses were perceived during pregnancy, and how they and their later biographers wrote of their experiences.

Actresses' marital status could influence the meaning of their pregnant bodies. Frequent childbearing within marriage, for example, was expected.[62] Marital status also changed actresses' social standing and shaped their experiences as economic and artistic agents. On the one hand, marriage could help women forge advantageous connections to powerful individuals in their profession, in turn offering access to training, more lucrative contracts, or new or larger roles in the company.[63] On the other, under the system of coverture, married women lost their individual legal status and had no right to divorce. In cases of extreme cruelty, a woman might pursue a legal separation (a divorce *a mensa et thoro*), but this was often a prohibitively expensive option. All property a woman brought to marriage—including her body—also became her husband's; her earnings, too, were typically at his disposal. With the exception of Susannah Cibber, the married women in this study were theoretically subject to these legal limitations for their entire married lives despite sometimes being the dominant or sole earners for their families.

Despite these legal realities, historian Joanne Bailey finds that women expected to actively contribute to their family's stability and success, including through wage earning.[64] When they took their husbands to court, it was often because the husband was not contributing his proper share. A complaint against a husband for failing to provide (or locking away food or money) damaged a man's reputation and was seen as indicative of laziness and neglect, which could in turn impact his standing in a community: "male credit depended upon both wider community trust and the individual reputations of the household."[65] Bailey ultimately proposes a model of co-dependency in marriage, in which both partners were to meet a firm social expectation of providing for the family. Thus, when actresses—married or not—performed while visibly pregnant and returned to the stage after the births of their children, they were publicly signaling not simply diligence in their profession but also adherence to gendered cultural norms. Economic and reproductive labor was not exclusive, for material provisioning was a form of good mothering.

Bailey's work also usefully expands our understanding of women's honor beyond a focus on sexual activity: "The sexual double standard was not rigidly applied in everyday life. Husbands were subjected to criticism for infidelity from their wives and peers and their personal sexual behavior had an impact on their reputation. Equally, women's honor was defined by their labour, household position and charitable works, as well as by their sexual reputation."[66] This is crucial when considering the myriad domestic arrangements in which the women in this study lived. Two women in this study—Susanna Mountfort Verbruggen and Sarah Siddons—were stably married throughout their reproductive years. A third, Susannah Cibber, was married during her first three pregnancies but was separated from her husband and living with a lover by the time of her fourth. The remaining three women—Anne Oldfield, George Anne Bellamy, and Dorothy Jordan—never married. In some cases, they did not have the option: Bellamy's second partner John Calcraft was already married, and Jordan's second long-term relationship was with a member of the royal family.[67] In other cases, remaining unmarried may have been a matter of preference for the demonstrated legal advantages it offered women. Oldfield, for example, did not marry despite having had two long-term relationships and accumulated considerable wealth and property. After her death, a biographer praised her for preserving the inheritance of her first son, Arthur Maynwaring Jr., by not marrying her second long-term lover Charles Churchill. Remaining unmarried enabled her to retain control over her earnings, business dealings, and property rather than surrendering them under the practice of coverture in English common law.[68]

Regardless of marital status, people in the eighteenth century had access, if they could read and afford it, to an increasingly large library of advice on how to conceive, understand and manage the adverse symptoms of pregnancy, prevent and treat miscarriages, prepare for and give birth, and navigate the postpartum period. In 1774, the publication of William Hunter's *Anatomy of the Human Gravid Uterus* offered an unprecedented view into the process of fetal development in a series of highly detailed engravings for a specialized medical audience.[69] Written advice manuals aimed at a lay audience, meanwhile, were written by those in the nascent field of obstetrics and experienced midwives.

Expectant parents, especially mothers, also received advice about pregnancy, childbirth, and recovery from their immediate circle of family and friends. This advice reflected both cultural norms and individual experiences. Sarah Churchill, the Duchess of Marlborough, for example, warned her granddaughter against both traveling on bad roads (a widely acknowledged source of miscarriages) and "reaching out your arm to whip the horse" while driving a chaise. This less typical and very specific warning came from the duchess's belief that such an action had brought about one of her own miscarriages.[70] Family and friends, more than published sources, could provide reassurance about what was normal based on their own experiences and on intimate knowledge of the pregnant woman. When Churchill's granddaughter believed she was pregnant but was concerned about her size, for example, the duchess soothed her by suggesting, "It is not natural for any great bigness to appear in four months, when a person is very tall and very lean" and instead recommended attending to changes in her breasts as a more reliable marker of early pregnancy.[71] The intimacy of these relationships also allowed childbearers to share their impatience, their discomforts, and their fears. In 1782, Sarah Napier (Lady Sarah Lennox) wrote, "I have been three weeks in hourly expectation of being confined, have been very uneasy, & very *cross* as you may guess at not getting over this tiresome business."[72]

In addition to personalized advice and support, Judith Schneid Lewis's study of aristocratic women's letters between 1760 and 1860 demonstrates how much familial tradition and attitude might impact the management of pregnancy and birth, from the very strict to the highly individual. She shows how often printed advice manuals and even the pleas of spouses and family members were disregarded in less conservative homes in deference to a powerful belief that happy women had healthy pregnancies. One might urge restrictions, patience, and rest, but mental as well as physical health was important to a successful pregnancy and many women continued to attend parties, ride horses, visit friends, and otherwise participate in public life nearly up to the moment they went into labor. For actresses, this translated to general acceptance of their working bodies with recommendations that they, like any other working woman, retire about a month before birth.[73] Of course, guessing a pregnancy's progress from external signs was subjective, but a woman's size, perceived effort of movement, and markers such as the "rising of the apron"—a stage at which a woman's belly was obvious and causing the front hem of her clothing to rise from the floor—were observable to audiences watching gravid performers. Clothing could thus play a role in women's calculations of their due dates, and in perceptions of their pregnancy's progress.

Dressing for Pregnancy

Managing pregnancy, on stage and off, was also about dressing the body. Most women wore their existing clothing, making alterations and accessorizing as needed to accommodate their changing bodies.[74] This is clear in a 1774 cartoon, "The Man of Business," in which a man's wife appears to be asking him to confront a bevy of women he has impregnated. Each woman wears the basic outfit of the day with the addition of scarves or aprons (Figure I.1). This is because very few specialized maternity garments existed. One exception is maternity stays, which laced at the sides and were easier to

Figure I.1. M. Darly, *The Man of Business* (June 1, 1774). Courtesy of The Lewis Walpole Library, Yale University

adjust around a growing belly. The aim was not to "straight-lace" or minimize the appearance of pregnancy, but to provide support and create a foundation for overclothing. During one pregnancy, Elizabeth Leathes wrote to thank her parents for securing her a larger pair of stays: "[They] have relieved me from a deal of pain which I suffered by wearing the others. I suppose you will be surpris'd to find that I am so much increased in size since my return from Town, as to be obliged to leave them open three inches behind notwithstanding I let them out as much as they will allow on each side. This makes me apprehensive that I shall be confined sooner than I first expected."[75] In this case, Leathes used her stays to mark the progress of her pregnancy. Short stays, which ended a few inches below the breasts, were an alternative to longer maternity stays, and both options could be paired with gowns made to fit more loosely and which therefore would require less alteration. There were also more improvised outfits, such as that which Sarah Churchill recounted in a letter to her granddaughter in 1735: "I remember when I was within three months of my reckoning, I could never endure to wear any bodice at all; but wore a warm waistcoat wrapped about me like a man's, and tied my petticoats on the top of it. And from that time never went abroad but with a long black scarf to hide me. I was so prodigious big."[76] Scarves, kerchiefs, and aprons were "characteristic" accessories associated with pregnancy.[77] On stage or off, pregnant women sought comfort and support in their garments, but many also attempted to retain their fashionable wardrobes with adjustments and accessories.

As the century progressed, the open-front gowns, short stays, and neoclassical styles of the final decade probably made a difference to what people were seeing as "visible pregnancy," but it would be legible in any era. For example, for much of the century a woman with an "H" or "A" shaped opening to her overgown instead of a fashionable "V" shape might be pregnant; so might a woman sporting an oversized shawl or apron, or exchanging normal styles for sack-back gowns, riding cloaks, or other flowing and capacious garments.[78] Thus, even attempts to mask or conceal the body could draw attention to it. Just as an actress today being filmed only from the waist up, carrying an excessively large handbag, lamp, or houseplant, or perpetually in a coat might alert us to pregnancy, so eighteenth-century observers were familiar with a whole range of

Figure I.2. Isaac Cruikshank after George Moutard Woodward, *Cestina Warehouse or Belly Piece Shop* (London: S.W. Fores, 1793), © The Trustees of the British Museum

modes in which the body became legible as pregnant. A short-lived fad in 1793 even had women wearing cork bellies under evolving neoclassical gowns. While the idea was to create a silhouette reminiscent of classical statuary, it became the subject of much hilarity for making women appear pregnant.[79] One satire on the trend, "The Cestina Warehouse" (1793), shows women selecting from padding representing each month of pregnancy; the smaller pads are tied at the waist below the stays of the woman on the left, while the woman on the right in the back wears a bigger piece that begins immediately below her bosom (Figure I.2). "Frailties of Fashion 1793" (1793), meanwhile, shows a park full of women sporting belly pads, including a small girl and her doll (Figure I.3).

Pregnancy, of course, looks different in different bodies (something both cartoons represent). Taller and leaner women or those carrying low might have their condition concealed by capacious skirts for longer than those who were shorter or carrying very high. Some no doubt sought to hide their bodies and succeeded; but

Figure I.3. Isaac Cruikshank (1756–1811?), *Frailties of Fashion* (London: S.W. Fores, May 1, 1793). Courtesy of the Library of Congress

equally, by miscalculation or choice, performers sometimes remained onstage until the day, hour, or even minute they went into labor, making it highly unlikely their bodies were not legible to audiences. Most married adult women spent a decade or more of their lives pregnant and were surrounded by friends and family doing the same. For us, it can still be unusual for an actor to combine performance work with pregnancy; for those in the eighteenth century, pregnancy across ranks and professions was a familiar sight.

Pregnant celebrity actresses in the long eighteenth century were not anonymous to their audiences; and they were the first nonroyal, nonaristocratic, nonfamilial, working pregnant bodies to which a significant cross-section of the population had almost daily visual and/or print access. As such, they were at once deeply familiar and utterly new, both reflecting and modeling the changes, symptoms, behaviors, and fashions of pregnancy for women in the audience. Often lacking an advantageous legal position, these women instead relied on the power and influence they could garner as celebrities to shape and protect their careers. Stage celebrities, trading on the appearance of public intimacy, melded public and private, persona and person, and domestic and professional labor in the context of larger social, medical, and political conversations about gender, sexuality, pregnancy, and motherhood.

Structure

The strengths of the chronological structure of this book are twofold. First, it allows maximal clarity around the limits and opportunities of the archive in the period, for the extent of available evidence varies considerably between 1689 and 1800.[80] Second, this structure attends to the immediate context in which each woman was living and performing, acknowledging changes in obstetric practice, the size of theaters, presence of celebrity news in papers, and so forth. Such an arrangement could easily suggest that there is a straightforward "change over time" narrative around this topic; this is true only to a limited degree. Certainly, greater newspaper interest in the lives of performers, the explosion in theatrical portraiture after 1770, and the popularity of theatrical biography changed much in terms of self-fashioning possibilities, though the basic mechanics of celebrity as articulated by Roach and others arguably remained stable. Cultural shifts toward sensibility and domesticity no doubt impacted cultural scripts around pregnancy and motherhood, though scholars are also continually revising the timelines on which such shifts occurred.[81] The workings of the theater around pregnancy and childbearing, such as lengths of leave and repertory accommodations, were remarkably steady, however, belying a simple progressive narrative. Finally, at the end of the day (despite John Hunter's successful artificial insemination of a client in 1785), there was still only one way to get pregnant in the eighteenth century. Thus, the visible, rumored, or known-to-be pregnant body throughout the time period existed on a relatively stable spectrum of cultural meaning from sex to sentimentality. The ensuing chapters sketch contexts for individual performers while offering many connections between the lives and careers of women across the long eighteenth century that enrich our understanding of them as people, as actresses, and as representatives of celebrity culture.

Chapter 1, covering 1689 to 1730, follows the careers of Susanna Mountfort Verbruggen and Anne Oldfield. Mountfort had one child a year, always in the spring, from 1690 to 1693 with her husband William Mountfort. After his murder during her fourth pregnancy in 1693, Susanna supported their two surviving children alone until her remarriage in 1695 to another actor, John Verbruggen. She died from complications of childbirth in 1703, and several of her roles passed to the young Oldfield, another promising comedienne. Oldfield became hugely popular in both comedy and tragedy and had several children during two long-term relationships with political figures. Like Mountfort Verbruggen, Oldfield was pregnant and the sole provider for her children in 1712–13, when her lover Arthur Maynwaring died. For both women, pregnancy aided the development of a new line of business: for Mountfort Verbruggen, playing character parts that capitalized on the grotesque comic potential of the pregnant body; for Oldfield, portraying noble tragic heroines whose stoic natures enabled her to construct her pregnant body as classically contained.

While chapter 1 takes a genealogical approach, chapter 2 considers two women bound together by competition, both of whom faced challenges to integrating pregnancy into their professional work in the age of sensibility. The chapter covers the years 1736–1761, focusing on Susannah Maria Cibber (1714–1766) and George Anne Bellamy (ca. 1731–1788). In 1736, Cibber's pregnant body, like that of Oldfield, aided in her rebranding herself as a tragic actress. After she endured two sensational trials for adultery in 1738 and 1739, however, Cibber's pregnant body transformed from a source of charismata to one of stigmata. While she successfully rebuilt her career in the 1740s by casting herself as the tragic victim of an abusive husband, she found visible pregnancy (the result of her ongoing extramarital relationship with a married man) incompatible with this celebrity image and withdrew from the stage entirely during her final pregnancy in 1749. In doing so, Cibber demonstrated the extensive control she wielded over her career and displayed what I am calling tenebrism, a strategy of concealment that masquerades as transparency.[82] The beautiful, impetuous Bellamy performed maternity on stage and reflected on it in a memoir, *An Apology for the Life of George Anne Bellamy* (1785). Initially, her onstage performances of maternity were popular, but growing disapproval of her private life and the perceived ill treatment of her children ultimately undermined their attractive power. Years later, Bellamy's memoir attempted to reconstitute her theatrical and maternal authority by showcasing the affective possibilities of her nurturing body at key moments in her narrative and using her maternity to aid her performance of social class.

Chapters 3 and 4 look at another pair of contemporaries, Sarah Siddons (1755–1831) and Dorothy Jordan (1761–1816). While the archive around each of these women is too large to allow for discussion within a single chapter, the chapters function as a pair, examining similarities and differences in reception and self-fashioning for two women living very different lives. Siddons (chapter 3) was a monumentally successful performer and married mother to seven children. A significant part of her success came from her ability to synthesize her on- and offstage performances of maternity into a powerful celebrity persona that granted her considerable agency in her backstage dealings with managers. This chapter traces the integration of her stage performances of Lady Macbeth with the public imagination during her very public 1785 pregnancy, contrasted with her significantly less sensationalized final pregnancy in 1794, meditating on the reasons why this shift in audience response took place, and connecting it with a series of miscarriages and larger social and political events.

Dorothy Jordan (chapter 4) gave birth to thirteen children and was pregnant at least eighteen times in the course of her thirty-year career in England. Her many pregnancies were both a logistical and financial challenge to theater managers, but Jordan's box office appeal allowed her to steadily secure more lucrative contracts and flexible performance schedules to accommodate her private life. Unlike Siddons, however, Jordan's repertoire did not offer an easy conflation of her on- and offstage life; instead, her story showcases the flexible narratives and complex semiotics of the pregnant body that allow us to reflect again on the experiences of women who came before her. This chapter draws on Jordan's own writings, satirical prints, and extensive newspaper and periodical research to illuminate the ways changing responses to Jordan's pregnant body were a bellwether for public sentiment about her private character.

The conclusion draws out the major implications of this work by meditating on the connections between these historical cases and pointing to further parallels with the stories of pregnant professionals today. It prompts us to consider how far (or not) we have come, and how we think through artistic labor and childbearing in our own time, when access to reproductive control is far greater than in earlier periods. We have long understood that when women entered the theater, their presence made fundamental changes to both writing and performance. They also changed managerial practice, space, and cultural ideas of womanhood and performance. Part of this was their difference, their bodies. Attention to historical women's bodies, and the ability of those bodies to visibly reproduce, opens new understandings of British theater history. As numerous historians have pointed out, the history of women in British theater from the Restoration forward is bound up in and often limited by narratives of actresses' sexuality. Women's bodies are often construed not as tools and instruments of their stage profession but as the site of male desire and earning potential offstage. From the moment the first actresses entered the commercial marketplace, they faced challenges to controlling the perception and meaning of their bodies and identities. Perhaps this is another reason why women's reproductive lives are only sporadically addressed in our current scholarship. Doing so feels too much like reducing these women to their sexuality and biology. But understanding the systemic impact of pregnancy offers not only a more complete view of women's lives but also information on topics that form the basis of our knowledge of eighteenth-century theater, including repertory planning and managerial practice. My study, therefore, not only details pregnancy's impact on theater but also suggests ways that we can use pregnancy to further our understanding of the theatrical world.

1

INHERITING GREATNESS

Susanna Mountfort Verbruggen and Anne Oldfield

Actresses Susanna Mountfort Verbruggen (1666–1703) and Anne Oldfield (1683–1730) illustrate the extremes to which readings of the pregnant body may be taken: from a sign of domestic probity to unrestrained sexuality, and how those readings intersect with celebrity identity. Such readings can push women to the polar cultural positions of a "Madonna" or a "whore" as the body is seen to indicate—exclusively or in oscillation—the sentimental or the sexual.[1] Scholars have often assumed, particularly in the context of narratives linking actresses with sex work, that the sexual interpretation was, with some exceptions, negative or detrimental and the sentimental positive or beneficial. The case is not so simple. These actresses capitalized on different readings of the pregnant body to the same end: career advancement. In the context of stable marriage, Mountfort Verbruggen leveraged the grotesque comic potential of her pregnant body to expand a repertoire built on astounding transformations; at a time of personal crisis, the unmarried Oldfield used her performances in a new line of tragic heroines to elevate her gravid body above its associations with uncontrolled sexuality. Thus, the combination of each woman's reputation and repertoire during pregnancy contributed to the expansion and maintenance of their celebrity power. These women are bound together not through rivalry—nearly always the story we tell about female performers—but through legacy: when then Mrs. Verbruggen died from complications of childbirth in

1703, her roles were given to other members of the company, including Anne Oldfield. In significant ways, Mountfort Verbruggen's obstetric tragedy set Oldfield on the path to the dominant position she would hold until her death in 1730.

Susanna Percival Mountfort Verbruggen

> "Nothing, tho' ever so barren . . . could be flat in her Hands."
>
> —Colley Cibber, *Apology for the Life of Colley Cibber*

Susanna Mountfort Verbruggen (1666–1703) was born Susanna Percival in the summer of 1666. She was the daughter of Thomas Percival, a minor member of the Duke's Company, and his wife, Anne Terry. By age twenty, she was a promising comedienne in the United Company where she met playwright and fellow actor William Mountfort. They married on June 22, 1686, and had four children.[2] William Mountfort died in December 1792; a little over a year later, Susanna married her second husband, John "Jack" Verbruggen in early 1694. Shortly thereafter, the United Company fractured when a faction led by Thomas Betterton, Elizabeth Barry, and Anne Bracegirdle successfully petitioned to start their own company and set up at Lincoln's Inn Fields. After some consideration, Susanna and Jack remained at Drury Lane for the increase in status and repertory lines.[3] While Jack eventually left for Lincoln's Inn Fields, Susanna remained at Drury Lane until her death in 1703, which followed the birth of her only known child from this marriage. We have few direct sources for her life and career. The sixty-two roles we know she played, for example, are likely far from the full picture for two related reasons: the majority of our repertory records in these years are tied to new play premieres and performances at Court; and she died just as theaters began to regularly place advertisements in London newspapers.[4] Despite these difficulties, Mountfort Verbruggen's known repertoire and references to her in print—particularly in the autobiography of Colley Cibber—vividly define her line of business and onstage persona.

Mountfort Verbruggen's great skill was comedic transformation, prompting bookseller and theater historian Thomas Davies to label her "the female Proteus in acting."[5] She undertook a variety of comic parts from an early age and found success in them all, from ingenues and coquettes to breeches and travesty parts, and eccentric character roles. We have no surviving likeness, but playwright and actor Anthony Aston described her as "the most pleasant Creature that ever appear'd . . . she was a fine, fair Woman, plump, full-featur'd; her Face of a fine, smooth Oval, full of beautiful, well-dispos'd Moles on it, and on her Neck and Breast."[6] With her first husband, William Mountfort, she developed a line of "gay couples," with one partner—usually male—reluctant to enter into marriage and their witty love interest eventually winning them over, a type popularized by Charles Hart and Nell Gwyn in the mid-1660s. She also excelled in breeches roles and, according to Colley Cibber, "Her easy Air, Action, Mien, and Gesture, quite chang'd from the Quiof [*sic*], to the cock'd Hat, and Cavalier in fashion."[7] In the space of a week, one could theoretically see Mountfort Verbruggen cycle through her entire range of parts, each transformation bringing new delights.

Her protean powers made her appearance in character parts particularly popular. This led to a line of lusty older women, vulgar country girls, and female bawds, which Elizabeth Howe calls "grotesques," drawing on the word's associations with incongruity, absurdity, and exaggeration.[8] Colley Cibber describes Mountfort Verbruggen's approach to one such character: "She would make no scruple of defacing her fair Form . . . [in] *The Western Lass* . . . she transform'd her whole Being, Body, Shape, Voice, Language, Look, and Features, into almost another Animal; with a strong *Devonshire* Dialect, a broad laughing Voice, a poking Head, round Shoulders, an unconceiving Eye, and the most be-diz'ning, dowdy Dress, that ever covered the untrain'd Limbs of *Jane Trot*."[9] Mountfort Verbruggen's physical transformations became a key charismatic component of her celebrity. The variety and diversity of parts she played and the many shapes to which she bent her body created space for that same body to grow and change with age and pregnancy without hampering her popularity. Instead, this plasticity made her, in the words of one anonymous critic, a "Miracle."[10] In this chapter, I tie the initial development of her line of grotesques to yearly pregnancies in the early 1690s and contextualize these appearances with an overall view of her repertoire during pregnancy in 1693 and 1703.

The Mountforts had four children in rapid succession, one each spring from 1690 to 1693: Susanna on April 27, 1690 (christened May 11); Edward on April 1, 1691 (buried May 3); Elizabeth on March 22, 1692 (died March 30); and Mary, christened April 27, 1693. The shortest interval between her children's births was eleven months, the greatest thirteen, indicating a swift resumption of sexual activity after birth, prodigious fertility, and perhaps the use of a wet-nurse.[11] Today, we understand that short birth intervals increase the likelihood of premature birth, low birth weight, and mortality in infants, as well as the risk of late-stage bleeding and placental abruption in mothers.[12] That only the eldest and youngest of the four Mountfort children survived could indicate complications due to the short intervals between her pregnancies, or have myriad other explanations. In each case, she conceived in the early summer when theatrical business slowed. By the time she resumed her busy schedule in the fall, the fatigue and sickness of early pregnancy may have passed; she would likely be certain of her condition too, able to plan with her managers for her pregnancy, lying-in, and recovery in the ensuing season. Mountfort Verbruggen remained on stage at least through her second trimester during each pregnancy, and well into her third when pregnant with Mary. Her only confirmed child with her second husband, Lewis "Vanbruggen," was born May 16, 1703, just shy of Susanna's thirty-seventh birthday and at what we would today call advanced maternal age.[13] Mrs. Verbruggen remained on stage for the majority of this pregnancy but, according to Cibber, died of lingering complications in late summer 1703, followed by her infant son in October.

Private Lives, Public Stages

As a popular and versatile performer, many playwrights wrote parts for Susanna. William Mountfort created roles for her in *The Successful Strangers* (1690) and *Greenwich Park* (1691). Thomas Southerne crafted many parts for her, including Lucia/Sir Anthony in *Sir Anthony Love* (1690) and Charlot Welldon in *Oroonoko* (1695). She was William Congreve's first Belinda in *The Old Bachelor* (1693), and Thomas D'Urfey wrote Mary the Buxom for her in his *Don Quixote* trilogy (1694–95). In 1696, she was John Vanbrugh's Berinthia in *The Relapse* and performed two roles for Mary Pix: the eunuch Achmet in the she-tragedy *Ibrahim*, and the Governor's Wife in *The Spanish Wives*. She was the original Lady Lurewell in George Farquhar's *The Constant Couple* (1699), a repertory staple throughout the next century. In 1700, Catherine Trotter's *Love at a Loss* saw her as Miranda. For Colley Cibber, she was Narcissa in *Love's Last Shift* (1696), Hypolita in *She Wou'd and She Wou'd Not* (1702), and the initial inspiration for Lady Betty Modish in *The Careless Husband* (1704).

These writers wrote not just for her abilities or age but for her entire persona, including what audiences knew of her personal life. They made the most of her marriages, from the "gay couple" pairings with her first husband William to her casting as Berinthia in John Vanbrugh's *The Relapse* (1696), the young woman who tempts the reformed rake Loveless (played by her second husband Verbruggen) back into his philandering ways. Her yearly pregnancies in the 1690s also marked the texts she performed and suggest that audiences were regularly aware of her condition. At the end of Dryden's *Don Sebastian* (1689), for example, the Mountforts spoke a teasing epilogue in character as the play's lovers. They are presented as having second thoughts about their impending marriage, a knowing reference to the married actors. But when William's Antonio suggests they simply sleep together, Susanna's Morayma retorts, "One Night might cost me nine long months repenting."[14] She was about four months pregnant with their first child at the time. Whether this was known already or possibly revealed in performance with a wink or a gesture, the liminal space of the epilogue allowed private information to increase comedic effect and create intimacy with audiences.[15] Play texts also contain possible references. Thomas Southerne's *Sir Anthony Love*, in which Mrs. Mountfort acted the title breeches role during her second pregnancy in 1690–91, contains the following exchange:

> *Ilf.* Sir *Anthony*—Sir *Anthony*—a word with you—
> *Sir Ant.* Pr'ythee let me go; I am big with jest, and shall certainly miscarry with the first grave word you say to me.
> *Ilf.* Be deliver'd of your burden then, lay it to my door; I'll father it for a friend.
> *Sir Ant.* As some men wou'd a bastard, for the reputation of getting it.[16]

Even if not initially written as a joke about her pregnancy, by the time she acted this breeches role in her second trimester and beyond, it had become one.[17] Similarly, in 1703 her final new role, Mrs. Whimsey in *The Fair Example*, premiered about six weeks before she gave birth and contains a comment in the final scene about wives' (theoretical) ability to have children independently of their husbands. Mountfort Verbruggen's obvious condition made the comment into a specific visual joke, suggesting that clever Mrs. Whimsey has already duped her undesirable husband. These traces ask us to attend to the way doubly ephemeral performing pregnant bodies have left impressions on archival materials.

The Mountforts' fruitfulness may have contributed to the merry depiction of their relationship on stage by playwrights. Off stage, frequent pregnancies were probably a more complicated proposition. On the one hand, there may have been considerable satisfaction and pride that came from the expected duty of childbearing; on the other, it was difficult and dangerous and took considerable effort to battle through the many symptoms of pregnancy to engage in the physical labor of performance. Though marriage had clear advantages economically and an air of respectability that could aid a woman's career, those advantages came with a loss of bodily and economic autonomy. Legally, Susanna's body was not her own, and she would have no formal and little social recourse to enforce family planning if it was something she desired. We should remember this even as we celebrate the many achievements of the women in this study. In December 1692, William's sudden death left his wife the sole parent to one living child and pregnant with another. After a year of widowhood and single parenting on a salary of 50 shillings a week she married actor Jack Verbruggen on January 31, 1694.[18] Throughout both marriages, whatever her physical and emotional struggles, Mountfort Verbruggen enjoyed a stable and respectable reputation. Aston called her, "the best conversationalist possible: never captious or displeased at anything but what was gross or indecent; for she was cautious lest fiery Jack [Verbruggen] shou'd resent it as to breed a Quarrel."[19] This, as well as playboy George Etherege's testimony that she was a virgin when married and remained a "discreet" (meaning chaste) woman after, suggests a reputation that balanced her performances of transgressive behavior on stage with heteronormative femininity off it, and functioned as a form of charismata.[20]

We know Mountfort Verbruggen performed during her five known pregnancies. Between 1690 and 1692, there is no concrete evidence that she performed into her third trimester. References to pregnancy in epilogues and roles she acted, however, suggest that audiences were aware of her condition, and that authors might use her pregnancies to comedic effect. Her absence from surviving cast lists for new plays during the last three months of her pregnancies may indicate she entered temporary retirement before giving birth, or that she was left out of premieres as her projected birth date approached to minimize the risk that she would go into labor early and disrupt the run.[21] In the latter case, Mountfort Verbruggen may have continued to appear in the older plays that made up much of the day to day repertory of the company but for which we have few surviving records. Because of these archival limitations, I will focus on her pregnancies in 1692–93, when we know she continued to act in new play premieres until very shortly before giving birth, and 1703, when repertory records improve.

Pregnancy, Repertory, and New Play Premieres 1693 and 1703

In the 1692–93 season, Mountfort Verbruggen's roles in a series of new play premieres offer important insight into how pregnancy did—and did not—impact casting and performance (Table 1.1). Susanna Mountfort was pregnant with her fourth child in December 1692 when a young man, who was stalking the actress Anne Bracegirdle, murdered her husband.[22] Despite this catastrophe, pregnant, widowed Susanna was back onstage in January. William Mountfort's death was followed shortly by that of another member of the company, the comedian Tony Leigh. This double blow delayed the premieres of two new plays (Southerne's *The Maid's Last Prayer* and Congreve's *The Old Bachelor*) as Mountfort and Leigh's roles were recast and rehearsed: "We are like to be without new Plays this month or the next; the death of Mr. Mountfort, and that of Mr. Leigh soon after him being partly the cause of this delay."[23] When the new plays were finally brought out in February and March, Susanna was performing her impressive protean transformations well into her

Table 1.1. Susanna Mountfort Verbruggen's Repertoire, 1692–93

Date	Part	Play
Unknown[1]	Nell	*The Devil of a Wife*
Unknown	Lucia	*Epsom Wells*
Unknown	Harriet	*Man of Mode*
Unknown	Leonora	*Sir Courtly Nice*
Unknown	Feliciana	*The Successful Strangers*
November 1692	Eugenia	*The Volunteers**
2 January 1693[2]	Prudentia	*A Duke and No Duke*
Late February 1693	Lady Susan Malepert	*The Maid's Last Prayer**
9–24 March 1693[3]	Belinda	*The Old Bachelor**
Late April 1693[4]	Annabelle	*A Very Good Wife**
May 1693	Catchat	*The Female Virtuosos**

*Indicates premieres.

[1]The editors of *The London Stage* include lists of speculative revivals at the top of each season based on reprintings of plays.

[2]Mountfort Verbruggen held the part of Prudentia in her early days (1684). If she still did, this would be her first known appearance after her husband's death.

[3]Peter Holland dates the premiere from a March 11 letter from Richard Boyle, Earl of Cork, to Congreve's father (*The Ornament of Action: Text and Performance in Restoration Comedy* [Cambridge: Cambridge University Press, 1979], 156). The play ran fourteen nights, ending March 24 if acted six nights per week.

[4]The *LS* gives late April because *The Gentleman's Journal* April issue (printed May) notes that it has already been acted five times. It was probably acted five times in a row, so the very end of April or beginning of May is possible. The play was published in June.

third trimester. After Mary's birth in late March or April, Susanna participated in two further premieres, offering us a chance to compare her prenatal and postpartum casting in a single season (Table 1.1). This is useful because Mountfort Verbruggen's pregnancies in the early 1690s are reasonably well known, but speculation about how they influenced her career has been narrow, confined to analysis of singular examples of casting that leave aside a more holistic view of her experiences.

Her first new part was the title role of Lady Susan Malepert in Thomas Southerne's *The Maid's Last Prayer, or Any rather than Fail* in February, a typical grotesque. Performance historian Gilli Bush-Bailey believes her condition is vital when considering the play's original cast: "*The Maid's Last Prayer* provides an unusual array of colourful characters for the company's leading actresses. Elinor Leigh plays the exotic Siam, while Mary Betterton is unusually cast as

Wishwell, a bawd. Susannah Mountfort was heavily pregnant, which may explain her casting as Lady Susan Malepert, the maid of the title and a character part of a foolish old woman—probably a useful disguise to cover her pregnancy and accommodate any restriction of movement."[24] This reasoning is practical and the attention to embodied experience welcome.[25] But I want to think through how the role might not be aiming to conceal the body but to take advantage of it.

Bush-Bailey's reasoning relies on a complex set of assumptions: the largest are that pregnancy, more than ability, dictated Mountfort Verbruggen's casting in the play and that disguising the pregnancy was a priority. The latter, in turn, presumes that the audience or managers (or both) would object to her pregnant body in a role that required youth and beauty because of concerns about verisimilitude and/or the assumed unattractiveness or indecorousness (the grotesqueness) of the pregnant form.[26] Mountfort Verbruggen's facility with character parts, however, made the role of Lady Susan well within her line of business regardless of her physical condition. As a grotesque part, moreover, incongruity and absurdity would theoretically be a boon rather than a liability. If we allow Mikhail Bakhtin to shade our understanding of the grotesque, we can further appreciate how pregnancy might function as an asset rather than a detriment in the role. Bakhtin describes the grotesque body as "that which protrudes from the body, all that seeks to go out beyond the body's confines . . . it outgrows its own self, trangress[es] its own body, in which it conceives a new, second body."[27] Drawing on grotesque narratives of the gravid body—its swelling convexity that pushes out into the world and refuses to be contained, its associations with sexuality, leakage and bodily fluids, its visible creation of a second body—the pregnant body of the actor becomes one that metatheatrically enhances the character body of Lady Susan Malepert (whose last name points to impudence and brazen disrespect), underscoring her excesses to comic effect.

Lady Susan is described as "that youthful virgin of five and forty, with a swelling rump, bow legs, a shining face, and colly'd eyebrows."[28] This emphasis on the lower stratum of her body reinforces her grotesque status. Her legs and rump are misshapen and large and her movement impaired, for "she hobbles worse than *Abigall* in the Scornful Lady, when she has broke her Crupper"

(1.1.74–76).[29] Desperate for a wedding night yet skittish about her reputation, Lady Susan flatters and deludes herself about the intentions of the men around her. She makes what she thinks are subtle indications of her interest in the handsome Granger (written for William Mountfort), but "she speaks too plain to be understood: She may be in earnest, upon this subject, to herself; but she will always be a jest to me" (3.2.11–13). Independently of Mountfort Verbruggen's pregnancy and the character's lust (which of course audiences might read metatheatrically), she is a grotesque character verbally, peppering her text with loud, compulsive exclamations (O law! Jesu! O Crimine!). She is also grotesque socially—always present, always persistent in forcing her way into any entertainment: "She'd no more miss a Ball, than the curling her little finger, when she eats" (1.1.73–74). Lady Susan overflows the limits of her own body in her size and movement, and of her sex and breeding in her speech and attempts to ensnare younger sexual partners. Though a virgin, she is rapacious socially and sexually, transgressing the bounds of politeness or sense. Though Mountfort Verbruggen would undoubtedly have made a meal of the role regardless of pregnancy, in this case her body natural could enhance and comment on the character body, underscoring Lady Susan's fundamentally grotesque and excessive nature.

Crucially, while this new role may have capitalized on grotesque associations with pregnancy, the next makes it clear that this was not the only way her pregnant body could be read. In March, Mountfort Verbruggen starred as Belinda in William Congreve's highly successful *The Old Bachelor*. Belinda is in the vein of another specialty: pretty and witty young women who profess to detest marriage for most of the play, only to end happily with their faithful gallants at the end. Belinda is described with a dizzying list of adjectives pointing to the mercurial skill Mountfort Verbruggen brought to the role. She is "too proud, too inconstant, too affected, and too witty, and too handsome for a wife."[30] That Mountfort played the part so late in her pregnancy—not more than a month before giving birth and likely much closer to it—suggests that there were no insurmountable objections to her body from the playwright, management, or the public, and that she was capable of adequately playing a beautiful, virginal character despite her visible pregnancy.

One might argue that this is all down to the extraordinary circumstances of the season, and perhaps especially an awareness of the financial precarity she may have faced in the wake of her husband's loss. But while delays to the premiere may have made her condition more obvious, she would still have been about seven months pregnant during a January premiere of *The Old Bachelor*. Mountfort Verbruggen's condition did not cause Congreve or the managers to reassign Belinda to a different performer, even though they had to recast the play anyway after Mountfort and Leigh died.[31] Before she lay in, then, Mountfort Verbruggen created two new parts: if Lady Susan took advantage of her pregnancy for comic effect, inviting the audience to laugh at it, Belinda, as an ingenue, did not and audiences presumably understood they were to ignore it. After Mary's birth, Susanna's casting in new plays continued to emphasize her varied lines of business. She created the new breeches role of Annabella in *A Very Good Wife*, a role clearly involving bodily display, and finished the season with another grotesque, Catchat, in *The Female Virtuosos*. Her repertoire of new parts immediately before and after the birth of her daughter show the elasticity of her full range unhampered by pregnancy: two plucky young heroines and two older comic women. Analyzing pregnancy's impact without a complete analysis of the actress's repertoire can create a false sense of the priorities and considerations at play for authors, managers, and performers.

Mountfort Verbruggen's range is again on display in 1703 when we have a more complete sense of her repertoire, including roles in stock plays and revivals. In the four months before she gave birth to her full-term son in May 1703, Mountfort Verbruggen, now in her midthirties, performed her full slate of comic types: breeches roles like Charlot Welldon in *Oroonoko* and Hellena in *The Rover*; witty young women like Hillaria in the new play *Turnbridge Walks* (premiered early/mid-January); attractive older women like Lady Lurewell in *The Constant Couple*, the clever wife Mrs. Whimsey in another new piece, *The Fair Example* (premiered mid-April); and the grotesque Gillian Homebread in *The Bath, or The Western Lass*. While the spotty repertory records for her earlier career make it uncertain, Mountfort Verbruggen's 1703 repertoire may well reflect her common practice: to remain on stage throughout pregnancy, visibly balancing professional and maternal labor.[32] Looking at her career across time, we can see how such practices became integral to her career's development by helping her cultivate this line of grotesque characters even while she continued to act her other specialties.

Pregnancy and the Development of the Grotesque, 1690–1692

As previously noted, playwrights capitalized on Mountfort Verbruggen's personal circumstances, including marriage and pregnancy, to enhance comedy. Pregnancy, in particular, could facilitate the transformation of Mrs. Mountfort into a grotesque like Lady Susan. And there are reasons to consider Lady Susan a culmination rather than a beginning of this trend.

During her second pregnancy in 1690–91 (when she also acted the eponymous breeches role in *Sir Anthony Love* while pregnant), Mountfort Verbruggen performed Phaedra in Dryden's *Amphitryon*, an uncouth peasant who cuckolds her husband with the god Mercury and dreams of making her eldest illegitimate daughter a King's mistress. That year or the following, she also acted the incorrigible, aging Abigail in Beaumont and Fletcher's *The Scornful Lady.*[33] Abigail (described as a "skin full of lust" and a "foul familiar") attempts to seduce any man who crosses her path.[34] Young Loveless declares, "She offered me once to know her: to this day she loves Youth of Eighteen. . . . She lov'd all the Players, in the last Queen's time, once over: She was struck when they acted Lovers, and forsook some when they played Murtherers."[35] Abigail is insatiable, preying on young men and running through entire companies of players. She is also imperceptive: she neither sees the repulsion she causes nor can she tell the difference between fiction and reality in the playhouse. Given the joke in *The Maid's Last Prayer* about Lady Susan's similarity to Abigail, Mountfort Verbruggen almost certainly played the part before the February 1693 premiere of Southerne's play. Since she was visibly pregnant for much of 1690–91, 1691–92, and 1692–93 she likely also appeared in the role while pregnant, metatheatrically enhancing the character's grotesque and excessive sexual desire. Indeed, the reference in *The Maid's Last Prayer* may suggest that Mountfort Verbruggen's performance of Abigail inspired Lady Susan, and that pregnancy enhanced her performance of both roles.

During Susanna's third pregnancy in 1691–92, we are on firmer ground with repertory records. That season, Thomas Southerne's experimental comedy *The Wives' Excuse, or Cuckholds Make Themselves* premiered in December, three to four months before Mountfort Verbruggen gave birth on March 22. She played the role of Mrs. Wittwoud, a lecherous older woman.[36] Wittwoud, like Lady Susan, is associated with excess: in this case, her pimping ways, which give men access to "as many [women] as you please, and as often as you have occasion."[37] She noses into and gossips about the business of those around her, and aims at the downfall of two virtuous women in the play. Theater historians Judith Milhous and Robert D. Hume theorize her casting as follows:

> The role of Mrs. Friendall was created by Elizabeth Barry, a piece of casting which raises some questions. Barry was about thirty-three. . . . She had done some highly pathetic roles . . . but by this time the authors were generally casting Barry in more lurid parts. . . . A more obvious choice for Mrs. Friendall . . . would have been Susanna Mountfort (then twenty-four). . . . Finding Mrs. Mountfort cast as Mrs. Wittwoud—a tough, scheming female rake, rather long in the tooth—is a surprise: Barry would seem to have been a natural for the role. We have no evidence about Southerne's casting plans when he wrote *The Wives Excuse* in early 1691, but . . . by the time of the premiere in December Mrs. Mountfort could not plausibly have taken the part of the younger, trimmer Mrs. Friendall: she was five months pregnant.[38]

There are assumptions about age and appearance in this assessment, just as in Bush-Bailey's account of *The Maid's Last Prayer*, that may or may not be relevant to how casting unfolded. After all, Mountfort Verbruggen was also five months pregnant when she acted Sir Anthony Love the previous year. Given her later appearance as Belinda just prior to Mary's birth in 1693, and the possible continuation of her stock roles throughout each of her pregnancies, the imperative of plausibility is also questionable. The suggestion that the casting changed as a result of her pregnancy may not be false—physical accommodation of pregnant performers is certainly a significant consideration—but there are also reasons to consider that the play was performed as its author always intended.

In many ways, it makes sense to cast a woman with success in tragedy (like Barry) as the ill-starred Mrs. Friendall, whose dubious "happy" ending is a painful separation from her husband that leaves her isolated and unable to remarry. Putting Mountfort Verbruggen in the role would use almost none of her comic talent. It is not, furthermore, as surprising to see Mountfort Verbruggen a female rake if we consider that this is similar to the part she played successfully in *Sir Anthony Love* the year before. Add to this the plotting in *The Wives' Excuse* that reveals the Mountforts' characters *in flagrante* to both their disappointments at the end of the play and the casting may be less concerned with making allowances for a pregnancy than with best deploying the company's talents. The part, in fact, may be explicitly playing up the comic potential of Mountfort Verbruggen's pregnant body by casting her as a woman adept at pawning illegitimate pregnancies off on unsuspecting husbands. In act 2, scene 1, her cousin Teazle warns her, "You may have occasion for an Husband, when you can't get one, Husbands are not always to be had at a month's warn'ng, to finish another Man's work."[39] In short, if Mountfort Verbruggen's pregnant body played a part in the casting, it does not necessarily follow that the decision or the result was punitive for the actress or her career; it seems to have become an advantage.

From 1693 onward Mountfort Verbruggen began adding grotesque characters to her repertoire regularly regardless of pregnancy, but each of the initial forays into this line of business came during a pregnancy in its second or third trimester. While many of the plays surveyed here were not successes, her facility with grotesque parts encouraged further opportunities to pursue this line of business. In 1694–95, her success as Mary the Buxom in Thomas D'Urfey's *Don Quixote* contributed to the play's eventual expansion to three parts, with the finale featuring Mary's marriage. Though premiering a play with a pregnant actress might be a greater financial or practical risk than performing a stock play, the example of *The Old Bachelor* in 1693 as well as the diversity of parts Mountfort Verbruggen played in 1703 should caution against making generalizations about the treatment of the pregnant body on stage. Taken together, what we know of her casting throughout these pregnancies suggests that rather than restricting or sidelining Mountfort Verbruggen, pregnancy opened and enhanced new avenues for her singular talents.

Mountfort Verbruggen died in the late summer of 1703, followed not long after by her son, tragedies standing in stark contrast to the comedic lives she had lived on stage but all too familiar to many of her auditors and compatriots. Unlike the outpourings of grief at William Mountfort's death, we are left to wonder in her case if audiences experienced personal griefs again when they learned of her death. Did pregnant women who had seen her perform feel additional anxiety for their impending deliveries? Did they mourn her loss? One of her popular roles was Charlot Welldon in *Oroonoko*, which Drury Lane performed on October 21, 1703, not long after her death and that of her son. Did audiences think of the lost Mrs. Verbruggen when Oroonoko (at Lincoln's Inn Fields, the possession of her widowed husband) mourned over the body of pregnant Imoinda? Who acted Charlot, competing with Mountfort Verbruggen's memory? Her death and other changes to the theater meant the loss of many of the roles she made popular, including the line of grotesques initially yoked to her annual pregnancies in the 1690s. Some of what she excelled at survived, however, including witty heroines and breeches roles that passed to other women in the company. One of those women was Anne Oldfield, who had been sharing the stage at Drury Lane with Mountfort Verbruggen for four years.

Anne Oldfield (1683–1730)

> Her Person was infinitely graceful, her Nature majestic, her Behaviour so inchanting, and her Conversation so agreeable, that, during her whole Life, She was in the highest Esteem with Persons of the greatest Wit and Quality in the Kingdom.
>
> —*Authentick Memoirs of the Life of That Celebrated Actress Mrs. Ann Oldfield*

Anne Oldfield was born in Pall Mall in 1683, daughter of Anne Oldfield the elder and her husband. Supposedly discovered by George Farquhar while reading a play out loud at the Mitre Tavern, she joined the Drury Lane company in 1699.[40] In later life, she was

Figure 1.1. Edward Fisher after Jonathan Richardson, *Anne Oldfield* (ca. 1760–1785), © National Portrait Gallery, London

described as tall and beautiful with dark hair, "speaking" eyes, pale skin, and an aristocratic mien (Figure 1.1).[41] Oldfield began chiefly in comedy, and her merit was recognized with prologues and epilogues and the granting of a benefit. According to Colley Cibber, however, she did not receive what we might call her "big break" until she inherited valuable parts after Susanna Verbruggen's death in 1703, including Leonora (*Sir Courtly Nice*), Narcissa (*Love's Last Shift*), Hellena (*The Rover*), Florella (*Greenwich Park*), Elvira (*Spanish Fryer*), Celia (*Volpone*), and Lady Lurewell (*The Constant Couple*).[42] These were vital to her development as a performer—opportunities to draw audience attention, demonstrate range, and distinguish herself from other players. She attained ascendency in sparkling, witty fine ladies of comedy early in her career, and by 1712–13 was building a reputation in tragedy as well. That year, like Susanna Mountfort Verbruggen before her, she found herself performing, pregnant, after the death of a partner. In Oldfield's case, her unmarried status, rumored sexual history, and professional success opened her to moral attacks that aimed to render her grotesquely sexual in print publications. She largely countered these attacks from the stage, where every new part that season cast her as a classical heroine of unimpeachable virtue worthy of admiration.

Though rumored to have had other affairs, two long-term relationships with political men dominated Anne Oldfield's romantic life.[43] The first, beginning about 1703, was with writer and Member of Parliament (MP) Arthur Maynwaring, friend and sometime secretary to Sarah Churchill, Duchess of Marlborough. Oldfield and Maynwaring were reportedly devoted to each other, and he wrote epilogues for her to perform and perhaps aided her career through his social connections to playwrights, managers, and proprietors.[44] They remained together until Maynwaring's death in 1712 and had at least two children: Arthur Jr., born in July or August 1709, and a stillborn or short-lived child in May 1713.[45] In 1709 Oldfield, because of the pregnancy, disputes with managers, or both, stopped performing in mid-April when about five months pregnant.[46] In 1712–13, in contrast, she remained on stage nearly until the birth; it is this pregnancy I will focus on. Sometime in 1714, Oldfield began a relationship with Lieutenant-General Charles Churchill, illegitimate nephew of the Duke of Marlborough. This relationship lasted until her death in 1730 and, along with continued successes in the theater, this period of her life brought additional social prominence and acceptance. The couple had one son, Charles, in 1720, and Oldfield—the same age at which Mountfort Verbruggen had died after giving birth—took an extended hiatus during this pregnancy.

Oldfield's relatively low birth rate and long birth intervals may suggest she engaged in family planning. As an unmarried woman with her own household, her sexual and reproductive labor was not the legal property of either of the men with whom she had long-term relationships, nor was she dependent on them for a place to live. Remaining unmarried also meant the money Oldfield earned was hers and could not be coopted by her partners, an additional form of agency and independence. That she retired at age thirty-seven during her 1720 pregnancy indicates that for reasons of personal preference, propriety, health, or comfort, she had the economic resources not to return to the theater until after her son's birth.

Though there were rumors Oldfield and Churchill had married, she acted as a *feme sole* in the disposal of her considerable estate in her will when she died a wealthy woman in 1730. She was interred in Westminster Abbey beneath the monument to William Congreve, one testament to her prominence. After her death, biographical publications quickly appeared and helped further solidify and affirm her celebrity status and identity. The anonymously authored *Authentick Memoirs of the Life of That Celebrated Actress, Mrs. Ann Oldfield* (London, 1730) was eight pages in its first edition, but nearly fifty by its third. The second, *Faithful Memoirs of the Life, Amours, and Performances of That Justly Celebrated, and Most Eminent Actress of Her Time, Mrs. Anne Oldfield* (London, 1731) came from bookseller Edmund Curll, using the pseudonym William Egerton. Margaret Saunders, to whom Curll dedicated the book, was a companion to Oldfield and likely the biography's primary source. This memoir was reissued in 1741 under the name *Memoirs of Mrs. Oldfield* (authorship attributed to William Oldys) and also appended to "Thomas Betterton's" (Edmund Curll and William Oldys's) *The History of the English Stage, from the Restoration to the Present Time.* Both early biographies should be used cautiously but attest to Oldfield's popularity and the versions of her life and celebrity that the sellers thought would be most profitable. Oldfield also features prominently, and perhaps more accurately, in Colley Cibber's *An Apology for the Life of Mr. Colley Cibber* (1740).

One remarkable font of Oldfield's celebrity power was her apparent ability to be or become the parts she played. Her transformations were of a slightly different order than Mountfort Verbruggen's shapeshifting, however, for the commonalities between Oldfield's characters (namely their refined wit and elevated social status) suggested that these were elements of the woman herself. Oldfield bolstered this image by taking the unusual step of wearing her costumes straight through from the pre-performance dinner onto the stage, and then to the parties and entertainments she attended afterward. Her most popular roles also encouraged this conflation. Oldfield's signature comic role, for example, was Lady Betty Modish in Colley Cibber's *The Careless Husband* (1704). Lady Betty is a witty woman of fashion who positively rejects the idea of marriage with her faithful suitor, Morelove. After a complicated plot to rouse her jealousy, however, Lady Betty sets aside her fears of losing her independence and agrees to marry. Like many a dramatic heroine, love tames Lady Betty's forward ways and circumscribes her safely into the bounds of patriarchal marriage. Begun with Susanna Mountfort Verbruggen in mind, Cibber initially set the play aside after her death until Oldfield's performance of Leonora in *Sir Courtly Nice* (inherited from Mountfort Verbruggen) inspired him to finish the play. In its final form, it was modeled directly on Oldfield: "There are many Sentiments in the Character of Lady *Betty Modish*, that I may say, were originally [Mrs. Oldfield's] own. . . . Had her Birth plac'd her in a higher Rank of Life, she had certainly appear'd, in reality, what in this Play she only, excellently, acted."[47] As Lady Betty, Oldfield's penchant for fine clothing, her wit, and her natural gentility encouraged the conflation of actress and character. Curll declared: "It was not the Part of Lady *Betty Modish*, represented by Mrs. OLDFIELD; but it was the real Mrs. OLDFIELD, who appeared in the Character of Lady *Betty Modish*."[48] Though Oldfield did not marry—and thus retained her financial and sexual independence—she did seem to have Lady Betty's hidden depths of feeling and true loyalty during both of her extended romantic partnerships.

Loyalty was a key virtue in the line of tragic parts Oldfield began to develop in earnest around Maynwaring's death. Her moving performances of grieving and repentant women fostered tolerance toward her private liaisons and were credited with providing the audience with moral instruction. As a performer and prominent public figure, Oldfield possessed what Felicity Nussbaum calls "exceptional virtue . . . a new kind of double standard for a commercial age in which the extraordinary talent of star actresses opportunely substituted for respectability."[49] Contrary to notions of feminine virtue dominated by the idea of chastity, actresses laid claim to something "closer to masculine *virtù*, marked by natural judgment, by the ability to deliberately carve out an autonomous identity, and to make appropriate ethical decisions based upon personal convictions."[50] After her death, for example, one of Oldfield's biographers praised her for *not* marrying Charles Churchill: by sacrificing the respectability that would come with the position, she preserved the inheritance of her elder son. Oldfield's maternal sacrifice, based on her personal ethical code and bolstered by her performances of loyal noblewomen onstage, rendered her more respectable than women who remarried with no regard for their children.[51] Oldfield's comedies brought her fame and fortune; her tragic roles lent depth and a measure of respectability to her nonconventional relationships.[52] Here, I focus on Oldfield's pregnancy with the posthumous child of Arthur Maynwaring born in May 1713, which paralleled both her first sustained, successful forays into tragedy and highly sexualized slanders of her circulating beyond the theater. In acting tragic noblewomen roles in the wake of Maynwaring's death and her pregnancy with his final child, Oldfield's stage performances of classical containment countered attacks that aimed to render her stigmatically grotesque.

Pregnancy and Tragedy, 1712–13

The road to Oldfield's eventual status as leading lady in both comedy and tragedy was neither easy nor swift. Her abilities were not in question, but sustaining a tragic line was difficult before 1712.[53] Oldfield had joined Owen Swiny's company at Queen's in 1706–07 (supposedly leading to Anne Bracegirdle's retirement), returned to Drury the following year, then left again in the spring of 1709 after a managerial dispute, rejoining Betterton's company at the Queen's. She returned to Drury Lane in 1710 under the new management of Colley Cibber, Thomas Doggett, Robert Wilks, and Owen Swiny, and remained there the rest of her career.[54] The splitting, combining, and reconfiguring of the companies in these years meant additional competition and conflicts around part assignments, as well as periodic opportunities. For example, Oldfield benefited from the exit or absence of other tragic actresses: Anne Bracegirdle retired in 1707, Elizabeth Barry retired in 1710, and while Jane Rogers lay in with her fourth child in 1709 Oldfield was the replacement who acted the Countess of Rutland in *The Unhappy Favorite* and Imoinda in *Oroonoko*.[55] Barry's retirement brought a more permanent assignment, Anna Bullen in *Virtue Betray'd*, but a new role, one that could be entirely her own, was elusive. Lacking this, making a mark as a tragic performer was a formidable challenge, for audience memory and expectation were shaped by the other women's embodiment and interpretation of character. This is one manifestation of the phenomenon Marvin Carlson refers to as "ghosting," whereby the audience's accreted memories of performers, texts, spaces, and other material influence reception and interpretation of a performance.[56] When staking a claim to tragedy, a new role would allow Oldfield to circumvent direct comparison with more established tragediennes.

Oldfield's stutter-steps into tragedy finally resolved in the spring of 1712, when she was given—or perhaps stole—the title role in Ambrose Philips's *The Distrest Mother*.[57] Philips's play, an adaptation of Racine's *Andromaque*, was a huge success at its premiere on March 17 and joined Lady Betty as a signature role for the rest of her career. The play and the character were puffed in *The Spectator* for being of a superior order, for "we have seldom had any Female Distress on the Stage, which did not . . . flow from the Weakness rather than the Misfortune of the Person represented: But in this Tragedy you are not entertained with the ungoverned Passions . . . the Character which gives Name to the Play, is one who has behaved her self with heroic Virtue in the most important Circumstances of a Female Life, those of a Wife, a Widow, and a Mother."[58] The assertion that the play did not indulge "weakness" and "ungoverned Passions" is important. Oldfield was not playing a morally compromised character swept away by love or lust that might invite parallels to her private life. She was playing a character of "heroic Virtue" and idealized femininity. In his memoir of Oldfield, Edmund Curll singled out the part for particular praise: "What harden'd Heart wept not with *Andromache*? What Mother did she not instruct in Maternal Love when *Astyanax*'s Danger wrings her Soul?"[59] More than simply appealing to the audience as a piece of fiction, Curll suggests Oldfield's performance taught women in the audience what true maternal grief looked and sounded like. Written retrospectively, Curll's observation takes in the totality of Oldfield's performances and personal story, not simply her first appearances. Deeply relevant to this were her repetitions of the part after Arthur Maynwaring's death, which helped her claim the status of grieving widow and refute characterizations of her body as contaminated and grotesque even as it became ever more visibly pregnant.

The Distrest Mother

The Distrest Mother is set in the aftermath of the Trojan War. Pyrrhus, the Greek hero, coerces the Trojan princess Andromache, Hector's widow, into marrying him in order to secure her son's birthright to the throne of Troy. In this arrangement, which pits maternal love against wifely fidelity, Andromache spies a loophole. She plans to die by suicide immediately after the wedding, fulfilling her part of the bargain while remaining loyal to Hector and trusting that Pyrrhus's honor will force him to abide by their arrangement concerning her son. Meanwhile, Hermione, daughter of Menelaus and Helen of Troy, loves Pyrrhus and is beloved by Orestes. When Hermione learns of Pyrrhus's plan to marry Andromache, she persuades Orestes to kill Pyrrhus on the wedding day. Ultimately, an angry mob of Greeks murders Pyrrhus at the wedding altar, Hermione dies by suicide, Orestes runs mad, and Andromache resumes her throne as regent until her son, Astyanax, is of age. The boy's youth and innocence are emphasized throughout the play, suggesting he is too young to be aware of his father's death or the machinations of those around him and perhaps justifying the fact that he makes no appearance on stage. Though maternal distress is the primary pathetic display within the play, it ends with only the promise, not the realization, of a reunion between mother and son.[60]

In 1712–13 Oldfield acted Andromache frequently, on September 27, October 18, November 25, December 22, February 10, and April 13. These performances spanned her entire pregnancy, from the earliest days of possible awareness through illness, fatigue, breast tenderness, and amenorrhea to growing certainty as November approached; quickening by the performance in December; a likely growing belly and loosening hips, perhaps with the return of energy and appetite, and a need for adjustments to costuming in February; and finally to changes in movement, growing fullness, and diminished lung capacity in April. Her performances were universally advertised as audience requests, "by desire" or "particular desire" of "several Ladies" or "Persons" "of Quality." Such requests sanctioned Oldfield's performance of nobility by those best able to judge its validity. Her performance on November 25 was especially poignant, as it was also her first appearance after Maynwaring's death. This event enters the historical record powerfully in both of Oldfield's posthumous biographies and is noted in Joanne Lafler and J. D. Phillipson's analyses of Oldfield's life and pregnancies.[61] Here, I want to add a more sustained consideration of how repetitions of the play, including the comic epilogue largely ignored in Lafler's and Phillipson's analyses, mattered to Oldfield's reputation in the short and long term.

In his *Faithful Memoirs* (1731) Curll observes that after Arthur Maynwaring's death, "*The Distressed Mother* seemed now to be the Case of Mrs. Oldfield both on, and off, the Stage."[62] *Authentick Memoirs* (1730) goes further, claiming Oldfield actually brought three-year-old Arthur onstage while delivering the epilogue on November 25, offering audiences the closure denied them in fiction by uniting mother and son while highlighting the continuing tragedy of Anne and Arthur's offstage loss. Her auditors, supposedly "charm'd herewith, because there was then some Similitude between the Circumstances of *Andromache* and herself, both having lost a Friend and Patron," responded strongly.[63] While there is no corroborating evidence for this anecdote, the story is a powerful testament to the affective potential of public performances of maternity, whether fictional, real, or some combination of both. In both eighteenth-century biographers' accounts, a fictional role frames and draws attention to a private tragedy, generating audience sympathy and support for Oldfield's condition as a single mother. In the story of Arthur's appearance, Oldfield actively manipulates the threshold space of the epilogue, reinforcing the public/private conflation already central to her celebrity. Drawing a parallel between her own situation and that of the fictional character raises herself from a political mistress to a widowed queen and her illegitimate young son to a prince. Arthur's presence changes both play and epilogue, but even if he never appeared, her pregnancy might do the same. At each repetition of *The Distrest Mother*, particularly the final one in April 1713 when she was eight months pregnant, Oldfield's condition became more and more visible. Visible pregnancy added viscerally to the plight of the character Andromache—who now confronts the horror of sacrificing herself *and* her unborn child to save Astyanax—and of Oldfield herself—who is facing everything from financial uncertainty to a death in childbirth that would leave Arthur orphaned. In 1712–13, pregnancy helped solidify and enhance the conflation of public and private in Oldfield's tragic performances of Andromache just as her wit, fashion sense, and relationship with Maynwaring had encouraged conflations with Lady Betty Modish.

The play's epilogue was exceptionally popular, "greatly contribut[ing] to the Run" of the play at its premiere and always "insisted on" at subsequent performances.[64] The piece celebrated Andromache's triumph over Pyrrhus and subsequent coronation as queen of Troy. It was a major tonal shift from the play itself—noble she-tragedy to arch sexual comedy—but one that capitalized on Oldfield's specific talents. Particularly at her first performances of Andromache, the epilogue allowed Oldfield to draw on her established success with witty comedy even as she sought new ground in tragedy:

> I Hope you'll own, that with becoming Art
> I've play'd my Game, and topp'd the Widow's Part.[65]
> My Spouse, poor Man! could not live out the Play,
> By dy'd commodiously on Wedding-Day:
> While I, his Relict, made at one bold Fling
> My self a Princess, and young Sty a King.
>
> . . . .
>
> 'Twas a strange Scape! Had Pyrrhus liv'd till now
> I had been finely hamper'd in my Vow.
> To die by one's own Hand,[66] and fly the Charms
> Of Love and Life in a young Monarch's Arms!
> 'Twere an hard Fate—ere I had undergone it
> I might have took one Night—to think upon it.
> But why, you'll say was all this Grief exprest

For a first Husband, laid long since at Rest?
Why so much Coldness to my kind Protector?
—Ah Ladies! had you known the good Man Hector!

. . . .

At length howe'er I laid my Weeds aside,
And sunk the Widow in the well-dress'd Bride.
In you it still remains to grace the Play,
And bless with Joy my Coronation Day:
Take then, ye Circles of the Brave and Fair,
The Fatherless and Widow to your Care.[67]

Epilogues, especially those performed by women, commonly poked fun at the play and/or the character played by the epilogue's performer. This one drew on Oldfield's woman-of-fashion persona and her position as a sexually active and attractive woman. Unlike Andromache, Oldfield would have taken "one night" with Pyrrhus to "think" before making her noble sacrifice. Defending the decision to pair a saucy comic epilogue with a tragic play, its author Eustace Budgell insisted, "The Moment the Play ends, Mrs. *Oldfield* is no more *Andromache*, but Mrs. *Oldfield*."[68] Oldfield's performance afforded the ability to see this transformation from grieving widow and self-sacrificing mother to vivacious and alluring actress, which in turn made the skill of both more legible.

If and when Oldfield brought her actual child onstage, however, and more importantly when the audience was acutely aware of Maynwaring's death and her developing pregnancy, the theoretically clear shift from character to actress blurred. The speech's ending is considerably more sober when considered in light of the visual spectacle of Oldfield and Arthur as relicts of the deceased Maynwaring (Hector). What was normally a bit of comic relief, teasing the audience with the difference between Oldfield and Andromache, now allowed their similitude to dominate. The "Fatherless and Widow" were not abstract or fictional concepts, but two—increasingly, three—living entities suffering a recent bereavement. Similarly, it is not truly the *play* that the "Circles of the Brave and Fair" are being asked to care for, but the actress and her children.

This new iteration of familiar material—what Lisa Freeman calls the palimpsestic layering of repeated events into the memories of those present and into the archival record—suggested that it was not the comic epilogue that best showcased the "real" Anne Oldfield, but instead the performance of Andromache: the principled woman who abjures a conqueror's bed and will sacrifice herself to save her son.[69] What was typically a conventional bid for support of the author and his play or an opportunity for the leading lady to flirt with her audience became far more urgent and also more tragic. If each iteration of the *Distrest Mother* and its epilogue were ghosted by her previous appearances in the part, yet also accumulated meaning as her circumstances or performances changed, then it is possible Oldfield herself conveyed an entirely different reading of the epilogue intentionally, playing up the tragic rather than the bawdy subtext of references to "the good man Hector" and the "Fatherless" child she now carried. Perhaps, regardless of the literal truth of the anecdote about young Arthur, she created such a powerful sense that the personal was on display through her pregnant performances that it later seemed possible her young son—at the time of those reflections the only Maynwaring child living—had been standing on stage beside her. That she was praised for her clear-eyed, selfless maternity and loyal dedication to her romantic partners in biographies decades later is not solely the by-product of a desire to capitalize on her death or rewrite problematic narratives, but also years of creating and reinscribing such narratives on and off the stage. Her pregnant performances in the wake of Maynwaring's death were crucial to defining both her repertoire and her reputation.

Pregnancy, the Grotesque, and Oldfield's Rhetorical Performances

Oldfield's performance of the faithful wife and tragic widow asserted a nobility to her status as grieving partner that powerfully countered calumnies that circulated about her after Maynwaring's death. These highly sexualized attacks were further refuted in the other tragic roles she undertook: more heroines drawn from neoclassical sources whose filial loyalty and stoic resolve in the pursuit of honor and justice are their defining characteristics. Though not all were successful, they are important examples of the "didactic nature" of Oldfield's stage roles which, in Felicity Nussbaum's words, "[help] to balance her personal inadequacies."[70] In the 1712–13 season,

Oldfield's tragic roles attempted to capitalize on the success of her portrayal of Andromache while giving her myriad opportunities to display a character body–body natural hybrid on stage that stood in direct opposition to grotesque readings of her body in published attacks. In these parts, the skill she displayed relied on mastery of both passionate emotion and her increasing pregnancy, presenting classically controlled and contained character bodies fused to her disciplined body natural.

Oldfield took two weeks off after Arthur Maynwaring's passing on November 13.[71] In the wake of his death, rumors—perhaps spread by Tory enemies of Maynwaring's—began that Oldfield had given him a fatal venereal disease. In response, she ordered an autopsy in front of several witnesses, seeking and receiving medical proof that Maynwaring's body (and hence her own) was not corrupt.[72] These attacks revived accusations from the previous spring that had appeared in a document entitled *The Justification of the Letter to Sir John Stanley*. Stanley had served as a secretary in the Lord Chamberlain's office for a nearly fourteen years and was involved in helping mediate actor-manager disputes. In *The Justification*, the author suggests unfair bias toward Oldfield that has left two favorites (Letitia Cross and Jane Rogers) off the stage.[73] The insinuation that Oldfield is receiving preferential treatment quickly turns sexual and vicious. The author refers to "having once felt the stinging effects of her Love" and wishes that "Dr Wall" (a pock-doctor) were still alive to "[purify] the whole mass of her blood, which had been corrupted by a series of complicated distempers."[74] He claims that failing the assistance of this doctor Oldfield had to go to the extreme of trepanning, a dire treatment for late-stage syphilis that had impacted the bones of the skull.[75] Finally, hearing her benefit is shortly to take place, he advises her to ask a crown of each of her lovers, "by which means, if the House were a good deal larger than it is, she would be always sure of its being full."[76] Here Oldfield's body is the worst kind of grotesque: her blood corrupted, her brain swelling and leaking from her skull, "stinging" disease in her lower parts, and so insatiably sexual she could fill a theater with her lovers. When similar rumors revived in the fall of 1712, they suggested Oldfield was not the respectable widow she tried to play, but a monstrous figure misruled by appetite and disease.

The attacks did not stop after the autopsy. The day before her February 10 performance of Andromache, Oldfield's sexual conduct was called into question in the Tory paper *The Examiner*. It had recently come to public attention that Maynwaring had made Oldfield the executrix of his estate, essentially bestowing on her the status of lawful widow, exactly the role she was performing in Andromache.[77] *The Examiner* countered by reading this validation not as the result of trust and affection, but lust for "a *Celebrated Actress*, who is too much admired upon the Stage, to have any Enquiry made into her conduct behind the Curtain."[78] Maynwaring's Whig compatriots were no better, defending him against numerous accusations but conceding his relationship with Oldfield was misguided and lamentable. A little over two months later, in April, more attacks on her sexual health appeared again just as the theater strove to squeeze every shilling out of Joseph Addison's *Cato* before Oldfield went into labor.

Noting the vehemence of these attacks, biographer Joanne Lafler suggests Oldfield remained on stage that year during her pregnancy because she no longer cared for her reputation once Maynwaring was gone. Phillipson disagrees, as do I, arguing the attacks would come regardless of what she did and that remaining on stage was a deliberate strategy to counteract them. Oldfield was a high-profile figure in her own right and had recently been accused of sleeping her way to the top within the company, slights these accusations built on. Her relationship with Maynwaring exacerbated her visibility and its political stakes, for he was the favorite of the now-disgraced Marlboroughs; there also was a volatile political situation that year with Queen Anne's failing health and rumors of Jacobite plots which exacerbated tensions between political camps. For Oldfield, maintaining her position in such circumstances ensured a continued salary and enabled her to counter attacks outside the theater with her performances inside it. Oldfield's performances in tragedy fused her body natural to classical, heroic character bodies: rather than displaying contamination, greed, and excess, she offered contained, controlled, proper feeling.

The first of these fusions was Andromache. Three others followed, all new parts. The first two roles were adapted from French sources and thus in the neoclassical vein. The third was Marcia in Joseph Addison's phenomenally successful *Cato*. I have already noted that the attacks on Oldfield, perhaps not coincidentally, corresponded with her repetitions of Andromache. They also corresponded with her appearances in these new parts. She played the title role in Cibber's tragicomedy *Ximena, or The Heroick Daughter* in late November after ordering Maynwaring's autopsy, and debuted Emelia in the near-tragic *Cinna's Conspiracy* in mid-February just after the attack in *The Examiner*.[79] In April or May, a lewd poem on the popularity of *Cato* included the accusation that Oldfield had gonorrhea.[80] Her stage roles intentionally or incidentally, then, functioned as responses to the attacks. I will return to Marcia in a moment. Ximena and Emelia are daughters whose attempts to avenge their fathers' deaths put them in conflict with either their love interest, the current ruler, or both. Though each play offered a romantic pairing for Oldfield's characters, these romances were subsumed to questions of honor and filial duty. Oldfield's new heroines inclined to Bakhtin's classical body, exercising exacting restraint and discipline around matters of chastity and honor, and standing as exemplars of an idealized femininity that recognized and submitted to rightful patriarchal control. Audiences repeatedly watched Oldfield discipline her sexual and romantic passions in fiction and her pregnant body outside it.

This theme of bodily discipline was reinforced by Oldfield's mastery of the Augustan performance style, rooted in control of the passions and the ability to move between them swiftly and clearly. Joseph Roach describes it thus: "As long as rhetorical theories of acting prevailed, the esteem in which an actor was held by his public seems to have depended on the degree to which he was perceived as capable of keeping his bodily powers in check . . . the actor/orator of the seventeenth century sought to acquire inhibitions."[81] Helen Brooks argues that while such conceptions of acting ability are almost always coded male, women's roles, particularly in she-tragedy, involved similarly complex displays of control and restraint. Though Oldfield's tragic heroines were often passionate, buffeted by fate and pulled apart by the conflict of love and honor, the refined power such displays required "paradoxically . . . demonstrate[d] her agency and exceptional physical skill and control."[82] Emilia, the heroine of *Cinna's Conspiracy*, for example, begins the play describing the wild emotions she is subject to as she meditates on her enemy, Augustus, and the man she loves, Cinna, who has vowed to help her in her revenge:

Abandon's then to my impetuous Rage,
I meditate a thousand Deaths on *Caesar*,
Yet in the transports of a Wrath so just,
I *Cinna* love, more than I hate *Augustus*. . . .
When on the frightful Dangers I reflect,
On which I may precipitate my *Cinna*,
My self I irritate against my self.[83]

In performance, the tempestuous nature of Emelia's passion relied on Oldfield's carefully planned and executed changes from rage to love to fear to agitation. *Ximena*, the more successful of the two plays and Oldfield's choice for her benefit that year, faces an even more impossible quandary: she believes the man she loves has killed her father, and honor demands she seek his death in recompense.[84] Though the decision is agonizing, she does as honor dictates and chooses filial duty over passionate love, mastering the desires of her heart and body.

Oldfield's burgeoning tragic career was marked by displays of fidelity and control. Even her stock parts in comedy could contribute, demonstrating (as the flip from tragedy to comedy did at the end of *The Distrest Mother*) the self-possessed facility with which this actress moved from role to role, genre to genre, and passion to passion. Oldfield's tragic roles positioned her as the possessor of an exceptional virtue rooted in bodily control, filial loyalty, patriotism, and a dual vision of virtuous maternity stemming from her performances of Andromache and from the spectacle of Oldfield the working mother, persistently visible as her pregnancy progressed. In fact, though her condition could be associated with wantonness or grotesque corporeality, the belief that excessive sexual activity—especially with multiple partners—made conception nearly impossible might also serve to counter those same accusations.[85] Her pregnant body could be read in a multiplicity of ways; the question was how and to what degree Oldfield and her allies were able to control the narrative.

Pregnancy and British Tragedy

Marcia in Addison's *Cato*, Oldfield's final new part of the 1712–13 season, shows yet a third daughter setting filial loyalty above personal happiness. *Cato* opened on April 14, 1713, the day after Oldfield's last appearance as Andromache. Written by Addison and embraced by both his fellow Whigs and the Tories, the play was an unprecedented success, running a record-setting twenty consecutive nights, excluding benefit nights.[86] Unlike the French adaptations she starred in earlier in the season, this was an English tragedy and, as Lisa Freeman has shown, presented as a cleansing corrective to foreign influence on the stage.[87] Oldfield's portrayal of Marcia put her once again in the role of the unflinchingly loyal daughter who disciplines herself against passion. In this case, the extended run of the play also (and increasingly) showcased the discipline Oldfield was able to exert over her body natural as she appeared to be staving off childbirth to please the public.

The play is set at Utica and centers on Cato the Younger, who elects death by suicide rather than bow to the tyrant Julius Caesar. Cato's stoicism and love of country are his dominant characteristics. Intersecting with this larger political plot are two romantic subplots between Marcia and Juba, a Numidian prince allied to Cato, and Marcia's brothers Marcus and Portius, who both love her friend Lucia. The play ends with Cato's death, Caesar's imminent arrival, and the pairing off of Juba and Marcia and Portius and Lucia. Christine Dunn Henderson and Mark E. Yellin have recently argued that the love scenes, derided by some eighteenth-century critics, are crucial to understanding Addison's purpose.[88] Rather than holding up Cato as the unequivocal hero, they suggest Addison is actually critiquing his inflexible stoicism, showing us a variation of his principles inflected by sociability that can function more successfully in the real world. In uniting Juba and Marcia, both credited with embodying many of Cato's most distinctive traits, we receive a version of Cato's principled stance "tempered by the 'softer' ties of love and affection and reworked into something closer to the type of polite and sociable character endorsed in *The Spectator*."[89] Marcia, then, is meant as an exemplary character for her audience both because she disciplines her passions, but also because she possesses them.

Deeply principled and exceptionally loyal, Marcia is a paragon of virtue and the steely emotional control evinced by her father, which will not allow her to encourage Juba's love without her father's consent and in the midst of political crisis. She stands in contrast to the softer Lucia, who cannot relate to Marcia's "Constancy of Mind" because "Nature . . . Enfeebled all my Soul with tender Passions. . . . Pity and Love, by turns, oppress my Heart."[90] In act 4, Oldfield had an opportunity to powerfully display rhetorical control just as Marcia's emotions slipped their bounds. The turncoat Sempronius dresses as Juba to abduct Marcia. He is foiled by Juba, who kills him and briefly leaves the stage. Marcia enters, and believing the corpse to be Juba, bursts forth into a torrent of lamenting and raving. Juba, overhearing, reveals himself and she moves from amazement and pleasure to confusion and finally joy. In the final scene, Cato gives his blessing to their union as he dies and Caesar's army approaches, again offering Oldfield the opportunity to display rapid shifts of emotion.

The scene in act 4 was one of the few involving the love plots singled out for praise as this pillar of Roman virtue "her secret Thoughts no more conceals/Forgets the Woman, and her Flame reveals."[91] In this analysis, the "woman" is the disciplining stoic who controls her "flame," rather than being inseparable or particularly susceptible to it simply for being female; womanhood, in Marcia's pattern, is capable of attaining the control and containment of the classical body. Elsewhere, the incident was praised as "natural as well as necessary, so that it takes away all Indecency unfit for the Daughter of Cato."[92] Marcia is overwhelmed by her passions only at the moment she believes them impossible to act upon. The daughter of Cato cannot be unruly or grotesque sexually, and in playing her convincingly, the actress can perhaps borrow these virtues as well—Marcia as written by Addison "takes away" stigmatic indecency.[93]

Published accounts of this remarkably popular piece never directly used the rupture between actress and character Oldfield's pregnancy created to ridicule the actress or the piece, despite the fact that it was apparently obvious by the end of the run.[94] Philosopher George Berkley testified in a letter to his friend Sir John Percival on May 7, 1713 that "Mr Addison's play has taken wonderfully, they have acted it now almost a month, and would I believe act it a month longer were it not that Mrs Oldfield cannot hold out any longer, having had for several nights past, as I am informed, a midwife behind the scenes, which is surely very unbecoming the character of Cato's daughter."[95] Berkley suggests the consequence of attending too closely to the actor body: the undercutting of Marcia's character by

Oldfield's pregnancy. And yet, as Phillipson points out, it is the midwife, not the pregnancy itself, which is the issue because her presence signals the inevitable loss of control that will trigger the end of the run.[96] The presence of the midwife may have raised awareness of the distinction between Oldfield's condition and the character she played, but it also created a sense of urgency around each performance and drew attention to the professional labor and dedication—economic and artistic virtues—that Oldfield displayed by continuing to appear. In this way, Oldfield is a forerunner of women like Sarah Siddons (chapter 3) and Dorothy Jordan (chapter 4), whose professional dedication was sometimes equated with their willingness to perform while pregnant.

Throughout the 1712–13 season, Oldfield demonstrated the ability to discipline her pregnant body using the rhetorical performance style of Augustan tragedy. This was crucial to her development of a tragic line of noble heroines and enabled her to counter the grotesque readings of her body as transgressive and contaminated. Negative attention to Oldfield's pregnant body that year persistently read that body as purely sexual, never maternal. But maternal was exactly the image Oldfield projected for that same body as Andromache, while her later, virginal tragic heroines emanated rhetorical and bodily control in the face of increasing pregnancy. Her final demonstration of the controlled classical body was the holding back of the inevitable process of labor to facilitate the continued run of *Cato*. On May 9, two days after Berkley's letter was written, *Cato* closed for the season because Oldfield could not or would not continue. While Oldfield may not have prevented or wholly refuted attacks upon her body and sexuality that season, she certainly offered a powerful competing vision to her audiences, a stoical and devoted mother. As her biographies attest, over the course of her continued career, Oldfield's vision won out.

Conclusion

In the context of her offstage reputation, Susanna Mountfort Verbruggen's total transformations suggested a mercurial, lively, and humorous persona untainted by sexual slander, allowing her to perform a wide variety of roles throughout pregnancy. As Cibber so evocatively put it, “nothing, tho’ ever so barren . . . could be flat in her Hands.”[97] Her behavior was potently and clearly performed, however, not innate. She shed her skins with aplomb and verve, and this was the basis of her celebrity. As a performer, Anthony Aston tells us that audiences continued to call for her performances in breeches roles even as she grew stout and would have been more comfortable giving them up; the plasticity of Mountfort Verbruggen’s body in performance seems to have accommodated many physical changes: weight gain, pregnancy, and aging.[98] Oldfield, on the other hand, seemed to retain a core of her celebrity identity within each character: whether Lady Betty or Andromache, she was beautiful, alluring, confident, sophisticated, intelligent, but principled. She had range, but she also had a recognizable brand which suggested that the commonalities between her characters reflected her true identity. If Mountfort Verbruggen washed the slate clean each time, building her celebrity on total transformation, Oldfield slowly gathered layers and built hers on an exceptional virtue combining her stage heroines with her offstage life. In this way, their entire careers can, to some degree, be understood in the context of the ever-changing and boundless grotesque body and the stable and clearly delineated classical body.

Despite differences in celebrity identity, marital status, and repertoire, neither Oldfield nor Mountfort Verbruggen’s careers suggest that pregnancy resulted in punitive casting decisions, enforced retirement, or the permanent derailing of their careers. Instead, for both, pregnancy came at key moments in their professional development and productively intersected with their self-fashioning labor. Mountfort Verbruggen capitalized on grotesque associations with pregnancy to enhance her vulgar characters with safety because of her offstage reputation for stable marriages. Oldfield’s task was to disrupt and counter grotesque readings of her body offstage with opposing performances of bodily control and containment on it. Pregnancy could enhance these aims in one arena of a career (grotesques, tragic roles like Andromache) while being largely neutral in its impact on other arenas, such as the ingenue roles in comedy both women continued to play alongside these newer lines.

I began this chapter with the idea of legacy, and so I end it. Susanna Mountfort Verbruggen’s death in childbirth was a personal and professional tragedy, and she was neither the first nor the last performer to lose her life this way. She left a legacy in the parts written for her; as Elizabeth Howe argues, "The history of Restoration drama must be seen as partly the history of its female players. Such drama can never be properly understood unless we take account of which actresses were available at each and every stage of its development."[99] But Susanna Mountfort Verbruggen also left a legacy of a different kind: a daughter who took to the stage around the time her mother died.[100] Susan Mountfort acted both with Betterton's company and later with Drury Lane, playing roles originally belonging to her mother. Her presence on the early eighteenth-century stage offered the eerie afterimage of a dead favorite. For some older audience members, she might even conjure memories of seeing her mother perform while pregnant with this daughter or one of her siblings, and perhaps even in some of the same roles. In 1712–13 exactly ten years after Mountfort Verbruggen performed throughout a pregnancy and died, Oldfield found herself in the position of doing the same while performing alongside this daughter. How did the presence of Susanna's daughter in the company at the same time raise the specter of her mother's fate for Oldfield and/or the audience? If it did, it would seem to only add to the tragic plight of Oldfield and her characters.

Oldfield's 1712–13 performances, too, left a legacy beyond that of her posthumous reputation: that of Andromache as a "pregnancy part" for tragic actresses. After Oldfield, Susannah Cibber, George Anne Bellamy (chapter 2), and Sarah Siddons (chapter 3) all acted the part while pregnant. Why? On a practical level it packs considerable pathos into a reasonable amount of stage time without requiring violent physical business. On an emotional level, the excruciating choice Andromache faces is only heightened when she weighs not simply her son's life against her own, but against herself and that of the unborn child she carries. Such resonances do not require changing the text; the body speaks for itself. Perhaps these great actresses sought to recapture the striking power of Oldfield's performance, to allow their own bodies to be haunted by her celebrity, to suggest that they too were "Distressed Mother[s] both on and off the stage" and hence worthy of the fame and fortune that attended Oldfield's career. This ephemeral performance by Oldfield's ephemerally pregnant body—an artifact of Diana Taylor's repertoire—echoes down through the entire history of the eighteenth-century British stage.[101]

Women throughout the century used combinations of their private circumstances, onstage performances, and celebrity personas to prevent or dispel undesirable responses to their pregnant bodies. While not all were successful, understanding the strategies they employed is integral to understanding female celebrity and nuancing our perceptions of the ways maternal and theatrical labor intersected. Susanna Mountfort Verbruggen and Anne Oldfield enable us to begin to theorize the ways pregnancy impacts audience perception, from bolstering the fictional narrative (Mountfort Verbruggen's grotesques, Oldfield in *The Distrest Mother*), to creating a narrative that exists in parallel (Mountfort's widowhood contrasted with comic performance), to relative neutrality (ignoring the body in ingenue roles, for example). Pregnancy can be, and has often been, presented as solely grotesque and unruly or controlled and contained; this is the binary that many celebrities seek to resist, challenge, or control, sometimes by embracing these associations and sometimes by presenting contrasts, combinations, or oscillations of these two extremes. When such self-presentation is within the control of the performer, directly or in collaboration with managers and/or playwrights, such associations can be turned to positive ends; when the celebrity loses this control, extratextual narratives can have detrimental effects. In the next chapter, we will see two examples of women whose private lives presented significant challenges to their attempts to incorporate their maternity into their stage careers, Susannah Maria Cibber and George Anne Bellamy. These challenges arise in the context of a culture of sensibility that promoted affective ties between player and audience and a burgeoning emphasis on domesticity, which placed renewed value on maternity as the pinnacle of female life. In the final two chapters, we will return to echoes of the idealized, classical pregnant body in the career of Sarah Siddons and its grotesque counterpart in the career of Dorothy Jordan in the wake of these cultural changes.

2

PREGNANT SENSIBILITY

Susannah Cibber and George Anne Bellamy

In chapter 1, we saw how the visibly pregnant body's associations with the grotesque might be turned to comedic advantage in Susanna Mountfort Verbruggen's career, particularly in the context of her contrasting domestic life. We also saw pregnancy's ability to evoke pathos in Anne Oldfield's repeated performances of the eponymous *Distrest Mother*. As that pregnancy progressed, Oldfield's roles in new plays were an opportunity to perform bodily control and classical containment that defied grotesque readings circulating beyond the theater. Ultimately, Mountfort Verbruggen and Oldfield navigated their pregnancies in ways that contributed positively to their careers while remaining on the stage. This was not always possible. In this chapter, we will see how pregnancy's relationship to character and celebrity identity in the mid-eighteenth century manifested in configurations that complicated women's abilities to turn their condition to advantage. Susannah Cibber (1714–1766) and George Anne Bellamy (ca. 1731–1788) held similar lines of business, specializing in pathetic tragic heroines who moved audiences to enraptured tears. Unlike many of the other women in this study, however, Cibber and Bellamy could lay only limited claims to domestic probity to justify and bolster their stage careers. Susannah Arne's marriage to Theophilus Cibber ended in public trials for adultery and she lived the last thirty years of her life with a married man; George Anne Bellamy's whirlwind romances led to sham marriages, interruptions to her career, and public conflict. These case studies move us beyond the theater, into other spaces in which celebrity and performance operated: in Cibber's case, into the court room; in Bellamy's case, into the composition of a tell-all memoir. In the face of events that challenged public perceptions of their status as worthy subjects of approbation, both women sought the means to control audience understandings of their offstage lives, including their pregnancies. Cibber did so from the stage through a carefully curated repertoire of roles and temporary retirement; Bellamy did so through reflective life writing long after she ceased performing.

Both women's celebrity, and the strategies they used to control their public image, should be understood in the context of the "culture of sensibility" that arose in the mid-eighteenth century—a culture that valued the open expression of emotion and receptivity and sympathy to the suffering of others as a sign of moral worth.[1] Janet Todd describes sensibility as a "pedagogy of seeing" that taught the viewer how to respond appropriately—physically and emotionally—to what they saw or read.[2] Connected to the rise of sentimental literature in England and the moral sense philosophy of David Hume and others, sensibility described values that permeated all aspects of eighteenth-century life and made the expression of refined feeling a worthy goal for both sexes.[3] Within this culture, playgoing was an opportunity for the communal expression of emotion, a chance for audiences to demonstrate appropriate responses to pathetic displays on stage.[4]

The influence of this culture on the British theater is well studied, with scholars finding many connections between theater and other disciplines as critics and artists of the time sought to explain how sensibility was understood and operated within the theatrical space. Jean Marsden, for example, connects the emotive space of the theater to moral philosophy focused on fellow-feeling and sympathy, priorities that guided the structure and content of play texts and influenced acting styles.[5] Matthew Kinservik also considers acting styles, showing that critical and popular texts of the time proposing theories of acting "[Began] to assert that the performer must possess a 'sympathetic imagination' that allowed the actor intuitively to feel and behave as would the character being represented . . . to be 'transformed' into the character."[6] Joseph Roach, meanwhile, has highlighted the connections between acting theory in the age of sensibility and eighteenth-century understandings of medicine. One example is eighteenth-century polymath Sir John Hill's translaptation of François Saint-Albine's acting treatise *Le Comedien*, published as *The Actor* (1755), which lists sensibility and understanding as the two essential qualities for a star actor.[7] Drawing on understandings of communicable diseases, Hill asserts that actors must feel the emotions they seek to convey before they can transmit them to the audience: "By working up his own imagination to the scene he is to play, he commands also ours, and we are affected with him: not equally, but more strongly. The contagion is like that of many diseases, which shew themselves more powerfully in those who receive them, than in the person who has communicated the infection."[8] To understand emotion as communicable in less pathological terms, theorists often drew from electrical and musical metaphors, imagining the actor as a conduit for lightening-like passion or as a string whose vibrations caused the audience to resonate in harmony with them, an effect amplified by their numbers. As Marsden puts it, "the performer and the audience create[d] a symbiotic connection between the desire to feel, the communal situation, and the social validation of demonstrations of feeling."[9] Sensibility, then, can be thought of as a beneficial form of bodily permeability: rather than the excess and aversion of the permeable lower strata of the grotesque body, the sensible body's contagion was focused on the upper strata of the body: the moved heart, the impressionable mind, and physical symptoms like tears, fainting, and sighs.

If understandings of sensibility suggested audiences felt a heightened version of what performers felt, the moved audience member became a testament to the authenticity of the actor's feelings and their worth as a performer. But sensibility varied from person to person and depended on circumstance. Performers with a "general sensibility," such as Hannah Pritchard (1711–1768), could tune themselves to a wide range of frequencies and be effective for audiences across genres.[10] Other performers had narrower bandwidths. They might be unremarkable or unsuccessful in some situations, while in others their sensibility became overwhelming. George Anne Bellamy and Susannah Cibber found their greatest power in performances of pathetic, distressed femininity—the kinds of spectacle considered most deserving of sympathy. Residing in different companies, their sensibility marked them for the same kinds of roles, offering audiences the ability to compare the force and expression of their sensible bodies.

While theories of sensibility often speak of removing blocks and releasing emotion on all sides, unrestrained feeling was truly only the purview of audiences, and discerning judgment was crucial to all involved.[11] Playwrights and managers needed judgment to identify and use actors' natural and acquired strengths—to understand the conditions under which their sensibility resonated most strongly. For actors, judgment helped shape their passions and performances for maximum effect, playing upon audiences as upon a musical instrument. Audiences, meanwhile, judged the worthiness of actors and plays. This was often based on the ability of performers and texts to elicit spontaneous emotional responses, but it was also connected to whether or not the actor was an appropriate representative for what they played. Audiences, as Lisa Freeman puts it, "were keenly aware of how public and private 'character' either converged or diverged in performance."[12] If the culture of sensibility fostered a desire for the melding of actor and character that facilitated the audience's expressions of feeling, then intrusive disruptions to this diminished an actor's worth. In short, actors in the age of sensibility facilitated the creation of sensible subjects by becoming—or seeming to become—appropriate and appropriately sensible objects. Both Cibber and Bellamy's extra-marital pregnancies could raise questions about their status as worthy recipients of sympathy and therefore necessitated careful management.

Susannah Maria Cibber (1714–1766)

> "All that Corregio executed by the pencil we see in real life from Mrs. Cibber, the strength of lights and shadows, of the glaring and the obscure. . . . The dignity of sorrow, and the natural and unaffected graces which that artist gives to his madonas[*sic*], this Lady diffuses over the whole figure in the tragic scene."
>
> —John Hill, *The Inspector*

Susannah Maria Cibber's story is one of sensation, downfall, redemption, and triumph. Spanning her career, her pregnancies demonstrate some of the beneficial effects we saw in chapter 1, as well as challenges that could arise for women living unconventional lives. Born Susannah Arne in 1714, she began her career as a singer and made a transition to acting during her second pregnancy in 1736. Cibber appealed to aristocratic audiences, who found her genteel and refined—not least because she played genteel and refined characters on stage. She was pale, with dark hair, large eyes, and a body that readily expressed emotion (Figure 2.1). On stage she wept, trembled, blushed, and sighed; strong emotions acted on her body visibly because she was, and remained, quite slim and small, "preserv[ing] all the appearance of youth long after she had reached to middle life."[13] Her portrayal of emotion, manifesting readily in physical signs, fed into the culture of sensibility rising in public taste and became the valuable cornerstone of her celebrity. If charismata describes celebrity strengths and stigmata their vulnerabilities, it was in fact Cibber's readily expressed emotional and physical vulnerability that was her greatest strength. At the height of her career, she was the highest-paid actress of her day, and she had total control over her repertoire from 1747 onward.[14] Like Anne Oldfield, she was reportedly "dear to persons of the first quality of her own sex," patronized by wealthy married women despite an unconventional private life.[15]

Though many of her onstage roles were passive, innocent victims of cruel men, she was offstage a passionate and dedicated professional. David Garrick testified to her tenacity when he declared, upon hearing of her death, "Then half of tragedy is dead! She was the greatest female plague belonging to my house . . . whatever was Cibber's object, a new part or a new dress, she was always sure to carry her point by the acuteness of her invective and the steadiness of her perseverance."[16] It is always difficult to identify or confirm the degree to which theatrical women were able to control their own careers and celebrity identities, but an evaluation like this offers a crucial clue. Leslie Ritchie's *David Garrick and the Mediation of Celebrity* (2019) has shown how thorough and capable a manipulator Garrick was of press and personnel; we should not underestimate a woman who successfully defied his attempts to control her.[17] She once wrote to him, "I have often heard, that the only way to make a coward fight, is to make him believe you think he has courage . . . I

Figure 2.1. Print made by John Faber the Younger (ca. 1695–1756), Netherlandish, active in Britain, after Thomas Hudson (1701–1779), British, *Mrs. Cibber*, Mezzotint, Yale Center for British Art, Paul Mellon Collection, B1974.12.425

suspect you are trying if flattery will have the same effect in this light; but I am sorry to tell you it won't do."[18] A later attempt at manipulation led her to break with Garrick for four years and move to the Covent Garden company. Though Cibber never fulfilled her ambition of becoming a theater manager, the high salaries she commanded and the added financial security of her long-term partnership with landowner and minor politician William Sloper gave her unprecedented control over when, if, and for whom she would perform.[19]

Like Anne Oldfield, Cibber was seen as always acting some version of herself: "Mrs. Cibber is plainly Mrs. Cibber, whether she act Alicia or Indiana."[20] She was for this reason confined to a smaller range than some of her compatriots, like versatile Hannah Pritchard, but in actuality this better served her celebrity self-fashioning: every character reinforced the perception that audiences had direct access to the real Mrs. Cibber. The culture of sensibility encouraged this. As Cibber enacted sweeping, powerful emotion, she supposedly transmitted her own feelings to her auditors, and they felt what she felt, validating the authenticity of her performance. There was skill in this for the actress, and, for audiences, the indulgent thrill of being overcome. In *The Rosciad* (1761), poet and satirist Charles Churchill referred to her as follows:

> Mistress of each soft art, with matchless skill
> To turn and wind the passions as she will;
> To melt the heart with sympathetic woe,
> Awake the sigh, and teach the tear to flow;
>
> . . . .
>
> When poor Alicia's madd'ning brains are rack'd,
> And strongly imag'd griefs her mind distract,
> Struck with her grief I catch the madness too.[21]

In descriptions of her acting style, writers repeatedly emphasize her sensibility: her skill melts the heart through a reciprocal sympathetic response; she arouses sighs and elicits tears, deftly pulling all the physical manifestations of sensibility forth from the bodies of her spectators. And while most often praised for her tenderness and pathos, the sympathy she creates between herself and her audiences makes them vulnerable to the stronger emotion of madness, impressing the "imag'd griefs" of a character on the minds of the audience. In response to her acting style, there was a frequent emphasis on audience tears, sighs, and silences. Cibber did not necessarily move her spectators to wild cheers so much as stun them into reflexive displays of sensibility.

Julia Fawcett suggests that observers read women's performances in this era as "always confessional, never professional."[22] Rather than resist this, Susannah Cibber took full advantage of it after the scandalous breakdown of her marriage, using stage characters to narrowly define her public persona. Through her repertoire, she suspended her life at the height of its emotional climax: the distressed, beleaguered wife; the romantic heroine making a doomed bid for freedom; the moment at which the transgressor repents, runs mad, and dies. She told the story of what was, in actuality, only about five years of her life over and over again, to great acclaim, while living a very different life offstage. To understand Cibber's tactics, I am using the metaphor of tenebrism, a specific, heightened form of chiaroscuro in painting. Like chiaroscuro, tenebrism uses exaggerated contrasts between light and dark, but in tenebrism darkness dominates, with backgrounds painted partially or mostly black. Against this, a powerful, singular source of light spotlights a figure or group of figures in high relief. Unlike chiaroscuro, in which darkness and light primarily create the illusion of depth and volume, in tenebrism darkness is used to control the viewer's gaze.[23] In performing a repertoire that placed what audiences already knew (or thought they knew) of her private life on glaring display, Cibber was able to throw a concealing darkness over its realities. Leaving the stage for the 1749–50 season during her final pregnancy preserved this carefully nuanced separation between public and private.

Susannah Cibber had four children, two by her husband Theophilus Cibber (1735, 1736) and two with William Sloper (1739, 1749/50). During the first two years of her marriage, Susannah Cibber's pregnant body established her as part of the Cibber dynasty, heightened the pathos of her stage performances for audiences, and made her maternal and professional labor visible to all. Pregnancy helped create a symbiotic relationship between her public and private life. In 1738, however, a public adultery trial recast her pregnant body as proof of sexual guilt. While she was able to reestablish her career, it depended on carefully controlling the audience's gaze and perception. In 1749, her last pregnancy drew attention to associations and meanings potentially detrimental to her career. Consequently, she exercised her celebrity power and economic stability to enter temporary retirement. Cibber allows us to consider absence as a form of agency, the action of one who asserts their subject position and preserves their celebrity power by controlling when and how they become the object of the public gaze.

Pregnancy, Dynasty, and a Changing Career (1736)

Susannah Arne began her career as a singer in the early 1730s. She was known for her extremely expressive—though not particularly powerful or skillful—voice, a talent that translated well to her later career in tragedy. In 1733–34 she and her brother, the composer Thomas Arne (most famous for writing *Rule Britannia!*), were part of the English Opera Company performing at the Haymarket. A group of young rebels from Drury Lane joined them, led by actor, playwright, and recent widower Theophilus Cibber, Colley's son. Theophilus fell in love with the young singer and brought her back to Drury Lane with him in the spring, where she received a contract for the following season. The pair married in April 1734 and had two children: Susannah in February 1735, and Caius Gabriel in April 1736; neither lived for more than two weeks. The rapidity with which these two children arrived, and their failure to survive, mimicked the reproductive history of Theophilus's first marriage. This history is worth unpacking, for it was during this marriage that Theophilus established much of the reputation that would sway public opinion during the breakdown of his later marriage to Susannah Cibber.

Jane Johnson (1706–1733), called Janey, was a successful actress in comedy and tragedy. She married Theophilus on May 22, 1725, and bore four children in eight years: Colley George (April 18, 1726) and Catherine (August 18, 1727) were named after their grandparents and died early; the elder two survived and were Jane, known as Jenny (July 13, 1729) and Elizabeth, known as Betty (January 18, 1733).[24] Jane Cibber died from complications of childbirth a week after Betty's birth. During this marriage, Theophilus had acquired a reputation for unconstrained, excessive behavior, spending his time and money gambling, racking up debts, and being seen "as often in bagnios [brothels] and taverns as the stage."[25] Because of his behavior, the pair even separated for a time between the births of their last two children. As he gained unsavory notoriety, Theophilus began to be aligned with one of his signature stage roles: the swaggering but cowardly Pistol in *Henry V*. Thomas Davies described Theo's Pistol as a "peculiar kind of false spirit," given to "uncommon blustering" and "loud and grotesque vociferation," all of which could and did describe his publicity stunts and endless public quarrels with actors, managers, critics, and his wives.[26] Despite this widely known reputation, Theophilus felt no compunction about trying to rewrite history whenever he thought it might benefit him financially.

During a dispute that culminated in the Actor's Rebellion of 1733, Theophilus accused manager John Highmore of withholding Janey's salary and suggested that his first wife's theatrical labor led to her death: "Mrs *Cibber*, to the Hazard of her Life, play'd the laborious Part of *CAELIA*, In the Perjured Lover, not a Month before Her Death . . . tho' in a very bad State of Health, big with Child, and near her Time, [she] did attend her Business, both in Acting and Rehearsing, until the 15th of *December* last."[27] In this account (printed six months after her death), he accuses Highmore of abusing and overworking a pregnant woman. He makes no mention of any role he may have had as part of the management in Janey undertaking the "laborious" part of Celia, a pregnant woman who dies, abandoned by her lover, in a brothel. His claims may have had validity, but Theophilus was also opportunistic to a fault: dead, Janey validated his complaints about Highmore; alive, her pregnancy may have added to the tragic impact of a new role.

In the spring of 1734, a little over a year after Janey died, Theophilus proposed to Susannah Arne. Mrs. Arne and her brother, perhaps alarmed at his reputation, secured a prenuptial agreement requiring that Susannah's earnings go into a trust, part of which was to be invested and another portion of which was to be distributed to Susannah for her "sole and separate use."[28] Despite the fears for her well-being this suggests, the marriage had several advantages. Susannah would be hired at Drury Lane and increase her earnings, and she would ally herself and the Arnes with a powerful theatrical family.[29] Colley had retired from Drury Lane in 1733 but continued to be a prominent figure in the theatrical world. Theophilus was part of the management now too, and for all his faults, he had a certain genius of appealing to and exploiting audience taste; if his personal attempts at celebrity self-fashioning were largely unsuccessful, his wife may nevertheless have learned much from observation.

The new Mrs. Cibber had two pregnancies in her first two years of marriage and performed during both. In 1734–35, she had small roles in operatic afterpieces in the first months of the season. After the birth and loss of the baby in February, she forfeited the rest of her salary (then £100 and a benefit) and stayed home to recover. The following season she was pregnant again. This time, the couple's financial situation was more tenuous, for Theophilus was once again running up debts. Colley Cibber looked to his new daughter-in-law as a possible solution, and discovered in her a talent for tragedy: "In forty years' experience that I have known the stage, I never knew a woman at the beginning so capable of the business or improve so fast."[30] Just as financial concerns may have played a part in Mountfort and Oldfield's appearances in the late stages of pregnancy after the deaths of their partners, so the Cibbers's needs contributed to Susannah's pregnant appearances in 1736. In a more specific parallel to Oldfield, visible pregnancy would help Cibber pivot her career toward tragedy.

Colley Cibber, who had for thirty years worked with Oldfield, gave his daughter-in-law acting lessons while looking for a new play in which she might make her tragic debut. Playwright and acting theorist Aaron Hill's *Zara*, adapted from Voltaire's *Zaïre*, offered an appropriate vehicle and had already been positively received by a small coterie audience.[31] Zara is an innocent Christian captive who loves and plans to marry Osman, the Sultan of Jerusalem. When her brother, Nerestan (played by Theophilus), comes to court, Osman's misplaced jealousy leads to Zara's murder and his death by suicide. Susannah Cibber worked closely with Hill to prepare the role and made her tragic debut on January 12, 1736, when she was more than six months pregnant.[32] The performance was carefully framed by a prologue given by Theophilus that emphasized her "unschooled" and "natural" style as well as her status as his wife, upon whom his financial security rested. Given his reputation, the death of his first wife in childbirth, and accusations that overwork during pregnancy caused Janey's death, the prologue may have held more than a little undercurrent of exploitation. But Susannah was an immediate success in the role, appearing fourteen times in fifteen days despite the lack of a suitable Osman for the first week of the run.[33] Aaron Hill made his aims in writing and rehearsing the part with her clear in printed editions of the play: "I had, (of late) . . . been depriv'd of all rational Pleasure from the Theatre, by a monstrous and unmoving Affectation; which, choaking up the Avenues to Passion, had made Tragedy *forbidding* and *horrible!*"[34] Hill praised Cibber as the possessor of the kind of "unaffected Sensibility" that would reform tragic acting, and credited both her physical attributes and her heart for their unrestrained expression of emotion.[35] In contrast to the acquired inhibitions of Augustan acting, or perhaps their abuse by unskilled practitioners, Hill advocated the reform of the stage through the removal of such blocks. He credited his scheme to Frederick, Prince of Wales, to whom he dedicated the play:

> I saw your *Eloquence* of *Eyes* confess
> Soft *Sense* of BELVIDERA's deep Distress;
>
> . . .
>
> Oh!—*nobly* touch'd! . . . the *Stage*'s Anguish *heal;*
> And teach a languid People *how* to *feel.*[36]

The Prince displayed the discerning judgment and exquisite feeling of an audience member of sensibility, while Cibber modeled the kind of acting that could draw forth such responses. When the Prince and his new wife became avid fans of Susannah Cibber in 1736, they further sanctioned Hill's program and her status as an affecting and appropriate object upon whom audience members—even royal ones—could hone their sensibility.[37]

Hill's advocacy positioned Susannah as a new model for tragic acting. Each of her appearances in the spring of 1736 also emphasized her identity as the newest member of the Cibber dynasty, from the prologue that introduced her as Theophilus's wife to an appearance in one of her father-in-law's most popular plays, to her pregnancy with the next generation of the family. Her roles also drew on what audiences knew or could imagine of her marriage and private circumstances. Before her confinement, she performed Indiana in Richard Steele's *The Conscious Lovers* and Amanda in Colley Cibber's *Love's Last Shift*. Steele's Indiana is a foundling beloved of a wealthy young man, a kind of mirror for Theo's infatuation with a woman who brought little financial advantage to their marriage. Though the play is a comedy, Indiana was a good vehicle for Susannah's pathos: thinking that she will never be able to marry the man she loves, Indiana resigns herself to running mad and perpetual weeping immediately before the comic conclusion of the play. Colley Cibber's Amanda, meanwhile, is a woman impoverished by her faithless husband. She eventually regains his love through patient suffering and a bed trick in which she acts the part of a courtesan. Just as Susannah's Zara emphasized an innocence and chastity the actress retained in private life, Amanda hinted at the potential realities of Mrs. Cibber's marriage in a play written by her father-in-law. She added to her burgeoning celebrity brand on March 23, 1736, when she acted Anne Oldfield's signature role of Andromache in *The Distrest Mother* only two weeks before she went into labor. This choice set Cibber up to re-create and compete with Anne Oldfield's pregnant performances of the role in 1712–13 and worked to validate her new tragic line by positioning her as Oldfield's inheritor. Colley Cibber, as Oldfield's manager and Susannah's instructor, bridged the gap between the two women.

From her debut onward, Susannah Cibber specialized in overwrought tragic characters, victims of love or lust. When she appeared in comedy, these roles also inclined to the pathetic. Cibber's initial appearances in spoken drama came during a pregnancy in its third trimester, perhaps raising the specter of Anne Oldfield's tragic genius onstage, and/or the more recent memory of the first Mrs. T. Cibber, whom audiences had last seen alive heavily pregnant. If Susannah Cibber did not yet have a distinctive celebrity persona when she made her tragic debut, her husband certainly did, and her role both on and off the stage quickly became clear: the innocent, put-upon, suffering woman. In a different context she might have built a different persona; the one she did build was a product of both her natural talents and her material circumstances, including her pregnancy. Shortly, however, a formidable challenge to this public image arose.

Pregnancy in Court (1738 and 1739)

Susannah Cibber began her affair with William Sloper in 1737. They remained together until her death in 1766. Theophilus introduced them and encouraged the relationship, exchanging his wife's body and sexual labor for money to ease his gambling debts. When Cibber became pregnant with Sloper's child in 1738 and they wished to leave this ménage-à-trois arrangement, Theophilus saw his income slipping away and took the most public and sensational action possible: he sued Sloper for criminal conversation (adultery), ensuring that the whole sordid history would be revealed in a public court. In this trial, Theophilus's lawyers presented Susannah's pregnancy as unequivocal proof of her sexual guilt. But the trial also revealed extraordinary details of her life with Theophilus.

A trial for criminal conversation (crim. con.) was a trial between two men: the husband (plaintiff) and the wife's lover or attacker (defendant). The husband sued for damages, usually by claiming the defendant had deprived him of his wife's affection, time, and domestic and sexual services, including her reproductive labor. In this case Susannah's substantial theatrical salary was also in play. Ben Wilson writes of the standard legal strategy for criminal conversation trials: "The defendant . . . was obliged to present the object of his attentions as a low, debauched, corrupted woman who was worthless to the world. . . . The plaintiff, in order to secure a high payout, had to present his marriage as an unending festival of joyous love and his unfaithful wife as the best and most innocent woman in the world before the wicked seducer got his grubby hands on her."[38] Despite the almost universal absence of the woman in question—women could not testify at the trial and were often not present—such events placed their bodies and character at the center of the debate. The defendant's side read the absent wife as grotesque and worthless; the plaintiff as idealized and valuable. In the context of these trials, the disconnect between Mrs. Cibber's stage performances of innocence and her clear adultery off stage could have overwhelmed one source of charismata with stigmatic guilt; ultimately, however, the trials reinforced her reputation as a suffering wife, a reputation she would use to rebuild her career.

Cases of crim. con. could draw huge crowds, and this was no exception. The details of this trial and a second, less salacious one in 1739, were widely and frequently published, creating an even larger audience sustained over time.[39] The first trial included testimony from men Theophilus paid to spy on Susannah and Sloper during sex that went into such graphic detail that the judge ordered them to stop for, "we are not trying a rape."[40] In addition to eye-witness accounts of sex acts, Susannah's avowed pregnancy proved the couple's guilt. Testimony about her condition came from a Mr. Fife, who helped Theophilus abduct Susannah from Sloper's home in the summer of 1738: "When Mr. *Cibber* was in the Chamber in the Inn, she called her Husband a great many Villains, and said that now he had ruined her Reputation, she did not value it if all the World knew that she was with Child by 'Squire *Sloper*, and that she loved him dearly, for he was an honorable Gentleman."[41] Both the trial testimony itself and later publications of the proceedings relied on an ability to imagine the circumstances as attested to by witnesses. Imagining Susannah's absent pregnant body was presumably all the easier given the memory of her pregnancy on stage two years earlier. But imagining Theophilus's complicity was also easy: one writer urged audiences to remember Susannah's "*feigned Grief* in the Part of *Amanda*, in *Love's Last Shift* . . . for the Similitude it bears to the Cause of her *real* Sorrow."[42] In 1736, Susannah Cibber's pregnant body was bound up in her success as a tragic performer and the affecting pathos of her performances, part of which sprang from the "similitude" audiences might guess at between public performance and private life; by the time of the first trial in December 1738, pregnancy was proof of guilt, but this did not necessarily diminish sympathy for her. Clearly, the affair had indeed happened. Equally or more clearly, though, Theophilus was to blame, and the verdict reflected this: Sloper was ordered to pay £10; Theophilus had asked for £5000.

Despite technically winning, public sympathy was against Theophilus. When he attempted to perform on January 4, 1739, the audience hissed, jeered, and accosted him: "When the Scene came in which he was to appear, there was a dead Silence, till he popp'd his poor Head from behind the Scenes, then at once the Hurley-Burley began, Volleys of Apples and Potatoes, and such vile Trash, flew about his Ears . . . determin'd to go through the Play, he went through it amidst the greatest Uproar that ever was heard so long a Space in a Theatre."[43] Responses to Theophilus concur with Joanne Bailey's findings regarding expected and acceptable behavior for husbands of the period, despite their vastly superior legal position. Summarizing a wife's complaint in 1734, Bailey explains, "She had been his wife for some years, brought him a very plentiful fortune and was the mother of his several children, yet he was adulterous to a woman he brought into the house, to whom he made his wife act as servant."[44] The woman's testimony demonstrated that she had fulfilled all expectations of her as wife: she contributed economically to the family, ran the household, and bore her husband's children. Despite this, her husband offered her disrespect by committing adultery and robbing her of her rightful position of authority within her own home.

Though Susannah brought no dowry to her marriage, she earned several hundred pounds a year from Drury Lane. She had also appeared on stage during the final trimester of her second pregnancy, visibly performing social expectations that a wife would add to the couple's economic security and provide children. Despite these public performances of wifely duty, her husband was a spendthrift and adulterer who gambled to excess, stole her salary, and sold her stage costumes to pay his debts. The latter was not only cruel, it compromised her ability to make a living and thus her ability to be a good wife and mother. Furthermore, he had turned pimp to squeeze even more money out of her by exploiting his rights to her body. Susannah had clearly and publicly fulfilled her obligations to her husband prior to the affair, whereas he had violated nearly every obligation a man had to his wife. In addition to the abuses revealed in the trial, a publication entitled *Comforts of Matrimony* described Theophilus threatening his wife at gunpoint when she initially refused to sleep with Sloper, claimed he had given her a venereal disease, and reported that she was actively pursuing a divorce *a mensa et thoro*, citing sexual incontinence.[45]

Until she secured a legal separation from her husband, Susannah had a limited ability to avoid him, for she was, under law, his property. During the first trial, she went into hiding, where she remained until after the birth of her daughter Molly in February 1739. Unlike her two previous children, Molly survived. Biographer Mary Nash suggests Susannah's first two children died because she could not produce sufficient milk; if this were true, however, why not employ a wet-nurse? Sloper did hire one for Molly, however, so perhaps there is truth to Nash's claim. There is another explanation for the earlier children's deaths, however, one that connects directly to his first marriage and the accusation in *Comforts of Matrimony* that Theophilus "frequented Women of lewd Fame" and thereby gave his wife "*an injury*."[46] In a 1790 report in the *London Medical Journal* Thomas Denman, the popular accoucheur patronized by the Duchess of

Devonshire, wrote of symptoms in infants that later scholars have identified as syphilitic. After about two weeks of healthy life the infants would develop a heavy and often bloody discharge from the nose and no longer be able to nurse (not being able to breathe while doing so), quickly wasting away and dying.[47] It would be a horrific, distressing experience for any parent, all the more so for being largely inexplicable. If Theophilus gave Susannah syphilis during their marriage, it may explain why her early children (born in 1735 and 1736) failed to survive regardless of attempted interventions, while her children by Sloper (1739, 1749/50), born during the latent and vastly less contagious stage of the disease, lived.[48] A similar circumstance might explain the deaths of Theophilus and Jane's first two children and the survival of their final two. If Susannah did contract syphilis from her wastrel husband, it entered the latent stage before she began her relationship with Sloper and may have remained dormant during their relationship.[49] While the exact medical knowledge behind these suppositions dates to much later, the extreme danger and debility that could arise from sexually transmitted infections was well known at the time, and it was widely lamented that no amount of chastity in a wife protected a woman from her husband.[50] The accusation that Theophilus had given her "an injury," rather than reflecting negatively on her, instead reinforced the extreme, enraging behavior to which she and many other wives had been subjected.

Theophilus discovered his wife's whereabouts in September 1739 and sued Sloper again, this time for detaining her, which deprived him of her theatrical salary and company. The continuation of the affair was attested to by the midwife and wetnurses that attended Susannah and the child, whom Sloper had paid for. This trial was shorter but more serious, and Sloper was required to pay £500. Though still far less than the £10,000 Theophilus sought, it was clear that Theophilus would continue to sue Sloper whenever he found opportunity rather than consent to a legal separation. To avoid him, Sloper and Susannah took Molly and left the city, possibly the country. During the trial for criminal conversation, Theophilus presented evidence of his wife's pregnancy as a tactic for proving that Sloper had deprived him of his rightful use of Susannah's body. While this was accepted as fact, the memory of Jane Johnson, the extenuating circumstances surrounding her pregnancy, and the rumored venereal disease, coupled with her stage reputation for convincing performances of beleaguered and beset femininity and her husband's for lewd and embarrassing behavior, left Susannah Cibber more tragic victim than wanton siren.

Tenebrism and Triumph (1742–1749)

Susannah Cibber's first disappearing act happened at the end of this second trial. Her second came in 1742, when she made the remarkable decision to return to London and resume her career. Before this return she secured a legal separation from Theophilus. She also secured an agreement with the managers at both patent theaters that they would never hire Theophilus into the company she worked for, or even allow him to enter the building when she was present. She also tested the waters of audience response by acting for a season in Dublin, where, among other appearances, she sang the role of Samson in the premiere of Handel's *Messiah*. Her performance of the lament "He Was Despised" supposedly resonated so strongly with her private circumstances, and was so moving in its expressions of pain, that Patrick Delany, the chancellor of St. Patrick's Cathedral, rose from his chair and cried, "Woman, for this all thy sins be forgiven thee!"[51] She received similar expressions of public acceptance upon her return to London. Her first performance was Desdemona, the innocent wife wrongly accused of adultery in *Othello*. Considering the disparity between her personal life and that of the character, Desdemona was a bold choice, one that forced audiences to either accept the continuing narrative of Cibber as the wronged wife or condemn her as a guilty adulteress. The gamble paid off: the audience burst into spontaneous applause during Desdemona's protestations of innocence and pleas for mercy in act five.[52] Just as Felicity Nussbaum suggests Anne Oldfield's performances of repentance in roles like the eponymous Jane Shore and Calista in *The Fair Penitent* could substitute for actual repentance on the part of the actress, so Cibber's pleas for mercy applied to both herself and her character and were heartily accepted by her audience. With this acceptance, Cibber embarked on her campaign of tenebrism, which threw a blinding and seemingly all-exposing light on a singular aspect of her identity (the wronged and suffering wife), that best ensured audience sympathy and support as she pursued a lucrative and lauded career. What remained in the shadows during these performances, rarely acknowledged directly, was Cibber's ongoing relationship with a married man.

When Cibber became pregnant with her final child in the spring of 1749, the bodily changes that would accompany her condition threatened to make the shadowy background of her private life glaringly obvious. When Cibber acted tragic, often-repentant women on stage, protested her innocence, ran mad in punishment for crimes of passion, or gave up all for love, it was easy to allow the misery of her first marriage and her dramatic escape with Sloper to haunt and amplify these performances. But much of the effect depended on ambiguity. If audiences confronted concrete evidence of the continuing relationship between Cibber and Sloper, there was a contradiction between the on- and offstage self. Cibber was not suffering; she was, essentially, living as a wealthy, beloved wife and mother, usurping the rightful position of Catherine Sloper, William's actual wife and mother to his legitimate children. In this context, continuing to appear during pregnancy risked disrupting the crucial balance between exposure and concealment—light and shadow—upon which her career was now built.[53] Fortunately, Cibber enjoyed measures of celebrity power and economic resources that meant she was not dependent on her theatrical salary for security, nor was she concerned that a year's absence would cause audiences to forget her. She made the decision to refuse her contract for the year and avoid the stigmata of exposing her illicit pregnant body.

There were other reasons Cibber may have made this choice. She had lost, quite traumatically, her first two children, both born during her active career. Her only surviving daughter was born while absent from the stage. Facing this pregnancy at a more advanced age and in a tenuous state of health herself after a busy season, she may have removed herself from the stage primarily for health reasons rather than for reasons of celebrity. Indeed, she and Sloper spent at least some of this pregnancy at Bath, where the waters were thought to be restorative and healthful for pregnant women, and where she was mistakenly reported to be "so extreamly ill . . . that her life is despaired of" in October.[54] Professionally, her relationship with

Garrick had also soured in the spring of 1749 when he refused to believe her claims that she was too ill—perhaps, in addition to other complaints, because she was experiencing early pregnancy symptoms—to take on a demanding new role late in the season. Garrick's truculence on this matter helps to explain the break she made with Drury Lane, which had a profound effect on the patent theaters and led to rival productions of *Romeo and Juliet* in 1750.[55] In contrast to Garrick, John Rich, the manager of Covent Garden, had recently shown competent care of Sarah Ward, who moved to London and made her debut at seven months pregnant before taking a full eleven weeks off for her confinement and lying-in. Just as pregnant people today might base their behavior and expectations in a workplace on the experiences of those around them, so Rich's treatment of Ward may have counted for much in Cibber's mind when compared with Garrick's behavior. When she returned to London in 1750–51, she went to Covent Garden. The crucial point is this: whether Cibber left the stage during pregnancy for her health, to preserve her celebrity power, or some combination of both, the choice was clearly hers, and clearly made deliberately. Her absence was a form of agency, not the result of a manager forcing or shaming her out of her profession.

Upon her return, Cibber emerged, once again, unscathed from a pregnancy that could have marked her as guilty and unworthy of public support. During the tumultuous benefit season of 1750–51, which grew out of the persistent and pernicious competition between the two houses after the rival *Romeo and Juliets*, the Prince and Princess of Wales—happily married and now parents to seven children with another on the way—once again made known their support of Cibber as a favored actress. The couple who commanded performances of the young, newly married Mrs. Cibber in 1736 also commanded her benefit on March 17, 1751.[56] The play chosen was *Zara*, in which she had made her tragic debut. Fifteen years, two public trials, and two illegitimate pregnancies lay between the two events, but the role she performed and the status she held by virtue of her patrons was the same: once again, all that was stigmatic disappeared while her charismatic celebrity glowed as brightly as ever.

If, as Julia Fawcett argues, the culture of sensibility compromised celebrity performers' status as subjects, persistently casting them as objects, Susannah Cibber did not attempt to challenge this overtly; she instead used her financial power to appear and disappear as most benefited her, including during pregnancy. These disappearances were both literal (leaving the stage) and figurative (using tenebrism to conceal and while seeming to reveal). Cibber's tenebrism was a form of manipulation that worked with, rather than against, audience biases: *with* perceptions of her as a performer of "inimitable sensibility" who felt all she performed, *with* perceptions that cast her as the passive victim/object of pity, *with* her personal history, *with* the notion that women were "always confessional, never professional."[57] If we look past her admittedly effective disappearing acts, we can see these as the actions of someone who was, in fact, subject and not object. In the handling of her pregnancy, especially, we see that absence can be a form of agency; but Cibber's disappearing acts were successful in part because they did not prompt—and until now have only rarely prompted—scrutiny, leaving her carefully controlled public persona to dominate.

Elaine McGirr is one exception, and she highlights how effective such strategies are in their manipulation of audience predisposition to conflate personal and professional. Many writers of the eighteenth century and beyond position Constance in *King John* as central to Cibber's reputation despite her relatively scant history with the part, and indeed a dearth of maternal characters in general.[58] These writers explicitly tied Cibber's effectiveness as Constance—whose pained expressions of grief after being separated from her child were "never to be forgotten by those who heard it"—to the death of her son, Charles, in 1758; but in 1758 Cibber had not played the part for several seasons, and she never did so after Charles's death.[59] That later commentators connect Constance's fictional loss to Cibber's real one despite this shows the continued allure of wanting to believe that what one sees on stage holds truths beyond the dramatic representation.[60] Cibber capitalized upon exactly this desire in her tenebristic self-performances. When she acted the beleaguered Lady Brute in *The Provoked Wife*, the grieving mothers Constance in *King John* or Andromache in *The Distrest Mother*, the single-minded passion of Juliet, or the innocent victim Desdemona in *Othello*, audiences had leeway to meld Cibber with the character she played to whatever degree they felt comfortable in ways that ultimately benefited the actress. In 1749, a visibly pregnant body might have pierced that protective ambiguity, forcing private circumstances into the light and calling attention to the distinction between her onstage performances of passive victimhood and her offstage life. As in 1739, visible pregnancy risked calling Cibber's status as a suitable object for audience sensibility and support into question. That she could remove herself without harming her career, however, signals her powerful subject position. It is not unlike what Helen Brooks argues of Oldfield's acting style: mastery is what creates the illusion of a loss of control. By disappearing during her last pregnancy, Cibber preserved the powerful celebrity identity she had established in the wake of scandal.

George Anne Bellamy (ca. 1731–1788)

> "No woman ever excelled Miss Bellamy in the requisites from nature, and were but her love to the profession, her application to its necessary studies, and her patience . . . equal to her abilities, she would have few equals."
>
> —John Hill, *The Inspector*

Susannah Cibber did her self-fashioning labor throughout her career, using her stage presence and absences to reiterate and solidify a selective biographical narrative that maximally benefited her career. As part of this, she concealed her pregnancy from public view in 1749–50. In contrast to Cibber's carefully controlled tenebrism, George Anne Bellamy's self-fashioning during her career was inconsistent and disrupted. She later turned to retroactive exposure, publishing a multivolume memoir at the end of her life in an attempt to exert control over and resolve the sensational events and contradictions in her life and career. As her story unfolded in real time, however, pregnancy and childbearing initially allowed Bellamy to claim a status that Cibber could not in her later career: that of a "domesticated wife" and mother on stage and off.[61] It was the rupture of this image, in part, that she aimed to correct by telling all in her memoir, where she used pregnancy to engage in performances of maternal and moral authority.

George Anne Bellamy was the illegitimate daughter of James O'Hara, Baron Tyrawley, and Miss Seal, later an actress known as

Figure 2.2. F[rancis] Lindo (1714–1767), *George Ann Bellamy*. Courtesy of the Garrick Club, London

Mrs. Bellamy. George Anne spent about twenty-five years on the London stage. In her early days, she moved between Covent Garden and Drury Lane as a counterpoint to Mrs. Cibber. She was strikingly beautiful, with blue eyes, dark hair, and lively high spirits (Figure 2.2). In the course of her career, she was a great favorite of James Quin, a great frustration to David Garrick, and a great friend of Whig politician Henry Fox. Bellamy's gift for passion and pathos made her a popular performer, and for a time there was no doubt she was the "it" girl of her day. John Doran's description of Bellamy, written half a century after her death, is an evocative portrait of a career marked by continual revolution:

> she excited the wonder, admiration, pity and contempt of the town for thirty years. . . . To say that she was a siren who lured men to destruction, is to say little, for she went down to ruin with each victim; but she rose from the wreck more exquisitely seductive and terribly fascinating than ever . . . for this perilous charmer was unequalled in her day for the expression of unbounded and rapturous love . . . when she played some poor lady distraught through affection, the stoutest hearts under embroidered or broad cloth waistcoats, crumbled away, often into inconceivable mountains of gold dust.[62]

Like Susannah Cibber's sensible body, which displayed every wrack and torment of her characters, Bellamy had her own celebrity talisman: the passion that made her compelling onstage (charismata) and compulsive offstage (stigmata), creating an enticingly unattainable and unbiddable persona particularly susceptible to romantic love. When she acted those same emotions on stage, they penetrated and "crumbled" the hearts of her auditors, transfiguring sensibility to profit.

Bellamy had four children with two lovers: one in 1749 with George Montgomery Metham, later an MP, and three between 1752 and 1756 with John Calcraft, a close associate of Henry Fox. While she retired temporarily during her first pregnancy and her fourth child was born in late summer, she spent her two middle pregnancies on stage in front of audiences. These pregnancies introduced her reproductive life to public view and offered mergers of actress and character later bolstered by a line of maternal characters in which she enjoyed considerable success. When she left her children and her London career, however, critics called the authenticity of these earlier performances, and Bellamy's position as a worthy object of sympathy, into question. She spent the 1760s between theatres in Dublin, Edinburgh, and London before a permanent retirement in 1770.

Creditors increasingly pursued Bellamy for debt, and she was eventually imprisoned, during which time she authored a five-volume memoir likely dictated to (and perhaps embellished by) author Alexander Bicknell.[63]

Bellamy is the only actress in this study who attempted to publish her own life story. *An Apology for the Life of George Anne Bellamy* (1785), a title that echoes Colley Cibber's famous autobiography and its many imitators, is a tale of misadventure and distress.[64] Like many sentimental novels it takes an epistolary form. Bellamy presents herself as setting down a chronicle of her life with the hope of edifying her readers: "Happy shall I be, if the recapitulation of my errors and misfortunes should prove a beacon to warn the young and thoughtless of my own sex from the Syren shore of vanity, dissipation, and illicit pleasures, of which remorse and misery, as I too sensibly feel, are the sure attendants."[65] Part penance, part titillation, Bellamy claims that her worth will ultimately be proven by the exposure of her sensibly felt "remorse and misery," which endows her with a kind of moral authority. Throughout, Bellamy participates in the kind of self-fashioning Cheryl Wanko identifies in her study of thespian biography, creating a narrative of high and low, tragedy and triumph that aims to recapture audience interest, recirculate her presence and celebrity, and restore her diminished economic and cultural value.[66] She also attempts to explain and justify her various exits and reentrances to the market economy in London, a task Wanko identifies as particularly fraught for women who must prove at each reentry that their value has not been diminished by offstage sexual activity.

Kristina Straub sees the *Apology* as Bellamy's attempt to fashion herself into the heroine of a sentimental novel, portraying her various failed romantic liaisons not as transgressions but "as the fate of an unprotected innocence."[67] Even the act of writing the memoir, however, compromises the notion of her innocent distress: "At the heart of the spectacle of virtue in distress lies the assumption that virtue is never made into a spectacle by its own volition. . . . By making a spectacle of herself, Bellamy compromises the very credentials as sentimental heroine that she seeks to establish."[68] Julia Fawcett also focuses on Bellamy's failed self-fashioning in the memoir, understood through the lens of overexpression: "an autobiographical strategy that scrambles corpus and costume in order to secure the celebrity's right to self-definition."[69] Unfortunately, Bellamy's gender precludes success, for a woman's "public persona, no matter how exaggerated, will always be read as an extension of her private self."[70] Of evaluators of Bellamy's *Apology*, only Felicity Nussbaum suggests that it reflects some degree of success in self-fashioning. Rather than simply lamenting her maligned status, Nussbaum suggests that Bellamy attempts to claim a more masculine form of virtue by emphasizing her education, participation in politics, philanthropy, and often her superiority (in sensibility, earning potential, and knowledge) to her male colleagues and companions.[71]

The *Apology* is clearly a complex series of performances. Bellamy casts herself by turns as wise beyond her years, helplessly naive, erudite and religious, impulsively sexual, quiet and domestic, rash and full of rage. She is pious, charitable, materialistic, political, a trendsetter, a victim, an eccentric, and a natural philosopher. She sometimes aligns herself with tropes of feminine sensibility, and sometimes resists or questions those same expectations. She draws throughout on her various stage identities: the young impulsive lover, the suffering but noble tragic wife, and the distressed mother. She uses her pregnancies to periodically unite these three identities, giving Bellamy the opportunity to become a moralizing subject sanctioned by biological motherhood, economic power, and affiliations with aristocratic men and women. I will move through a consideration of Bellamy's four pregnancies and their representation in her memoir to demonstrate the impact of pregnancy on her career both in "real time," and as framed and discussed in the *Apology*.

Pregnancy in Print: 1749

When George Anne Bellamy came to London in 1748, she was one of two women John Rich hired to compete with Susannah Cibber at Drury Lane (the other was Sarah Ward, who made her debut at seven months pregnant). Bellamy embraced the comparison with Cibber, situating herself as a rival to this established and popular performer. In two short seasons, she rose to sufficient status to be Drury Lane's Juliet and compete head-to-head with Susannah Cibber in the rivaling *Romeo and Juliet* productions of 1750. Much of her success was due to her onstage performances of lovely, agonized heroines, but Bellamy's offstage life was already contributing to and bolstering her celebrity identity as the passionate and impulsive ingenue.

Toward the end of her 1748–49 season, for example, she claims to have been abducted—though happily—from the theater in the middle of a performance of *The Provoked Wife* by the handsome George Montgomery Metham. James Quin, her mentor, was left in the unfortunate position of apologizing for her but turned it to advantage by presenting the impulsive young actress as having fulfilled her character Lady Fanciful's desire for "an admirer *that was made on purpose for her*."[72] What could have been a sign of unprofessional behavior becomes, in this recounting, behavior that sanctions Bellamy's stage performances of passionate lovers, framing them as earnest performances of self. There is no contemporary comment on this event. If Bellamy did run away with Metham during *The Provoked Wife*, it was between February and April, the only times she played Lady Fanciful that year; any absence did not last long, for *The London Stage* records her presence in the company until the season ended in May. By that point, she was about two months pregnant. She stayed offstage and away from London for the rest of 1749.

Bellamy and Metham took a house in Yorkshire where she gave birth to her first child, George, in December 1749. In the *Apology*, Bellamy describes the months waiting for the birth of their child as full of her hopes for a settled, retired, and happy life. As her body expands, so does her sense of contentment. She takes religious counsel and enjoys the company of young women in an adjoining seminary, recalling her own early education in such a setting and using the presence of these women to attest to the respectability of her situation despite its irregularity. She presents herself in many ways as the ideal pregnant woman of her age: her mind is easy and free from agitation that could endanger herself or the child, sure of Metham's love and willingness to marry her, and moderate in all things. The young ingenue has achieved her aims, and Bellamy writes of feeling content to leave the stage and become a wife and mother. Metham, too, expresses an "earnest desire" for their impending parenthood.[73]

Bellamy's description of her labor with this child, which lasts eleven days, transforms her from the heroine of a domestic comedy to an object of agonized pity. She is in pained distress, fearful, and so modest that she initially refuses Metham's desire to bring her a man-midwife: "The apprehensions arising from my delicacy, prompted me to smother my pains, till my life was in danger; which in the end brought on a forced labour, and obliged me to have recourse to that assistance I had strove to avoid."[74] Bellamy calls the combination of her modest reluctance and fear of a male attendant her "delicacy," a term whose associations with female helplessness held erotic associations in the age of sensibility.[75] In casting herself as the entirely helpless victim who needs the guidance of masculine authority figures, she creates within this pitiable scene of childbirth a frisson of the erotic power of her stage performances of distressed femininity. Immediately after crafting this image of the pathetic-erotic object, however, Bellamy turns philosophical, admonishing her female readers not to allow modesty to lead them into danger during childbirth. In doing so, she employs a strategy of moving herself from the object position to the subject position that Julia Fawcett notes elsewhere in the memoir, claiming wisdom and authority as one who can instruct others, mother to mother:

> It is a matter of great surprise to me, that as female practitioners in midwifery are in general inexpert, women defer having an *accoucheur*, till necessity obliges him to be called in. Those who, out of a mistaken modesty, do this, not only risk the lives of themselves and infants, but, if difficulties render it necessary that a doctor should be called in, are informed by it of their danger, at a time when no addition ought to be made to their terror. And if, through their continued obstinacy, their lives should be lost, they are, in my opinion, guilty of self-murder.[76]

Bellamy's account of her first experience of childbirth synthesizes her stage identities of the young ingenue, the tragic heroine, and the distressed mother, but also becomes an occasion to reassert control over the experience. While Bellamy initially credits the unnamed accoucheur with saving her life, she then claims such authority herself, testifying to the dangers of women's modesty and the indispensability of male attendants. In doing so, she takes back the control of her body and labor sacrificed in the birthing room. Much like the inherent tension Kristina Straub sees between using sentimental tropes of passive femininity in the memoir and the active act of writing, Bellamy both desires to be the object of sympathy in this scene and struggles against it.

In the memoir, Bellamy's first pregnancy enables her to present herself as naturally inclined to quietness and domestic pleasures. When birth comes upon her, she crafts a scene of dramatic tension in which she embodies various aspects of her stage identity. This scene also involves a performance of social class, for Bellamy's first childbearing experience serves to place her on the forefront of a medical revolution. Metham privileges a male birth attendant over Bellamy's female midwife; while initially reluctant, Bellamy adopts this practice for her future children. In 1749 this would have been unusual, but by the time of the memoir's publication in 1785, an accoucheur was a fashionable choice for those who could afford them, spurred by Queen Charlotte's use of male attendants for all fifteen of her children's births. Thus, Bellamy's description of her 1749 birth puts her in the position of knowledgeable, high-status maternal authority figure and early adopter of what has become a much-sought-after medical practice. In essence, Bellamy informs her readers, she used man-midwives before it was cool. Bellamy uses her obstetric history to both claim a position of maternal authority and link herself with aristocratic and royal femininity through shared female experience, a strategy that will also play an important role in Sarah Siddons's career.

Bellamy spent almost the entirety of this pregnancy off the stage. Rather than damaging her career, this absence was timely and profitable because John Rich needed her back in London to help battle Garrick in Susannah Cibber's absence (Cibber was offstage having her final child, Charles). To help secure her return, Rich raised her salary to £7 a week, gave her backpay for the entire season (functionally bestowing on her paid maternal leave), and offered her a benefit without house charges.[77] Just as Metham's behavior around the birth of their son attested to Bellamy's value—she was both emotionally and economically worth the expense of a male attendant—Bellamy's first removal from circulation and reentry to the theatrical marketplace raised her economic value rather than diminishing it. Bellamy was back on stage at Covent Garden in late January 1750, almost exactly a month after the birth. It must have been exhausting, traveling back to London in a coach with an infant on rough roads shortly after giving birth and, upon her arrival, reestablishing a household and attending rehearsals. Even if the baby were with a nurse, her physical recovery would barely be complete before she was back to a full schedule of rehearsal and performance. Her health held, however, and she enjoyed a successful spring playing many of Susannah Cibber's most popular roles in the other performer's absence. The next year she moved to Drury Lane and rose to new prominence by making a successful stand against Cibber in Juliet. Commentators lauded her spontaneous and impassioned style, especially in the first half of the play, helped no doubt by the easy similarities between the actress and the character, both impassioned and impulsive young women ruled by love. After the contest, she settled into several years of steady success on stage. Her personal life became fraught, however, when Bellamy ended her relationship with Metham during the 1751–52 season.

A "Domesticated Wife": 1752–56

After Metham, Bellamy next and almost immediately became attached to John Calcraft, an army officer and later politician under the patronage of Henry Fox. Calcraft is a villainous figure in the *Apology*. He tricks Bellamy into accepting him as her lover during a fight with Metham by offering her a contract to either marry her within seven years or forfeit £50,000 pounds. Though this offer initially attests to her value, later in the memoir she discovers that he is already married and has no intention of paying her. In her depiction of the relationship with Calcraft, Bellamy finds herself at the mercy of an unscrupulous, unfeeling man, just as might the heroine in a sentimental novel. Calcraft's unnatural coldness is particularly on display during her pregnancies and while she is in childbed. Unlike the serenity that dominates her pregnancy with George Metham's child, Bellamy writes that emotional turmoil marks her pregnancies with Calcraft's children.

Despite these private woes, Bellamy's memoir claims Calcraft was widely believed to be her husband, or a close equivalent. In part, this was because Bellamy was sharing and running his household and remaining onstage during pregnancy.[78] She was also socializing with his patron, Henry Fox, and prominent members of Fox's circle, including his wife Lady Caroline. To audiences of the 1750s, Bellamy's story seemed to be one of an impulsive youthful indiscretion with Metham, followed by a prominent and legitimate relationship that could atone for the earlier misadventure (not unlike the Foxes themselves, who had eloped). Even while enjoying the benefits of this elevation in status, however, Bellamy had trouble sticking to the script with a partner she did not love.

Bellamy and Calcraft's first child was born in the winter of 1752–53 during her third and last season at Drury Lane. The child may have been stillborn or died early, for I have found no baptismal or burial records for them. Bellamy does not mention this pregnancy or birth in her *Apology* either, skipping from spring 1752 before the pregnancy to spring 1753 after her return to the stage. Instead, we know of this pregnancy because of the way it affected the theater. On November 20, 1752, Drury Lane's prompter Richard Cross notes in his diary that Miss Bellamy had "taken ill" after a performance of *King Lear*.[79] She remained off stage until February 1, when she acted Calista in *The Fair Penitent*. We can be certain this absence was for childbirth because Cross explains her return with, "Miss Bellamy has lain in & is up."[80] Bellamy, it seems, went into labor on or close to November 20, and returned to the stage a little over two months later. In the diary, Cross seems to have been anticipating her absence, for he records all the roles Bellamy acted that fall and the date of each appearance. In addition to Juliet, at the time her most popular role, she acted Leonora in *The Revenge*, Monimia in *The Orphan*, Imoinda in *Oroonoko*, Belvidera in *Venice Preserv'd*, Cordelia in *King Lear*, and Calista in *The Fair Penitent*. We do not know why Cross kept this list. He does not keep such lists for other pregnant performers, even those who gave birth in the midst of theatrical seasons, suggesting it was specifically important to track when and what Bellamy performed.[81]

A leading actress's pregnancy had a large impact on the season, shaping what plays could be brought out before and during her lying-in and sometimes the frequency with which a performer might safely appear. Bellamy, for example, played twenty-three times in the first two months of the 1751–52 season at Drury Lane, but only fourteen times in 1752–53 during the late stages of pregnancy. Unlike an unexpected death or illness, managers could prepare for a lying-in to some degree. This preparation could include identifying substitutes for some roles. In this case, Mrs. Davies and Miss Haughton briefly undertook some of Bellamy's parts in January. Cross's tracking could somehow relate to this, or to salary payments or contractual obligations; perhaps Bellamy and the managers had agreed on a lighter schedule prior to the birth, or a payment scheme for the year that relied on the number of nights performed. If "taken ill" means that she began to experience symptoms of labor, then the tracking could be because she—and the theater—were pushing the limits of her physical condition by keeping her onstage. She would not be the first to perform nearly up until the birth of her child. So far, every woman in this study has done so at least once. Regardless of the exact reason, Cross's attention highlights the importance such events had to the running of theatrical companies and affirms that Bellamy was, in fact, pregnant while performing that year.

It is even more frustrating that Bellamy skips most of the 1752–53 season in her memoir because she performed a pregnant character while she herself was visibly pregnant, a relatively rare occurrence in London.[82] On October 5 and November 2, she acted Imoinda in Thomas Southerne's *Oroonoko*. It was not a new role, having been in Bellamy's repertoire since 1748, but this is the only occasion we know of when her body natural matched that of her character. In Southerne's adaptation of Aphra Behn's novella, Imoinda is a white woman raised in Africa and sold into slavery to a plantation owner in Surinam.[83] Her husband, a captured African prince, is later sold to another man in the colony. They reunite and Imoinda and a friend persuade Oroonoko to lead his fellow captives in an uprising with Imoinda fighting alongside him. When the uprising fails and they face recapture, however, Imoinda insists that Oroonoko kill her and their unborn child to spare them enslavement.

The play was one of the most popular tragedies of the eighteenth century, and Imoinda's death was a particularly moving and sensational scene. We have seen the impact of visible pregnancy on a nonpregnant character with Andromache in *The Distrest Mother*, which invites audiences to elide the body natural of the actress and the character body of Andromache, implicitly heightening the pathos of the performance. But Imoinda's condition is at the crux of the play's tragic action and is overtly referenced in the text: it is for the sake of his unborn child that Oroonoko leads the uprising, and for the sake of the child that Imoinda chooses death over capture. In this case, Bellamy's condition did not add new stakes to her distress, as in *The Distrest Mother*, but rendered existing stakes more concrete. Within the play, Imoinda's pregnancy is certain, but not necessarily visible—it is first reported as a rumor among the enslaved women surrounding her. But Bellamy was in quite an advanced state of pregnancy when she played the role, first six and then two weeks before "taking ill" and retiring for the birth. Whether by silhouette, intentional or unconscious gestures, or changes to her gait and physicality, her Imoinda offered not the delicate, abstracted suggestion of pregnancy, but its palpable reality. It also added urgency to Imoinda and Oroonoko's plight: there is no time to wait for another solution, they must act before their child is born. Despite what we might be able to imagine of the effects of such a performance, Bellamy does not mention Imoinda in her memoir, and I have found no reviews or reactions to her performance in surviving contemporaneous papers or journals. What might fill this archival silence? Audience disapproval or discomfort? Heightened emotional weight for an already affecting play? Did it add to Bellamy's fame? Call her or Garrick's taste into question? We do not know, but such casting—and even the lack of commentary around it—stands in contrast to more familiar complaints about pregnancy's ability to undermine the fiction of a play, or the powerful but implicit impact I have suggested in *The Distrest Mother*.[84]

The following season, 1753–54, Bellamy returned to Covent Garden pregnant with her third child. She performed between November 20 and February 28 and then from March 28 to the end of the season.[85] This time she performed until the day she went into labor with her daughter Caroline Elizabeth, and lay in for only a month in comparison to the nearly two and a half months that she took in 1752–53. Absences of one to two months around birth are common throughout the century, and it is possible Bellamy simply needed a longer recovery period in 1752–53. But her shorter absence in 1753–54 may also have been a matter of timing. That year, the birth occurred close to the start of the benefit season. Bellamy's second performance back, in fact, was her benefit, a significant source of her income each year. Holding one's benefit early in the season (which generally ran from March to May or June) was a marker of status and helped ensure higher profits, for wealthy audience members would begin leaving town for their country homes as the spring advanced. Thus, Bellamy may have lain in for a shorter time so she could return and hold her own benefit earlier in the spring. During the late stages of this pregnancy, Bellamy played her established parts of Athenais in *Theodosius*, Monimia in *The Orphan*, Calista in *The Fair Penitent*, Eudocia in *Siege of Damascus*, Desdemona in *Othello*, and Celia in *Volpone*.[86] She acted neither Juliet (gifted to young Maria Nossiter, who played it for the full year) nor Imoinda (at Covent Garden, the possession of Mary Elmy). Like Oldfield and Cibber before her, however, she acted Andromache in *The Distrest Mother*, repeated six times in the last two months of her pregnancy.

She also acted the new part of Empress Fulvia (a Desdemona-esque character nearly killed by her husband's jealousy) in Philip Francis's poorly received *Constantine*. She had a new costume made for the event, which she describes as "showy and proper for the character," and which would also have been made to accommodate her pregnant body.[87] The costume was an expense borne by the theater, a visible investment in their star, yet Bellamy wore it only a few days before the run was interrupted "by the introduction of a daughter into the world."[88] Like Anne Oldfield in 1713, Bellamy's pregnancy dictated the length of the run of a new play. And like Susanna Mountfort Verbruggen or Susannah Cibber in 1736, Bellamy's pregnancy and execution of her theatrical duties showed a woman adhering to an important cultural script: contributing both her economic and reproductive labor to her household.

Even while engaging in successful performances of her value as a maternal and sensible subject, cracks in this facade were beginning to show. Bellamy made a late start to her season because of another upheaval in her private life. Richard Cross—still attentive to Bellamy's activities though she had left Drury Lane—reports in his diary for October 24, 1753, that, "Miss Bellamy, who engag'd lately with Mr Rich is off again—Mr Colthorp [Calcraft], who kept her, swears to kick Rich a great noise about it in ye Bedford Coffee house."[89] Bellamy signed a contract with Rich in October, later than normal, but then left her theatrical and conjugal ties to run away (once again) with George Metham. By November, six months pregnant and having missed the start of the season, she returned both to the theater and to Calcraft. Bellamy does not mention the incident, instead representing this as the year that she and Calcraft joined their households officially and she became, in her words, his "domesticated wife."[90] This may be true, but a fracas in a public coffee house, especially one so closely associated with the theater, was an excellent way to ensure personal gossip was spread far and wide. By leaving this event and her 1752–53 pregnancy out of her memoir, Bellamy effectively renders them invisible, effacing obstetric tragedy and inconstancy and focusing on the event that best sanctions her identity as a wife and mother.

Returning to the memoir, we find that the birth and subsequent christening of Bellamy's daughter in 1754 was, like George Metham Jr.'s birth in 1749, an important moment for social performance. Bellamy emphasizes the social ranks of the child's godparents, though her disdain for Calcraft is readily apparent:

> This event [the birth] seemed of more consequence to Calcraft than if he had been made master of the world. He imagined the Marmoset to be already the very likeness of himself; and was in hopes that this pledge would insure to him my affection in future. Lady Caroline Fox [after whom she was named], Lady Tyrawley, and Mr. Fox, stood sponsors in person. This circumstance put the certainty of my being married out of all doubt; as it was not to be supposed that I should have been so highly honored had it been dubious.[91]

Their daughter—whose paternity is clearly visible—raises Bellamy's affective value for Calcraft. The Foxes, despite the racy start to their marriage, were high ranking and largely respectable; their intimacy with the couple sanctions Bellamy and Calcraft's relationship, as does the presence of her father's wife, Mary O'Hara, Lady Tyrawley. The christening therefore further situates her pregnant performances within the bounds of respectability.

Bellamy's next and last child with John Calcraft, christened Henry Fox Calcraft, was born in September 1756 and baptized on November 4. His birth and naming further emphasized their intimacy with the Foxes in public, but Bellamy's memoir positions this pregnancy and birth as attended by nasty shocks in private that undermined her hopes for stability and respectability, if not love, with Calcraft. While pregnant, she recalls asking Henry Fox why he disapproves of their union, the excuse Calcraft initially gave for not marrying her. Fox expresses amazement that they are not married, assuring her that he and his wife were under the impression that they were. Given Bellamy's condition, however, he counsels her to avoid confronting Calcraft, as heightened emotion was considered dangerous for pregnant women. To be a good mother to her unborn child Bellamy must continue in a state of willing victimhood to a dishonest man, a pitiable position for any heroine. She manages this until after the birth. When Calcraft, displaying his lack of sensibility, tries to confront her about a bill less than a week into her lying-in, she challenges him with her knowledge of his shameful false excuses about not marrying her. Complaining after he has left to a companion about her untenable position, it is revealed to her that Calcraft—worse than simply lying about Henry Fox's objections—is already married. "Struck with instant madness," Bellamy rises from her bed to confront him, collapses "to all appearance dead," and remains ill most of the year.[92] In her recovery, she is overseen first by Dr. William Hunter (who was to deliver the child but arrived too late), and later by Dr. James Ford at Bristol. Both men would later attend the births of Queen Charlotte's children. In 1785 when she published her *Apology*, Bellamy's attendance by these now-royal doctors would powerfully signal her worth as a woman, a mother, and an authority for other childbearing women while emphasizing the extreme danger of Calcraft's callous behavior.

Though Bellamy is understandably furious with Calcraft in the memoir, she ultimately agrees to stay in the relationship if he will settle her debts. Over the next few years, before her departure from Calcraft and from London, Bellamy made several highly successful appearances in tragic maternal roles. These, like the assumed marriage with Calcraft and her performances during pregnancy, placed Bellamy within normative tropes of femininity and authenticated her offstage identity as a mother and wife with her onstage performances of tragic womanhood. Once audiences saw her leave Calcraft, her children, and her career for other relationships, however, the authenticity of her affecting stage performances became suspect, as did her status as an appropriate object of public sensibility and support. In her memoir, she seeks to correct perceptions of their relationship and her departure.

"Real Heartfelt Anguish": Maternal Distress, 1756–61

After the birth of her fourth child in 1756, Bellamy's repertoire began to shift strongly toward the maternal. In January of 1758 she played the title role in Elijah Fenton's *Mariamne* (1723), a mother who loses her child when he is made a political prisoner: "In the last two Scenes of the second Act, the Queen is persuaded to part with her son . . . the agonies of a mother, in such a pitiable situation, are finely realized by Mrs. Bellamy."[93] In an age of sensibility, that the audience was moved attested to her power and skill, as well as her status as a worthy representative of such a story. On April 17 of that same year she acted Constance in *King John*, one of Cibber's few maternal roles, in a benefit for some of her compatriots. The play includes an affecting scene in which, separated from her son, Lady Constance runs mad. Recalling her experiences in the part much later, after being separated from both her sons, she writes, "I have often performed [it], and when I performed have most susceptibly *felt* . . . the wailings of Constance, when she laments the loss of her beloved son."[94] Bellamy uses her successful stage performances of distressed maternity to attest to the authenticity of her private feelings and experiences.

The most important of Bellamy's maternal roles was the title character in Robert Dodsley's *Cleone* in December 1758. The play had an uneasy journey to the stage. Dodsley had written it several years before and tried unsuccessfully to get it produced at Drury Lane. Bellamy writes, "Mr. Garrick had declined the piece; but from what reason I could never guess" and further specifies that "Mrs. Cibber" had also rejected it, perhaps because the power she wielded over her repertoire would have or could have reversed Garrick's judgment.[95] Other observers suggested Garrick did not like the piece because it contained no star vehicle for himself, but the lead role was an excellent one for a performer like Bellamy. A plot laid by her brother-in-law forces Cleone to flee her husband's house with her young son, whom an assassin murders (offstage) as she attempts to make her way to her father. Cleone discovers the child murdered, and there are two scenes of her mad mourning over his body that reviewers found overwhelming: "The conclusive scenes of maternal agony over her murdered child harrowed the hearts of the audience with powers then at their height, and by many conceived of the highest excellence. . . . The distress is perhaps too horrible for female minds to bear—the maternal feelings are those which vibrate with the greatest keenness of sensation."[96] In combination, Bellamy's talents and Cleone's story created an intense sensorial experience for an audience in the age of sensibility. Dodsley's play was a major opportunity for an actress whose career was so often described in relation to Cibber's because of their shared repertoire. Here was an entirely new part—one Cibber was not interested in playing—for Bellamy to claim. In the memoir, she frames herself as determined to maximize the distinction between herself and other performers in her preparation, writing, "the language was simple, and I determined that my performance of it should be the same. It was an effort worth trying; as from its novelty, I should, at least have the merit of its being all my own."[97] Bellamy's performance, particularly in the mad scenes, was an enormous success that once again affirmed her value as a sensible subject. One spectator declared, "Never did a part more naturally become an Actress," and expounded,

> I had a pleasure which the Theatre has not afforded me this great while . . . the pleasure of relieving real heartfelt anguish by a flood of tears . . . the humanity of the whole audience burst into these overflowings several times during the representation. . . . Her attachment to her dear infant, the fixed position of her eyes, which shewed that every other object was excluded from her mind, her tender prattle to him, when she thinks him alive, and her lamentations over him, when again she thinks him dead, were traits of nature as finely performed by her, as they were difficult to be executed.[98]

Bellamy had grown from the embodiment of youthful passion into a fine performer of maternal roles. This spectator's "real heartfelt anguish," the "flood of tears" he unleashes, and the "humanity" of the whole audience, whose sensibility overflows throughout the piece, attest to the authenticity and power of Bellamy's performance. In part because she had performed while heavily pregnant, her widely known maternity was a boon, facilitating her skillful performance of a part that "naturally be[came]" her.

In the fall of 1760, Bellamy left Calcraft, London, and her children for Ireland, where she performed at Smock Alley in Dublin. The papers reported her positive experiences there and commented on her dresses and successes performing with Henry Mossop. Soon, however, she was singled out for criticism based on perceived neglect of her maternal duties in Edward Thompson's *The Meretriciad* (1761), a satiric poem criticizing the vices of various public figures, many of them courtesans:

> But here observe the *Juliet* of her days,
> Fall'n from the pinnacle of public praise
> Oft' with encomiums has the Playhouse rung,
> Enraptur'd with the music of thy tongue,
> Oft' has the Virgin sympathiz'd thy doom,
> And wept for *Juliet* in the silent tomb;
>
> . . .
>
> But if the *ties of mother will not bind,*
> How weak are women, ignorant, and blind!
> Not all the rhet'ric of a Courtier's tongue,
> *Or that of mother from thy tender young,*
> Were found sufficient to subdue thy lust,
> Tho' quite corroded, by corrosive rust,
> When *M**** had thee, such a deed as this
> Was merely modish, and became a Miss;
> But yet his tenderness, could not subdue,
> That thirst of dear variety in you:
> All he could say that itch could not destroy,
> *To bind the Mother to the loveliest Boy.*
> But since Old Time has worn the dimple sleek,
> And furrow'd wrinkles o'er the blushing cheek,
> Who would imagine you would play the whore,
> And fly in raptures to the *Irish* shore?
>
> . . .
>
> If e'er these lines should reach thy flinty heart,
> Fly to thy babes—and *act the mother's part*[99] (emphasis mine)

When Bellamy began to play maternal characters on stage successfully, she was adhering to a script like that proposed in the *Meretriciad*: older, wiser, and perhaps less beautiful, her foremost concern should now be her children, displacing the sexual exploits of earlier years. That this was only a shift onstage, not off, was problematic for the author. Thompson suggests that the public sanctioned Bellamy's relationship with Metham, and even with Calcraft, but her behavior since, and particularly a perceived indifference to her children, is wholly without excuse. Lust drives her to leave Metham, then Calcraft, and all her children to fly "in raptures" to Ireland. Lust (economic, professional, and sexual) displaces the maternal.[100]

Inclusion in *The Meretriciad* and accusations that she had abandoned her children degraded Bellamy's worthiness as an object of sympathy. She was not redeemed but further marginalized by her omission from Charles Churchill's *The Rosciad*, printed the same year and focused on performers. While not wholly complimentary, Churchill offers several long panegyrics to the foremost female performers of the patent companies, but Bellamy is not among them. Neither is she mentioned in the numerous responses and emendations to the original text. This absence may be because she was not performing in London at the time, but her inclusion in one (ridiculing) text but not the other (elevating) one suggests a downward slide, a move from the company of people whose stage abilities and prominence make them worthy of a discussion of their skills to those who can be judged on sexual behavior. The contrast established is that between a vision of the sexually profligate Bellamy and the ideals to which she might have aspired (Juliet, lauded celebrity, motherhood).

Despite opportunities to profitably enact maternal sensibility in the 1750s, Bellamy ultimately failed to sustain the part in real time or in her memoir. Unlike Anne Oldfield and Susannah Cibber, whose long-term partnerships and financial stability made it possible to provide for their children and keep them with them, Bellamy's relationships were marked by constant betrayals and upheavals that prevented her ability to act the mother's part both by depriving her of financial stability and of access to her children. She was unable to settle into domesticity, or into the daily work of building and maintaining her career and image in London. John Doran writes, "She had once almost shared the throne assumed by Mrs Cibber, but she wanted the sustained zeal and anxious study of that lady, and cared not, as Mrs Cibber did, for one quiet abiding home, by whomsoever shared, but sighed for change had it and suffered for it."[101] Slippage makes it unclear if Doran means a theatrical or a private home, but for Bellamy both were true as she sought fame, stability, and safety.

Conclusion

Felicity Nussbaum argues that actresses' celebrity was "imagined not as private property but as mutual, consensual, interplay. Individuality and its objectification in the marketplace operated as a kind of currency with fluctuating worth in an emergent credit economy as inner life was projected onto the stage."[102] Susannah Cibber and George Anne Bellamy have illustrated two very different responses to extramarital pregnancy in the context of the culture of sensibility and a commercial system in which the ability to project and elicit powerful emotion was a valuable commodity. Cibber concealed; Bellamy revealed. Both women's strategies aimed to assert or preserve the high value of their stage careers and celebrity, and both have had long-term consequences for our evaluations of their significance to theatrical history.

Cibber—who amused herself by teaching a parrot to spout tragedy,[103] who might have left the stage permanently but never did so, who settled for nothing less than complete control over her own career, who lived surrounded by the family she chose in defiance of the principles of honor and virtue that defined the lives of the women she played on stage—performed such a successful disappearing act that we are still struggling to find her centuries later. She played the victim on stage, but her decision to return to London, resume her lucrative career, and not be shamed into hiding suggests a woman who had had enough of being bullied. She did not return to remain silent on the sidelines: she goaded Garrick to buy the Drury Lane patent with her; when this failed, she corralled him and James Quin into the same company; out of work because of managerial disputes in 1745, she organized a charity performance for veterans and publicized it—and the bad behavior of the Drury Lane managers—with letters written in her own name to the papers.[104] Faced with disappointing co-stars, she directed them to improve the effect of her own performances and of the play upon the audience.[105] She translated from the French and produced a popular afterpiece called *The Oracle* (1753), taking full credit for every aspect of the performance rather than obsequiously thanking the managers as most writers did.[106] All of these actions—many of them public and/or clear from her surviving correspondence—suggest she was far from the characters she played on stage. Thus, when we evaluate her absence during her last pregnancy, we should be wary of assuming that, like one of her stage characters, she was hiding and hunted in distress.[107]

Even her stage characters, however, hint at more than passive lamentation. A thread of Cibber's celebrity often overlooked is how frequently rage figures into praise of her best performances. Churchill, for example, describes her as having "rival excellence of Love and Rage;" love is the passion that later commentators tend to privilege, but I would suggest rage was equally if not more important.[108] What might Susannah Cibber's rage have meant to the many women in her audience who faced violent or exploitative marriages? Did they see her only as the victim she often performed, or did they also see a figure of resistance? She carefully controlled her public image in the service of her continued career, but her private life was an open secret. Her career gave her financial independence, privacy, the power to control her story through stage performance, and an ability to keep her loved illegitimate children, something other married women had no right to do. Victimhood and resistance need not be mutually exclusive in our understandings of her: performing innocence after overwhelming evidence of one's guilt and being applauded for it suggests, powerfully, an acceptance and validation of the resistance her career signaled. Much of her power came from her unflinching consistency of persona and purpose; concealing pregnancy was a choice that preserved what she had built.

Bellamy, despite her lucrative career and sensational memoir, ended her life in poverty, a fact that tends to tarnish the assessment of her career. Though her pregnancies and status as a mother were a key form of charismata in the 1750s, in her *Apology* her children are never positioned as hers—George is given to Metham's sister, the Calcraft children are separated from her when the relationship ends—she feels pain at the loss of them, but also deeply resents her daughter for ingratitude. Bellamy is a picture of contented domesticity with Metham, but only ever doing a burdensome duty with Calcraft. Her desires to be free or to regularize their situation are complicated by her pregnancies and her debts, which limit her agency and force her to remain in a sexual relationship with a man who does not value her. Her mimetic performances of the wife and mother role are unconvincing and unsuccessful in this relationship; only those tinged with the earnest sensibility of the relationship with Metham enable her to recapture the success of her stage performances of maternal distress.[109] On the one hand, this supports her early celebrity persona of the passionate and impulsive young ingenue—the Juliet who gives all for love. On the other hand, it also sets her outside discourses of sensibility, which should make her particularly susceptible to her maternal feelings.

Both women's stories resonate with aspects of Anne Oldfield and Susanna Mountfort Verbruggen's experiences. Cibber in 1735 and 1736 and Bellamy in the 1750s performed while pregnant in the context of marriage; like Mountfort Verbruggen, their appearances signaled normative femininity. Both of these midcentury women also appeared in roles where pregnancy might heighten the pathos of the performance, including Andromache in *The Distrest Mother*. In doing so they positioned themselves as inheritors of Oldfield's greatness. Cibber's parallels to Oldfield do not stop there. Like Oldfield, she made a major career shift during pregnancy and rehabilitated an irregular private life through consistent public performances of her celebrity persona. Like Oldfield, she retired during a pregnancy that came at "advanced maternal age" and that retirement, whatever else it might be, was also a statement of value and worth: both women could afford (economically and professionally) to temporarily retire without diminishing their market value. Bellamy engages in similar performances of value in her *Apology* when recounting her 1749 pregnancy experience, which included temporary retirement and beneficial changes to her contract. Ultimately, however, Bellamy's disrupted and inconsistent performances of celebrity and maternity become a form of stigmata that overbalanced the charismata of her charm and the impulsive passion that first made her a sensation. She turned to memoir at the end of her life to recapture the power of her performances on stage through performances in print. Though largely unsuccessful, Bellamy's use of pregnancy and childbirth to emphasize her social status and relationships with prominent and even royal figures is an important forerunner to our next subject. We now turn to the celebrity who best exemplifies the ability to create a symbiotic relationship between maternal and theatrical labor: Sarah Siddons.

3
CONCEIVING GENIUS
Sarah Siddons

In the preceding chapters we have seen pregnancy's role in bolstering an expanding repertoire and productively changing or enhancing a celebrity's reputation (Susanna Mountfort Verbruggen, Anne Oldfield, Susannah Cibber). We have also seen pregnancy lend legitimacy to offstage romantic partnerships in print sources and on stage (Anne Oldfield, George Anne Bellamy). And we have seen strategies employed when pregnancy created conflicts with an existing celebrity persona (Susannah Cibber) and became a tool for retroactive self-fashioning in a later memoir (George Anne Bellamy). The final actresses in this study, Sarah Siddons and Dorothy Jordan, provide a second look at challenges others faced and successes they enjoyed. Siddons, for example, returns us to considerations of an actress with a stable domestic reputation nearly one hundred years after Mountfort Verbruggen, while her associations with maternity echo and surpass Oldfield's posthumous reputation and Bellamy's in the late 1750s. Jordan faces challenges and triumphs in her career similar to those that marked Oldfield, Bellamy, and Cibber's lives, but found different ways to overcome them.

Siddons and Jordan also form a pair that connect and reflect on one another. They were coworkers at Drury Lane for over two decades, appearing to stake out diametrically opposed positions: Siddons was famous for tragedy, Jordan for comedy; Siddons had a largely unremarkable private life, Jordan became a royal mistress in

1791. But they were also both women who raised children behind the scenes, nursed infants during breaks in rehearsals and performances, used their lucrative contracts to support growing families, and rose to and remained at the top of their profession for years. Their considerably higher number of known pregnancies, a greater archive of material from their lives and careers, and the significant critical attention they have received since make it necessary for each woman to receive her own chapter. Rather than extrapolating from limited records, these chapters require sifting and selection from an abundance of narratives and perspectives. In addition to the connections and context they offer earlier women's lives, Siddons and Jordan provide clear ground for understanding how their visible maternity and connections to the royal family shaped the significance and meaning of their gravid bodies in decades that, in Lisa Cody's words, came to "[treat] the successfully reproductive body as an aesthetic, cultural, and political ideal."[1]

Sarah Siddons (1755–1831), to a greater degree than any other performer in this study, succeeded in melding her on- and off-stage lives into an apparently seamless and symbiotic identity. Unlike the aspirational tragic heroines of Anne Oldfield, the tenebristic displays of Susannah Cibber, or the ruptured narrative of George Anne Bellamy's life, Siddons seemed to carry her complete, stable, and unchanging self onto the stage. Night after night, she played tragic women—queens, mothers, and wives—thrilling audiences with her sublime performances. Her popularity derived not only from the power of her acting but also from what her stage performances seemed to offer the audience of her real, private self. Siddons encouraged this impression through deliberate strategies of self-fashioning that tied her onstage career to her offstage identity as a wife and, even more importantly, a mother. Maternity was a key charismatic component of her celebrity throughout Siddons's London career, operating to increase the effect of stage performances, justify her substantial earnings, and promote Siddons not simply as a stage celebrity but as an icon of nationalistic and mythic proportion.

This chapter traces perceptions of and reactions to Siddons's pregnant body between 1785, her first London pregnancy, and 1794, her last.[2] In 1785, Siddons's well-documented pregnancy provides many insights into the way theaters might manage pregnancy for their prominent performers. Her condition was also a constant topic of conversation in the public papers, where opinions about what she should and should not perform were strong and reveal a variety of perceived relationships between Siddons's changing body and her stage roles. Most strikingly, the papers created a powerful connection between Siddons's pregnancy and the role of Lady Macbeth, a part in which she had recently made her first London appearance. Nine years later, Siddons's 1794 pregnancy grants us the opportunity to consider how performers and managers might apply knowledge from one experience of pregnancy to a later one and offers more access to Siddons's personal thoughts and reflections on her condition. In the papers, her 1794 performances—dominated by a spectacular revival of *Macbeth* to open the new Drury Lane theater—prompted expressions of goodwill, support, and appreciation but direct commentary on her condition is rare. In examining this pregnancy, I detail potential reasons for the turn away from active discussion of Siddons's pregnancy in public, using Lisa Freeman's concept of the palimpsestic performance, which accrues meaning over time. From personal tragedies within the Siddons family to tragedies on a national and international scale, Siddons's last pregnancy combined and intersected with a host of complicated personal and political threads that shifted the meaning of her gravid body as an individual and cultural signifier.

Born in Wales on July 5, 1755, Sarah Siddons was the eldest of an eventual twelve children born to Sarah (née Ward) and Roger Kemble, both actors and the leaders of a touring company. Young Sarah married William Siddons, also an actor, in 1773. During a time of seismic shifts in British culture, Siddons had at least ten pregnancies while building a staggeringly successful career. Her first two children were born as she and William acted in provincial strolling companies, Henry on October 4, 1774, and Sarah Martha (Sally) on November 5, 1775. Siddons was pregnant with Sally when recruited for Drury Lane's 1775–76 season, David Garrick's last as manager and leading actor. She made her London debut in December 1775, six weeks after giving birth, moving to London with her husband and two infants in tow, establishing her household, and beginning rehearsals. Mostly performing in comedy, and with a voice unused to large performance venues, she failed to capture audiences and returned to the provinces before settling in Bath in 1778. For the next four years, she flourished at the Theatres Royal in Bath and Bristol and gave birth to Maria (July 1, 1779), Frances Emelia (baptized April 26, 1781, died in infancy), and Eliza Ann (June 2, 1782). Four months after Eliza Ann's birth, she returned to Drury Lane. This time, she was a triumph. George, her sixth child, arrived on December 27, 1785,[3] at the height of what poet Anna Seward called "Siddonian idolatry." After three miscarriages in three years (1788–1791), Cecilia, the baby of the family, was born on July 25, 1794.

One challenge this project grapples with is the diversity of the embodied experience of pregnancy. It is difficult to recapture a sense of exactly what a woman felt and looked like when pregnant, in every performance and across her lifetime, for pregnancy manifests, and can feel, different each time. In Siddons's case, we are fortunate to have comments from those around her, and sometimes from the actress directly, that offer insight into her experiences. For example, we have consistent evidence that from at least her sixth month onward her condition was readily visible and easily recognized by audiences. When scouting for David Garrick in 1775, Henry Bate referenced her "big belly which mars for the present her whole shape" when she was six months pregnant with Sally. In 1785 and 1794, friends and colleagues wrote that she looked "very big" on stage, also around the start of her sixth month.[4]

These descriptors, of course, reference her actual or perceived size, and hence assumptions about the progress of her pregnancy and when she might expect to give birth. Historian Joanne Begiato, whose work focuses on marriage and the family, also suggests that such language operated metaphorically: "measuring and charting bodily increase" became "an attempt to impose some degree of certainty on the pregnant condition."[5] Finding a pervasive mood of apprehension during pregnancy among the women she studied (1775–1830), Begiato explores how language reveals these feelings and attempts to exorcise or transform anxiety—about due dates, for example, or the health of the child—into certainty. In April 1794, for example, around the time Hester Piozzi called her "very big," Siddons thought herself "so frightfully large and heavy" that she might be having twins.[6] In this case, her description slips easily from a comment on size to one that uses "the metaphor of weight [to convey] physical and emotional oppression," as Begiato puts it.[7] Siddons's size is "frightful" to her, leaving her uncertain of the number of children she carries, which in turn may generate doubt about the anticipated due date, difficulties of labor, and the likelihood that she and the child(ren) would survive birth. Like many women of the time, Siddons always remained aware of the dangers of impending childbirth and acknowledged these in her letters to both male and female correspondents.[8] The apparent, unequivocal visibility of Siddons's body, coupled with announcements of her pregnancies in the papers when she was about three months along meant that in both 1785 and 1794 audiences might be aware of her pregnancy even before her condition was visible. In both cases, however, by the time she was performing in London she was obviously in the family way. The visibility of her vulnerable, human experiences juxtaposed the near-mythic status she enjoyed in the public imagination and sparked considerable interest for audiences.

Queen of Tears: Siddons's Celebrity

Throughout her career, Siddons's tall, muscular figure, bold gestures, powerful voice, and expressive face, with her dark eyes, demonstrative brows, and distinctive profile reinforced her representation of powerful, almost superhuman heroines. Discussing her extraordinary celebrity, Joseph Roach describes Siddons as a "role-icon," one who seamlessly carried her onstage persona into private life and labels her the "Tragedy Queen."[9] This role-icon identity was regularly visible onstage in her performance of queenly roles, rendered in paintings and drawings, and made available for purchase in the form of prints and engravings. Among the many visual depictions of the actress, Joshua Reynolds's exquisite *Mrs. Siddons as the Tragic Muse* may be the most significant evocation of her Tragedy Queen persona. In this near-life-size representation, the actress is indeed a queen: seated in a floating throne, she is crowned, bedecked in a thick rope of pearls, and attended with figures representing Pity, holding a bloody knife, and Terror, bearing a smoking, poisoned cup (Figure 3.1).[10] X-ray evidence has shown that a putto formerly stood at her knee but that Reynolds removed it, probably to retain the tight focus on the actress. Her gold dress and reddish hair help

Figure 3.1. Sir Joshua Reynolds (1723–1792), *Mrs. Siddons as the Tragic Muse* (1784). Courtesy of the Huntington Art Museum, San Marino, California

this, receding slightly into the background and allowing the luminosity of her white skin and billowing sleeves to draw the eye.[11] She looks to the side and up, mouth slightly open and left index finger raising. She is literally above us, tantalizingly close but across a gap of sky and vapor we cannot traverse; we cannot even catch her eye. This sense of inaccessibility appears to have gone with her into private life; one of her biographers wrote, "Mrs. Siddons had a right to be painted as the Tragic Muse, for her very manner in society was marked by an abstractedness and reserve that were the result of her studiousness."[12]

The commodification of Siddons and her widespread visibility, coupled with this sense of elusive inaccessibility, enhanced her celebrity through the creation of public intimacy. Her pregnant performances and the display of her children on stage were also part of this balancing act, enhancing the feeling of intimacy between actor and observer. Visual representations of her were crucial in the creation of this persona, and Robyn Aselon credits Siddons more than any performer before her for successfully wielding the power of the static image.[13] Also integral, as Laura Engel and Shearer West have argued, were that Siddons's portraits aligned her not only with fictional or mythical queenship, but specifically with Queen Charlotte, another larger-than-life figure who combined royalty and maternity in her public image and remained engaged in her public career throughout her many pregnancies.[14] The connection was furthered by Siddons's rapid and highly visible adoption as the king and queen's favorite actress. In her first season alone they supported her with five command performances and later made her an official reader to the royal princesses. During Siddons's 1785 pregnancy, the royal couple saw her several times, privately and publicly. On one occasion the queen even sent Siddons a box of powders she took for her health, assuring her they were safe to use during pregnancy.[15] Patronizing her on and off the stage, Charlotte validated Siddons's performances of royalty, her worth as a public figure, and her status as a respectable woman.[16] These associations with the queen were further enhanced when Siddons elected to use royal accoucheur Dr. James Ford, whom we met briefly with George Anne Bellamy in the last chapter, to deliver her sixth child. In the papers, Ford became the subject of good wishes before the birth, and gratitude after when she safely returned to the stage. Siddons's celebrity compellingly blended the mythic with the domestic, the regal with the maternal, and she reinforced this blending both on and off the stage.

The power of Siddons's performances and her role-icon status contributed to the all-consuming experiences audiences had in the theater. When Siddons toured to Edinburgh, young men found employment at the theater helping to remove those overcome by her performances, a practice referred to as "carrying off the dead."[17] After seeing Siddons in *Isabella, or The Fatal Marriage,* travel writer Karl Gotlob Küttner found her vocalizations, particularly her mad laugh as she plunged a dagger into her breast, to be "truly harrowing, arousing unpleasant, distressing feelings . . . such sounds as cut me to the quick."[18] Sheridan Knowles swore he felt "the chill of the grave" and "smelled blood" while sitting in a stiflingly crowded upper gallery at Drury Lane, watching her in the sleepwalking scene of *Macbeth*.[19] Siddons's performances worked so powerfully on the imagination that they shaped the physical experience of self and of the theater space for her audiences. The effects of her performances were long lasting. After *Isabella*, a young woman wrote to her father that Siddons's "screams, two falls flat upon her face are too dreadful—as well as the madness with which she ends the play. . . . I am crazy for Dear Divine Angelic Mrs Siddons" and excused her scattered writing with "you see I am cracked."[20] While the anonymous author of *The Beauties of Mrs. Siddons* attested: "Her sorrows took possession of my soul. . . . [I] could only express my feelings by tears;—and, even now, my agitation is so great, that I must lay by my pen."[21] Even the memory of Siddons's acting could plunge one back into the physical extremes first experienced in the theater. Some audience members were cautioned—even forbidden—from attending her performances out of the fear they would be mentally or physically unable to withstand the emotions she would pull from them.[22] These reactions testify not only to the power of Siddons as an actress, but also to the culture of the time and the desire of audiences to participate actively in the fiction they saw onstage.

The psychosomatic impact of Siddons's performances was part of a culture that actively encouraged the expression of emotion by valuing sensibility, and that considered human passions contagious. "Sensibility" was a term whose use and associations varied across the century. For our purposes here, as I suggested in chapter 2, it is useful to think of it as a form of bodily permeability focused on the upper strata of the body (head and heart) rather than the grotesque permeability of the lower strata of the body (genitals and bowels); an "interpenetration of spirit and flesh" and an "openness through sensation to the world" that is spiritual and emotional rather than sexual or scatological.[23] Sensible bodies could share and communicate emotion through vibration and electrical impulse, creating sympathy between people. Siddons's performances acted on the bodies of her audiences through this sympathetic exchange: as she performed, she communicated strong emotions to an audience who also felt them. When audiences were overcome with emotion, then, it was not simply their own that they felt but also Mrs. Siddons's, shaped and sculpted to maximal effect by the actress, and those of people around them. As Jean Marsden puts it, "The thrill of the theatrical experience existed precisely in this experience of infection, in the individual's experience of being swept along on a tide of emotion, and this effect was enhanced by being part of an audience that watched other spectators perform their own experience of sympathy."[24] The sharing of emotion made for effective performances; for some thinkers, it also had larger implications.

David Hume argued that feeling was the ultimate arbiter of morality, while Edmund Burke specifically labeled sympathy, the ability to feel what another feels in oneself, a defining marker of the human condition.[25] Theater, specifically tragedy, encouraged the public experience of sympathy and expression of emotion and was therefore a potentially powerful moral force. Burke suggested, in fact, that rousing the pity of audiences in the theater would lead to greater charitable beneficence in society as audiences sought the catharsis they did not receive within dramatic fiction. One audience member echoed this idea after seeing Siddons act in 1784: "Good God! What a blessed Society we should be could we always feel and be influenced by those generous emotions which she excites, when she makes every heart ready to burst with social, friendly, & exalted Sentiments."[26] Crucial to Burke's thesis was the experience of the sublime, the greatest feeling of which humanity was capable.[27] That which awes, overwhelms, or terrifies arouses the sublime; along with the pain these feelings cause, however, comes pleasure. In Burke's understanding, the sublime generates tension and exertion within the body, strengthening one against the shocks and troubles of daily life.[28] The sublime combination of feeling the pain of others (enabled by sympathy and sensibility), the pleasure that encourages us to seek it out, and the satisfaction we derive from relieving that pain prompts ethical behavior. Though it was typically associated with the masculine, Pat Rogers, Heather McPherson, Christopher Reid, and Laura Rosenthal provide ample evidence that the label was applied to Siddons.[29] Her audience members experienced "the LUXURY of grief," fell into agonies of weeping and fainting in response to her acting, and struggled to put their experiences of her performance into words.[30] She was associated with a higher order of being, with Greek ideals and Shakespeare, and had masterful control over her body and expressions; on multiple levels, her body could be considered a closed and controlled classical body, but one markedly vulnerable to sentimental sensation.[31]

As epic in scale as her stage persona could be, and as sublimely masculine, Siddons also consistently framed her career as that of working mother providing for her many children, balancing, as Laura Rosenthal argues, "her masculine sublime with a specifically *maternal* beauty."[32] When she announced that she would be leaving Bath for a more lucrative contract in London, for example, she promised to give her audiences "Three Reasons" for her decision that became famous in her own time. On May 21, 1782, eleven days before Eliza Ann was born, Siddons became the fourth woman in this study to act the role of Andromache in *The Distrest Mother* while heavily pregnant. That evening, she replaced the play's popular comic epilogue (discussed in chapter 1) with a personal address during which she produced the promised reasons, bringing her three young children—Henry, age seven; Sally, age six; and Maria, nearly three—onto the stage. Her pregnancy further pleaded the urgency of her situation. In Siddons's address, the pursuit of a successful and lucrative career was an active form of good mothering. Such a claim was literally true and culturally advantageous, locating this economically and theatrically powerful woman within the "cult of prolific maternity" that emphasized affective motherhood as a lifelong, noble, and correctly and innately feminine pursuit in the latter half of the eighteenth century.[33] Judith Pascoe also emphasizes the importance of visible maternity to Siddons's celebrity, for "an audience could call on their knowledge of this safer Siddons [wife and mother] to allay any anxiety they might feel before the powerful performing one."[34] Rather than the balancing act between performed transgression and offstage reality I argued for in Susanna Mountfort Verbruggen's career, here Siddons's feminine respectability balanced and became part of her stage sublimity.

Lady Macbeth

Siddons played many popular maternal characters in her career, from Isabella in *The Fatal Marriage* (used for her second London debut, when she acted opposite her son Henry), to Euphrasia in *The Grecian Daughter* (who breastfeeds her father to save him when he is imprisoned), and Lady Randolph in *Douglas* (whose compellingly conflicted soul is agonized over the return and subsequent death of her long-lost son). But her performance of Lady Macbeth was the height of her tragic genius. From her first performance in London in February 1785 critics and audiences recognized Lady Macbeth as an ideal role for the actress: "We must commend her for fixing upon a part, to which, in figure, countenance, and manner, she is so peculiarly adapted."[35] All of Siddons's strength and power could be brought to bear in the "masculine ferocity of the heroine," along with moments of wrenching tenderness—her horror at Duncan's resemblance to her father, her care of Macbeth after the banquet—and the pitiful vulnerability of the sleepwalking scene.[36] She married her own celebrity (domestic, regal, maternal) with the character (ambitious and often seen as masculine), creating what Felicity Nussbaum calls an "interiority effect" that endowed the character with aspects of the actress and transformed a virago role into a tragic heroine worthy of pity.[37] That Siddons performed the role of Lady Macbeth while pregnant later that year and in 1794 is a circumstance Laura Engel, Judith Pascoe, and Ellen Donkin acknowledge, though only Engel hints at the dramatic possibilities of this evocative event.[38]

Siddons first played Lady Macbeth in London on February 2, 1785, for her benefit night, and what could have been a single appearance became a sensation. A review in the *Morning Chronicle and London Advertiser* enthused: "Her acting was by far the finest heroic, we have ever seen . . . when the sublime and terrible graces of Mrs. Siddons are before us."[39] Descriptions of her acting highlight the individuality and particularity of her interpretation, as well as her refined bodily control: "She works to her end with means all her own, an eye, a brow, a voice—all implying undaunted metal, and particularly impressing terror. In the Sleep, there is a display of more theory, perhaps than is evidence in any of her acting."[40] Long before her "Remarks on the Character of Lady Macbeth" were published in Thomas Campbell's biography critics recognized in her Lady Macbeth, and especially in the sleepwalking scene, not simply a compelling conception of the character, but a whole theory of performance. Siddons, for example, had observed actual somnambulists to prepare her performance. She also broke with stage tradition by dressing in white bedclothes for the scene and setting down the candle to better mime handwashing—an innovation she later says had Sheridan frantic backstage, so convinced was he that the audience would object to this departure from the great Hannah Pritchard's practice.[41] Siddons's performance was not simply an exceptional execution of a familiar role, but a highly individualized reinterpretation of the part, and recognized as such. Hannah Pritchard was famous for disappearing into each role she played, transforming utterly into the cold and furious virago. Siddons, in contrast, endowed and enhanced her Lady Macbeth with traces of herself to such an extent that Charles Lamb later complained, "We speak of Lady Macbeth when in reality we are thinking of Mrs. S."[42] As we will see, much like Anne Oldfield's pregnant performances of Andromache in 1712–13 left an indelible mark on the character, so, too, did Siddons's pregnant performances of Lady Macbeth in 1785.

Like many of the earlier women in this study, Siddons's career necessitated important balancing acts. Unlike Anne Oldfield or Susannah Cibber, however, it was not a case of using onstage performances of normative femininity to counteract extramarital offstage relationships. Rather, as Engel describes it, "Using . . . royalty and maternity as models for legitimate forms of theatrical display in her characterization of Lady Macbeth, in the building of her career, and in her representation of herself in her memoir, made it possible for Siddons not to appear to be too ambitious, too theatrical, or too independent."[43] Siddons's offstage reputation as a devoted wife and mother balanced her exceptional power in the theater and created a distinctive and effective persona. When she became pregnant in the spring of 1785, some of these seeming contradictions—especially within the character of Lady Macbeth—collapsed into one another, fusing Siddons's maternity to her stage performances in new ways and prompting unprecedented levels of press coverage and debate that foreshadow the tabloids and gossip sites of the late twentieth and early twenty-first centuries.

"Undaunted Mettle": 1785

Siddons was on tour in the summer of 1785 when news of her pregnancy reached the London papers. She was reportedly due at Christmas, and journalists began to speculate on the possibilities and dangers of her condition in the coming season of 1785–86. What is unique about this particular pregnancy is the confluence of surviving archival sources—financial records, the correspondence of Drury Lane insider Mary Tickell, and near-daily newspaper coverage—that offer a detailed view of how Siddons's pregnancy and impending absence were handled behind the scenes and thought of on and beyond the stage.[44] Together, these archival sources often point to practical considerations and concerns that dictated repertory planning that fall, meaning that through Siddons's experiences in 1785, we can perhaps glimpse the kinds of considerations and negotiations other celebrity women engaged in earlier in the century. These sources also reveal and revel in fantasies of what Siddons's pregnancy means for the future of the professional theater, and most especially her performances of Lady Macbeth.

Drury Lane was seriously dependent on Siddons's presence for its financial health. In her first season with the company (1782–83) she brought in about £254 per night, nearly doubling the £130 average box office on nights she did not perform.[45] She also helped the theater to net over £30,000 for the first time since Sheridan took over the management in 1776; this despite the fact that many of his mainstay celebrity performers, including Frances Abington, had abandoned him for Covent Garden between 1779 and 1782. Two years later (1784–85) box office receipts on nights Siddons performed were still averaging £242 compared to the £138 on nights when she did not.[46] If she remained healthy in the fall of 1785, the theater could rely on her presence until about a month before the anticipated birth. Assuming all went well and she lay in for the standard four to six weeks afterward, she would be absent two to two-and-a-half months, a period of time that could easily represent a loss of £2,000 or more in revenue. How to handle Siddons's pregnancy to maximize her appearances while preserving her health, and how to plan for her extended absence was, then, a serious question with real financial stakes.

Before her confinement, Siddons worked with the managers to balance the economic demands of her job with her needs as a pregnant woman. To assist the theater financially, for example, she began her London season a month earlier than normal, in mid-September instead of mid-October: "Mrs. Siddons's pregnancy makes it necessary that the Drury-lane Managers should reap their harvest while they can."[47] Between mid-September and the end of November Siddons acted twenty-three nights in eleven weeks. On a further three nights, she appeared as a tableau vivant of Reynolds's portrait of her as the Tragic Muse in a revival of David Garrick's afterpiece *The Jubilee*. Average box office for her twenty-three regular appearances was £233, compared to £136 on the twenty-four nights she did not appear, despite starting her season before many wealthy audience members returned to town. Her appearances earned goodwill as well as money and were seen as a sign of professionalism and devotion to her audiences: "The Siddons, with a chearfulness [*sic*] that does her and her husband great honour, has consented to play as often as possible between this and Christmas."[48] Emphasizing her "chearfulness" also suggested good health, for without the ability to look inside the womb at the child directly, the mother became primary guardian and indicator of a healthy pregnancy. A serene mind, moderate physical activity, and participation in regular daily life, particularly after the first tenuous months of pregnancy, were all considered healthy and desirable.

Of as much interest as how long and how often Siddons would perform before giving birth were questions about *what* she would perform. The management naturally wished Siddons to appear in as many of her most popular roles as she was able, among them Lady Macbeth, Desdemona, Lady Randolph in *Douglas*, Belvidera in

Venice Preserved, Mrs. Beverly in *The Gamester*, the title role in *Jane Shore*, Constance in *King John*, and Euphrasia in *The Grecian Daughter*. She also played the novice nun Isabella in *Measure for Measure* twice, the second time "By Command of their Majesties" on November 2, about seven weeks before giving birth. Their Majesties, it seemed, had no concerns about the disconnect between Isabella's beleaguered virginity in the play and Siddons's pregnant body. Rather than verisimilitude, physical exertion was the barometer by which her repertory was set. Despite its enduring popularity, for example, she did not play her other Isabella character, from *The Fatal Marriage* with its "two falls flat upon her face." Siddons's performance style could be incredibly physical, and she once wrote to a friend that she was as "sore in every limb as if I had been severely beaten" after a performance.[49] While considerations for women's safety appear to drive accommodations throughout the century, in Siddons's case there was particular attention from audiences, managers, and the actress herself not simply to the content of the part but to her particular approach and interpretation. Because of her status in the company, this meant that accommodating these concerns became the primary driver of the theater's repertoire in tragedy.

According to Mary Tickell, who acted as an unofficial producer and literary manager for the theater, Siddons exercised considerable control in the selection of her repertoire that season. As Siddons approached her confinement, Tickell wrote, "Mrs S . . . has declar'd she cannot with safety play any more of her Tragedy Characters. She plays Constance Tuesday, as the only easy one left—there have been great Enquiries after the Way to Keep him, & there is no doubt that before she lies in, we might [have] half a dozen thumping Houses to it."[50] Tickell's letter offers two tactics for keeping a popular tragic performer onstage, safely, as she nears her confinement: featuring her in less physically demanding tragic roles and, when this fails, swapping comedy (*The Way to Keep Him*) in for tragedy. Tickell reveals that Constance in *King John*, which Siddons played on November 22, was "the only easy [tragic part] left," meaning the subset of parts Siddons performed in preceding weeks represented those she considered safe enough to perform in late pregnancy. At some point, Siddons, alone or in consultation with the managers, must have decided which of her parts were "easy" and which were not, and used this designation to plan her repertoire.

Siddons's roster of roles in the fall of 1785 therefore offers valuable insight into the differing physical labor and exertion tragic parts demanded from performers, pregnant or not. Tickell's letter also suggests a hierarchy between tragedy and comedy, with comedy—at least of the sort Siddons was acting—considered less taxing (physically and/or emotionally) than tragedy and therefore a viable option for an actress more than eight months pregnant. This switch was planned in advance; Tickell tells us that Siddons had a new dress for the part and was in rehearsals for the piece earlier in the fall, demonstrating how a theater might proactively prepare accommodations for a pregnant performer.[51] Despite Siddons's poor reputation for comedy, Tickell was confident they would have "half a dozen thumping Houses" simply because people were so eager to see her before she lay in.[52] This eagerness must have been, in part, driven by the certain knowledge that each performance could be her last (until after Christmas or even, chillingly, ever). The managers emphasized the urgency of her situation by counting down her performances in advertisements, bolstering the near-daily updates on her condition.[53]

While the primary negotiations that year about how to navigate Siddons's pregnancy were conducted between the actress and the managers, periodicals played an important role in bringing the conversation about how Siddons's pregnant body should intersect with her professional work into public awareness. These public commentators positioned themselves as allies aiding the solving of a challenging puzzle, recommending specific plays and, when necessary, casting them with Drury Lane's available performers.[54] A common theme was a desire to see Siddons in more Shakespeare after her triumph as Lady Macbeth, with papers including requests for Ophelia or Gertrude in *Hamlet*, Beatrice in *Much Ado About Nothing*, and Queen Katherine in *Henry VIII*. Another theme was to identify roles that did not demand excessive physical exertion but still carried sufficient emotional weight and stage time to make them worthy of her efforts, such as Calista in *The Fair Penitent*, a role George Anne Bellamy played several times in her 1752–53 pregnancy. *The Distrest Mother*, surprisingly, was rejected outright. This may have been a matter of changing taste, or it may have been because Siddons was planning to play not Andromache but the role of the spurned princess Hermione, which one critic called "deplorable trash."[55] Audiences and allies could be hawk-eyed about protecting their favorites from overwork and mistreatment, taking to the papers to agitate for raises or the need for rest as they did for Isabella Mattocks in 1773. But this did not mean they wanted to see Siddons in just anything: while her health held, audiences sought roles that would preserve the magnetic and magnificent effects of her performances, the mixture of pleasure and pain central to the sublime. For a time, and in many parts, this seemed to work; as the pregnancy progressed, however, it became a more difficult balance to maintain.

In September and October, most commentary on Siddons's body focused on how well she appeared to be and on how indefatigably she was exerting herself for her employers and for the public. With the exception of Lady Macbeth, which we will return to in a moment, her body is not conflated with that of her fictional characters at this stage, nor is her pregnancy disruptive to the narrative fictions she performs; rather, it is a sign of professional devotion and reinforces her existing domestic celebrity. In addition to the sympathy audiences felt for the tragic plights of her stage characters, they felt sympathy and goodwill toward the actress who played them. In November, however, as her pregnancy advanced and the physical effort it took to perform became more apparent, audience members expressed concern for her safety and urged her to rest. After seeing *Jane Shore* on November 8—a role called for loudly in the papers earlier in the season—one anonymous commentator declared: "Mrs. Siddons ought not to appear any longer, and the managers should be reminded of the fable, by hazarding too much, they may lose all, and this may be the last golden egg she may ever bring them . . . our concern for the actress got the better of our feelings for the character she was to perform. . . . The audience seemed more than once frightened for her."[56] Such concerns suggested that, in some cases, Siddons's pregnant body natural could overwhelm or disrupt the fiction she was representing.

In Rowe's play, the titular former mistress of Edward IV is turned out into the streets to starve when she refuses to become Lord Hastings's mistress or support his disenfranchisement of Edward's legitimate sons. The part unfailingly caused an excess of response in Siddons's audiences, driven by the exquisite horror of Jane's slow death. The author of *The Beauties of Mrs. Siddons* (1786), recalling an earlier performance, found it "too shocking for human nature to support" and was particularly horrified at her convincing portrayal of Jane's "famishing."[57] Siddons's performance was not only emotionally powerful but quite physical, and at one point she flung herself face-first on the ground. While she altered this feature of the performance in late pregnancy, much to the audience's relief, those familiar with her usual approach appear to have felt additional anxiety in anticipating the danger of such a moment.[58] This dread, and the physical effort required to perform in her advanced state of pregnancy, distracted from the performance, centering attention on Siddons's body natural to the detriment of the character and story. Part of the power of Siddons's performances was in the anticipation of the sublime terror one would feel in her presence; during pregnancy, that same familiarity could prevent the mix of pleasure and pain of the sublime, instead generating only a painful anxiety. Rather than risk her health and worry the audience, the *Morning Chronicle* writer recommended she stop performing altogether.

A similar response was offered as the excuse for a poor house on the night in late November that Siddons acted her "easy" part of Constance in *King John,* the role of maternal agony that so affected Susannah Cibber's audiences: "The thinness of the house was as broad a hint as could be given to the managers, that the town thinks it is time for Mrs. Siddons to retire."[59] Here, the commentator suggests audiences are voting with their feet: communicating to the managers through the medium of the box office. Though Siddons played excellently, "the pleasure we at this time receive from her acting is considerably abated by knowing, at how dear a rate our pleasure is purchased.—It hurts us not a little to be drawn off from the *fictitious* sufferings of a dramatick personage to the *real* sufferings of the performer on the stage."[60] This author means physical suffering of an actress in an advanced state of pregnancy, suggesting that the effort of performing was becoming clear. Siddons's biographer James Boaden, however, suggested that the objection was to seeing Siddons enact maternal grief "a little month before her own confinement," putting the audience in the unpleasant but unavoidable position of anticipating potential real-life tragedy—of reading Constance's grief as a portent of Siddons's.[61] Boaden's comment suggests pregnancy could create a relationship between body natural and role that disrupted stage fiction, but that disruption could arise both from the disparity between actor body and character body *and* from its too-painful conflation. What a part like Andromache in *The Distrest Mother*—which we have seen pregnant tragic actresses turn to throughout this study—offers is the ability to mingle fiction and reality without an unavoidable confrontation between the two. In Siddons's hands, Lady Macbeth offered something similar.

Though there were dreams of seeing her in many parts and much appreciation for how often she played (if not always what she performed), nothing dominated the public imagination so completely as Lady Macbeth. From the earliest reports of her pregnancy, press notices link her condition to the text of *Macbeth*, and to what had rapidly become her most iconic role. Not to Isabella in *The Fatal Marriage*, Lady Randolph, Constance, Euphrasia, or any of the other maternal characters she played: to the woman who explicitly seeks unsexing, a stripping away of reproductive potential for the sake of political ambition. To say such a conflation was improbable if not for the effect of Siddons's specific brand of celebrity is supreme understatement.

Lady Macbeth and the Public Imagination

Shortly after her London debut as Lady Macbeth in February 1785, Siddons became pregnant with her sixth child. When the public learned of her pregnancy that summer her condition became an occasion for exploring and expressing the complex intertwining of varied strands of her celebrity in the minds of audience members: her maternity, her affinity with the character of Lady Macbeth, and her status as the Tragic Muse. From the stage, her visibly changing body was now literally performing both maternal and professional labor simultaneously. Press coverage of Siddons's pregnancy was continual and thorough, not unlike that of expectant celebrities today, raising her condition—itself arguably mundane—to an extraordinary event of national interest and importance. For the six months prior to George's birth, the papers explored associations between Siddons's pregnant body, the role of Lady Macbeth, and her status as queen of tragedy. Collectively, these created a Siddonian mythology that further elevated her image to something more than human, reinforcing her association with the heroic and sublime.

On July 29, 1785 the London-based *Public Advertiser* broke through the dull recitative of the movements of London actors and actresses on summer tours to comment on Siddons's pregnancy. After highlighting the practical negotiations her condition would require of the managers and suggesting William Siddons be jailed for crimes against public amusement, the writer offered a vibrant fantasy of the child Siddons might produce:

> To Her [*sic*] we will however say, 'Bring forth male children only!'—For with reference to her great talents—we hope will spring from thence the prodigies of some future age.
>
> 'Some mate inglorious BARRY there may rest,
> Some GARRICK guiltless of immortal fame!'
>
> Some who may act up to her Lady of Macbeth, and return all her excellence with equal force—And thus only can her talents flourish as they should do.

Here, the paper casts Siddons as a fertile version of Lady Macbeth and offers a nearly parthenogenic fantasy of the child she will create.[62] The fantasy is singular in focus: the creation of a man who can match her Lady Macbeth and therefore give free and full range to her great talents. For this had been a small blot from the outset: the extreme inequality in ability between Siddons's superb acting and that of William Smith as Macbeth. Much as Lady Macbeth takes the bloody daggers when Macbeth's will fails him, in this imagined future Siddons's reproductive ability allows her to rectify the problem of an insufficient partner herself. The imagined child will usher in some "future age" where time holds no sway—or perhaps will spring, Athena-like, fully formed from its mother—and Siddons can finally perform opposite a worthy partner, which can only be her son, the male version of herself. Barry and Garrick, held up as the exemplars of this child's potential, were both notable for having no successors.[63] Siddons—a female muse, hero, and mother—can do what both of these men (and Lady Macbeth) could not: she can reproduce and extend her sublime genius into future ages, imprinting her "undaunted mettle" on her child.

As we have seen, in the fall of 1785 Siddons's appearances as Jane Shore and Constance raised audience anxiety for her condition, her body natural either overriding the bodies of her characters and disrupting audience investment in the stage fiction, or inspiring too-painful conflations of her body natural and character bodies. Siddons's pregnant appearances as Lady Macbeth did not inspire the same reaction. References to Macbeth pepper reviews for other plays throughout the fall, and those references are consistently linked to her pregnancy.[64] Siddons played the part three times that fall, on October 1 and 29 and November 19. At her first appearance on October 1 reviewers reported no diminishment in the role's power:

> Lady Macbeth . . . is by far the best part she has yet undertaken on a London theatre.—She conceived the spirit of the Author, and seemed to feel almost every *minutia* of Lady Macbeth. We may say of her, partly in the words of Sir John Suckling:—
>
> Her tragic feelings so distinctly wrought,
> That one might almost say her Body thought.[65]

To describe a pregnant actress as "conceiving the spirit of the author" is at the least a Freudian slip, if not an overt reference to her physical condition. Like the earlier fantasy that Siddons could birth a worthy partner for her performances, this allusion suggests her potential for creating another Shakespeare. From the fantasy of the next Barry or Garrick to act Macbeth, Siddons's body may be shaping another wellspring of creative English genius. In fact, her performance of Lady Macbeth is now the cause of her pregnancy, a kind of Immaculate Conception through tragic genius. The author goes on to paraphrase John Donne (not Suckling) to describe what is so remarkable about the performance: that her "tragic feelings" and interpretation of character are so complete as to appear fully enmeshed in her physical body.[66] With no apparent distinction between actor and character, interpretation and performance, her body becomes that of the character. In drawing explicit attention to her body, moreover, the author suggests there is nothing untoward or disruptive about her pregnancy; instead it enhances her performance.

Siddons was six months pregnant at the time, and her pregnancy was readily visible. Mary Tickell saw her act *Tancred and Sigismunda* on October 6 and wrote to her sister, "Mrs Siddons contrives to make herself look wonderfully well from our Box, but in front they say she looks very big—she exerts herself amazingly, indeed I think rather to give one pain."[67] It was apparently a pleasurable pain, for after hearing that Siddons looked "very big" from the front boxes, Tickell wasted no time in inveigling invitations into these seats, especially when Siddons acted Lady Macbeth. For as savvy and calculating as Mary Tickell could be about theatrical matters, and even Siddons as a private individual, she was also, undeniably, a fan.

On October 29, Tickell called on a carefully selected friend to convince her to attend Siddons's Lady Macbeth performance that night so she might have access to a front box: "I had my Curiosity fully gratified by seeing Mrs Siddons in front last night, but I never wish again to see a play from my own Box."[68] Siddons's pregnant performances of Lady Macbeth, and specifically the view of her body that made it most obvious, was of significant interest to Tickell that season, and presumably to others. On November 19, when Siddons made her last appearance as Lady Macbeth five weeks before giving birth, Tickell and her family managed to reserve Garrick's box, and declared that she "never saw [Siddons] act better in my Life."[69] Though on this occasion she makes no explicit comments about Siddons's pregnancy, something about the circumstance prompted this superlative reaction: was it the view from Garrick's box? The success of the performance *despite* her physical condition? If so, did Tickell's own experiences with pregnancy (her third child was born in March 1785) influence her latent appreciation or awareness of this? Or was it Siddons's pregnant body—or the way she navigated the part in her condition—that enhanced the performance?

Tickell's avid interest in Siddons both as a stakeholder in the theater and as an audience member is underscored by the machinations she engages in around each performance of Lady Macbeth. Each time, she gains access to a more advantageous viewpoint that will bring the pregnancy more abundantly into view. By November, newspapers had begun to report on the disruptive potential of Siddons's body and print warnings to the managers about the risks of her overexertion, but they record no such response for Lady Macbeth. Something about Siddons's celebrity, interpretation of the part, or both, made her increasingly pregnant body an asset, something that seemed natural and aided the sublime performance, rather than something that sparked fear, anxiety, or disgust.

Lady Macbeth in Performance

In the course of her London career, Siddons performed Lady Macbeth while visibly pregnant sixteen times: three times during her 1785 pregnancy, and thirteen times in 1794. Of these pregnant performances, Laura Engel writes, "The double nature of her persona as the character and the pregnant actress must have collided . . . and helped to underscore Siddons's characterizations of Lady Macbeth as a potentially sympathetic figure."[70] I want to expand on Engel's observation, for the newspaper commentary and testimony of Mary Tickell I have already cited suggest that audiences did indeed read Siddons's pregnant body in conjunction with the character of Lady Macbeth, and such conflation holds radical implications for the play. Here, I introduce these implications so far as we might understand them regarding Siddons's 1785 pregnancy; in 1794, the palimpsestic nature of performance places some moments in a distinctly different light.

A pregnant Lady Macbeth reframes much of the play, even beyond her appearances on stage, and becomes a visible signifier of the dynastic implications of Macbeth's actions. The potentiality encoded in her pregnant body creates a new level of tension in the play not present if the couple is barren, perhaps adding to the experience of the sublime evoked by the performance. Beginning with the witches' prophecy that Macbeth will be "king hereafter" while Banquo will "get kings though thou be none," Macbeth's preoccupation with Banquo's dynasty becomes apparent: "Your children shall be kings," and "Do you not hope your children shall be kings?"[71] This preoccupation with the progeny Banquo will have and Macbeth will not is the first introduction to Macbeth's domestic life, before the audience has seen Lady Macbeth. If a visibly pregnant Lady Macbeth then appears, we understand both the prophecies and Macbeth's fixation differently. Her pregnant body becomes a vexed and troubling presence within the play, creating the tension and potential for terror that characterize the sublime. How will this *visibly* pregnant woman fail to get kings? What fate awaits her?

Visible pregnancy also radically changes the implications of Lady Macbeth's 'unsexing' speech, when she declares her intent to make the witches' prophecy that Macbeth will be king come true:

> Come, you spirits
> That tend on mortal thoughts, unsex me here,
> And fill me from the crown to the toe top-full
> Of direst cruelty! make thick my blood;
> Stop up the access and passage to remorse,
> That no compunctious visitings of nature
> Shake my fell purpose, nor keep peace between
> The effect and it! Come to my woman's breasts,
> And take my milk for gall, you murdering ministers. (1.5.39–47)

In a pregnant body, what is normally abstracted imagery becomes disturbingly localized and concrete. A pregnant woman asking to be "unsexed," filled "top-full" with cruelty (who is already "top-full" with a child), who asks for intervention in the normal workings of her body's "access" and "passages" and who desires to change her "milk for gall" is describing a process that would likely kill the child within her womb—or transform it into something other than human. The question of whether Macbeth would have become king without murdering Duncan is always a conundrum in the play; a pregnant Lady Macbeth explicitly raises a similar question about this speech—would she have safely delivered an heir if she had not asked to be unsexed?

In his 1827 biography of Siddons, James Boaden described the line "take my milk for gall" as follows: "A beautiful thought, be it observed; as if these sources of infant nourishment could not even *consent* to mature destruction, without some loathsome change in the very stream itself which flowed from them."[72] Having previously described Siddons's Lady Macbeth in the letter scene as demonstrating "the apathy of a demon," Boaden's contradictory statement suggests that there is a fundamental disconnect between Lady Macbeth/Siddons's body and the demonic forces she seeks to harness.[73] Boaden's description also lacks a specific subject—is he speaking of Siddons, of Lady Macbeth, or both? Thomas Campbell suggested that Siddons's inherently tender nature could not be suppressed when writing her "Remarks on the Character of Lady

Macbeth": "Mrs. Siddons, disposed by her own nature to take the most softened views of her heroine, discovers, in her conduct towards *Macbeth*, a dutiful and unselfish tenderness, which, I own, is far from striking me."[74] Like her audiences, Campbell suggests that even Siddons is inclined to endow the character with aspects of herself.

Much of this "tenderness" comes from Siddons's interpretation of her later "I have given suck" speech:

> I have given suck, and know
> How tender 'tis to love the babe that milks me:
> I would, while it was smiling in my face,
> Have pluck'd my nipple from his boneless gums,
> And dash'd the brains out, had I so sworn as you
> Have done to this. (1.7.54–59)

While often cited as evidence of Lady Macbeth's inherently evil nature, Siddons emphasized the extremity of the statement as a tactic to underscore her commitment to Duncan's murder, not as a literal threat against a child: "The very use of such a tender allusion . . . persuades one unequivocally that she has really felt the maternal yearnings of a mother towards her babe, and that she considered the action the most enormous that ever required the strength of human nerves for its perpetration."[75] Siddons, as her audience would be well aware even before this pregnancy, had "given suck" to many children. The actress had certainly felt "the maternal yearnings of a mother towards her babe," even if previous interpretations of this character had largely denied such feelings. Since there appears to be no living Macbeth child now, and a pregnant woman before us, the possibility of a repeated birth and loss is very much alive in this speech. Lady Macbeth's statement prompts a response from Macbeth that, regarding the witches' prophecy, is especially poignant if directed to a pregnant Lady Macbeth:

> Bring forth men-children only;
> For thy undaunted mettle should compose
> Nothing but males. (1.7.72–74)

Addressing this comment to his pregnant wife immediately after the witches have told him he will fail to have an heir suggests a belief that force of will can frustrate the witches' prophecy, temporary forgetfulness, or even a sense of hopelessness. While each of these readings is possible without a pregnant Lady Macbeth, a pregnant actress onstage provides a visible locus for Macbeth's hopes. It suggests a desire for imaginative impression, for words to shape the child within his wife's womb, just as commentators fantasized about the child Siddons's talents would create.

Thus, a pregnant Lady Macbeth helps motivate the killing of Duncan. After the murder, her urging of her husband not to "think so brainsickly" (2.2.45) on the act resonates with injunctions to pregnant women to avoid all scenes of distress or upset and all but the most calming and cheerful thoughts. From this point in the play, she carries the multiple burdens of her own guilt and Macbeth's alongside the veneer of cheerful calm her condition requires (which we might read metatheatrically as the kind of burden Siddons herself was carrying). In the banquet scene, what should be the height of their triumph as king and queen devolves into her desperate attempts to disguise Macbeth's growing instability once he learns that his latest attempt to avert the prophecy has failed, leaving Fleance alive. In the fall of 1785, this scene gained added prominence with a new costume for Siddons. Mary Tickell described it as "the richest I ever saw—my Mother says there are forty yards of purple sattin in it tho' the Petticoat is of gold Tissue."[76] The papers provided additional details: "It was a violet coloured satin, richly trimmed with gold fringe and sable. The petticoat was of gold tissue, ornamented in like manner; her head-dress consisted of plumage, interwoven with jewels. Her stomacher was also richly studded with gems."[77] The outfit, made to accommodate the pregnant actress, also signaled the theater's financial investment in its star.

Despite the many yards of fabric and flashy accessories, Tickell's testimony that Siddons looked "remarkably well" throughout the fall but "very big" suggests that concealing her pregnancy was not the aim; indeed, with it constantly in the news there would be little point. Rather, the rich and abundant fabric, delicate and expensive gold tissue, jeweled headdress and stomacher gave audiences an image of their player queen as close to literal royalty as the stage could bring her.[78] This investment in dressing Siddons's bump, as we might put it today—an investment that was notable for its unusual liberality—further highlighted her prominence and power in the company. Much as a queen's wardrobe is a national expense because her appearance is reflective of a nation's wealth, so Siddons's excessive new dress was both a testament to her value and a sign of the theater's fiscal health. The elaborate costume clothing the pregnant body also drew attention within the fiction of the play to how far the Macbeths have risen and how much they have to lose. Pregnancy once again helps raise the stakes at play for an increasingly unstable Macbeth: he has murdered Banquo but Fleance's escape means he has failed to avert the prophecy that Banquo's children, and not his own, will be kings. Macbeth's pregnant wife is still in danger. An audience complicit in Macbeth's foreknowledge that this pregnancy will not result in an heir may see that knowledge as a contributing factor in the deteriorating relationship between Macbeth and his wife in the play's second half and even his decision to kill Lady Macduff and her children after his second encounter with the witches in act 4, scene 1.

Before Macbeth's entrance in this scene, we glimpse the witches at work, adding ingredients to their cauldron suggestive of horrific parodies of childbirth and maternity. Among the first is the "finger of a birth-strangl'd babe" (4.1.30), a child killed at the moment of emergence. For the audience, this gruesome image could foreshadow a possible outcome for Lady Macbeth's pregnancy. When Macbeth requests the aid of the witches' masters, they "Pour in sow's blood that hath eaten / Her nine farrow" (4.1.78–79), an image of infanticidal maternity in which the living offspring are reintegrated with the body of the mother through a cannibalistic act. The staging of this scene calls for two children to serve as apparitions. The second apparition, "A Bloody Child" evokes ambiguous images of birth: a newborn covered in blood and amniotic fluid, a stillbirth, or, like Macduff, a child delivered by Caesarian section. The Bloody Child also prefigures Macduff's children, soon to be murdered, and Macbeth's own unborn child. The third apparition, "a Child crowned, with a tree in his hand," once again raises the idea of dynasty, but the crowned child is not to be Macbeth's, and his rage is awakened when he sees Banquo's descendants as the line of kings and learns of Macduff's flight. As if the series of images of bloody children have planted the idea in his mind, Macbeth vows to

> give to the edge o' the sword
> His wife, his babes, and all unfortunate souls
> That trace him in his line. (4.1.166–68)[79]

Knowing his own ambitions for dynasty are hopeless and Banquo's progeny beyond his reach, Macbeth vents his anger on the symbols of Macduff's legacy.

In the final act of the play, imagery that recalls her husband's visit to the witches fills Lady Macbeth's sleepwalking scene (Figure 3.2). When enacted by a pregnant performer, this imagery suggests doubled meanings for the audience: Lady Macbeth's obsession with the smell and appearance of blood creates associations not just with Duncan's murder but with pregnancy complications and miscarriage as well as the images of blood and childbirth in act 4, scene 1. The Thane of Fife's wife, a mother murdered along with her children, becomes a potential mirror for herself. Famously, this scene was one of Siddons's best and the effect on the audience was incredible: James Sheridan Knowles wrote, "Though pit, gallery and boxes were crowded to suffocation, the chill of the grave seemed about you while you looked on her;—there was the hush and the damp of the charnel-house at midnight; you had a feeling as if you and the medical attendant, and lady-in-waiting were alone with her; your flesh crept and your breathing became uneasy; you felt the tenaciousness of the spot which she was trying to rub out upon her hand; the scent of blood became palpable."[80] The last vision of a pregnant Lady Macbeth walking into the darkness offstage is haunting and provides a visual basis for imagining her death, signaled by a "cry of women" (5.5.8). With a pregnant actress performing Lady Macbeth the cry now implies, perhaps, a death in childbirth—a death that has been a possibility since Lady Macbeth's first appearance on stage. Alternately and worse, it could signify the suicide (as Malcolm claims) of a pregnant queen, an infanticidal maternity of the kind that provides the witches' magic in act 4, scene 1. From first to last, a pregnant Lady Macbeth enhances the sublime horror of the play, ratcheting up the tension around each decision and misstep the Macbeths make, adding the time pressure of impending birth to their actions, and, in Siddons's hands, enhancing the unlikely pity she drew from her audiences.

Figure 3.2. George Henry Harlow (1787–1819), *Sarah Siddons* (1814). Courtesy of the Garrick Club, London

Pregnancy and Creative Genius: The Jubilee

For all the readiness to read Siddons's pregnancy into and alongside *Macbeth*, and all the added horror and pity it could add to her performance of the play, Lady Macbeth's death meant it was not a role that could, itself, offer fulfillment of the hopeful parthenogenic fantasies of the summer, even if it seemed to be their target. That came with a closely related part. Beginning on November 18, Siddons appeared in a revival of David Garrick's afterpiece *The Jubilee*, a celebration of Shakespeare centered on spectacle and tableau that included most of the acting company. Her role in *The Jubilee* was that of the Tragic Muse, the female genius who inspired Macbeth and the other tragedies. In a break with previous tradition, Siddons's Tragic Muse was a tableau vivant of the Joshua Reynolds portrait. Heavily pregnant, she was drawn in state on a wheeled car.[81] As in the painting, she appeared enthroned and attended by figures representing pity and terror, wearing a crown and a golden dress made to match that in the portrait. Reynolds had made her into a muse and pagan queen, the font and origin of all tragedy, celebrating her performances of ennobled and distressed women. But he had done so before her greatest triumph. Now, she was inextricably associated with Shakespeare and what to some was his greatest creation: "In the grandeur of tragedy 'Macbeth' has no parallel, till we go back to the 'Prometheus and the Furies,' of the Attic stage."[82] Siddons was the point of connection between Attic greatness, the golden age of Shakespeare, and her own luminous genius. As she re-created Reynolds's static image with her living body while more than eight months pregnant, the synthesis of her celebrity—her status as the Tragedy Queen, the Tragic Muse, Lady Macbeth, and her maternity—was complete. The creative force of the muse, so often metaphorically linked to reproduction, was now literal and manifest. In re-creating the Reynolds's portrait, moreover, Siddons overwrote Garrick's original image of Shakespeare's tragic muse with her own. She also offered a vision of the incipient fulfillment of the fantasies articulated that summer and fall: that Siddons would birth a new tragic titan to partner her performances as Lady Macbeth or to become the next Shakespeare.

Siddons's 1785 pregnancy underscored her value to the theater, and the economic power she wielded in the company while adding considerably to her fame and status as a celebrity woman. The management attempted to buffer themselves against the financial blow they would sustain during her absence by starting her season a month early, featuring her in popular parts that prevented physical overexertion and outfitting her in expensive new costumes that awed audiences. They responded to Siddons's physical needs by altering her repertoire in late November to a less demanding comic role that she would not ordinarily play, but which was still a financially sound investment because the impending birth created demand for her presence. The revival of *The Jubilee* provided an additional opportunity to see Siddons without demanding further physical exertion from her and made her the complete Tragedy Queen on stage. Beyond the theater, her selection of royal accoucheur (and part owner of Drury Lane) James Ford as her birth attendant, and its acknowledgement in the papers, further reinforced associations with Queen Charlotte. Most strikingly, the summer and fall of 1785 demonstrate the powerful allure of reading her pregnant body in relation to her role-icon status and performance of Lady Macbeth. Pregnancy aided Anne Oldfield and Susannah Cibber in making career shifts into tragedy; for Siddons, pregnancy brought apotheosis.

Britannia Mater: 1788–1792

Siddons again played Lady Macbeth pregnant in a major new production in 1794. In the intervening nine years, her associations with royalty grew even stronger and took on new valances of meaning. By 1794 she was not simply the public's Tragic Muse, but an emblem of the nation and idealized, patriotic maternity for a time of war and uncertainty. Lisa Freeman writes, "She ascended to practically transcendent status as the sublime symbol of tragedy's flame, and she also achieved iconic stature as a symbol of both the majesty of the state and the nobility of the British nation."[83] To understand the effect this had on her 1794 performances it is helpful to employ Freeman's concept of the "palimpsestic performance": "the accretion and rewriting of layers of memory in the theatre of the mind over the course of years of witnessing the same actor in the same role."[84] Palimpsestic performance is similar to Carlson's concept of "ghosting" but allows for the disjunctions and discomforts that can arise as the body ages and conflicts with past memories, rather than focusing on memory as a suture that effaces physical change. I want to use this concept to consider how Siddons's pregnant performances of Lady Macbeth in 1794 contained not simply layered memories of her previous appearances, including during her 1785 pregnancy, but also her reproductive and maternal history (body natural), the expansion of her repertoire of Shakespearean heroines (character bodies), and her associations with royalty in light of events in France and innovations in the 1794 staging (celebrity body).

The years between 1788 and 1791 were difficult for Siddons personally and professionally. In three short years, she suffered three miscarriages and lost her six-year-old daughter Eliza Ann to sudden illness. Despite her brother John Philip Kemble's elevation to company manager and their highly successful pairings in tragedy, including as Macbeth and Lady Macbeth, tensions were high in the company.[85] She performed irregularly, both for health reasons and because of disputes with Sheridan over payment of her salary. It was also a span of time when much changed in the national and international landscape: George III had his first extended bout of mental instability, triggering a regency crisis in November 1788 that lasted for four months until his recovery in late February. Bookending this crisis, Siddons debuted two tragic maternal roles that further expanded her Shakespeare repertoire: Queen Katherine in *Henry VIII* and Volumnia in *Coriolanus*. When George III recovered, Siddons represented Britannia in a celebration gala at the King's Theatre. That summer, violence and upheaval in France broke out, leading to the execution of the French monarchs, declarations of war, and the Reign of Terror. Tracking Siddons's personal tragedies in relation to these national and international events demonstrates how her celebrity evolved in a time of turmoil and change. In turn, this helps us to understand how these factors mattered during her final pregnancy.

In April 1788 Siddons had her first of three miscarriages, events that called attention to the vulnerability of her body natural. Her friend and prodigious diarist Hester Thrale Piozzi dates the miscarriage as beginning on April 3, the night Bertie Greethead was to receive his first author's benefit for his presciently named *The Regent*, a new tragedy, in which Siddons played the lead Dionora.[86]

Performers typically took two weeks off for miscarriages, though these extended, painful, and dangerous events could result in longer absences. In a stark contrast to the silence that often surrounds miscarriage today, papers almost immediately reported the cause of Siddons's absence. Just as Siddons was recovering well enough to return (again under the care of Dr. Ford), her six-year-old daughter Eliza Ann suddenly fell ill and died. Siddons buried her daughter on April 18. On the same day, an "Ode on the Indisposition of Mrs. Siddons" appeared:

> O blest HYGEIA, come; and bid each heart rejoice!
> No partial call for private ends
> Thy salutary aid implores;
> Lo! At thy shrine a NATION bends![87]

This author imagines the entire nation suspended from daily activity to kneel in supplication for the restoration of a beloved public figure. In a few short months, similar odes and appeals would appear on behalf of the king. A grieving Siddons returned to work on April 26: "Saturday night Mr. Greatheed's Tragedy, the *Regent*, was performed for the fourth time, to a most crowded and brilliant audience, not a place being to be had in the boxes at the end of the second act. Mrs. Siddons never played with more genuine feeling, than on Saturday; her scenes with her child particularly, were so truly maternal and interesting, that tears flowed plentifully from every spectator."[88] Siddons's back-to-back losses stimulated interest and heightened response to her onstage performance of a maternal character, down to the slippage that makes the child "hers" (Siddons's rather than Dionora's).[89] Unlike the display of her heavily pregnant body that triggered audience anxiety in 1785, press notices of her return to the stage in 1788 stressed her resilience and appearance of health. Indeed, she played with new heights of "genuine feeling" when she feared for her child's safety, mourned his supposed death, and when they were joyfully reunited. For actress and audiences, the emotional weight of her reported losses increased the power and pathos of her stage performance.

The following year, Siddons added two important new Shakespearean heroines to her repertoire whose character bodies helped to reinforce her association with queenship. On November 25, 1788, she acted Queen Katherine in *Henry VIII*, the distressed queen whose husband moves against her for failing to produce a living male heir. Audiences had been clamoring to see her in the part since at least 1785 when critics recommended it during late pregnancy. Katherine has several magnificent moments of oratorical power as she defends herself as a true wife and rightful queen in a sumptuously staged trial scene, speaks passionately against her mistreatment at the hands of Cardinal Wolsey and others, and has a vision of her impending death. Siddons's first performance of the role came as the country entered the Regency crisis of 1788–89, and she repeated it eleven times as the crisis continued into February. In these months, rumors of the king's illness were escaping from Windsor, where his doctors sequestered him away from the queen, who nevertheless refused to leave him. As the crisis continued into December, opposition papers began to criticize and abuse Queen Charlotte, fearing Parliament would award her the Regency instead of the Prince of Wales. As a staunch Whig, Sheridan and his theater were associated with the Prince's faction. Siddons's association with Queen Charlotte, however, also offered through her performances of Katherine the view of a loyal woman and foreign queen maligned and cast aside by political enemies.[90]

Another new role came on February 7 as the Prince of Wales was poised to become Regent. Siddons acted Volumnia, the severely patriotic mother of the titular general in *Coriolanus, or the Roman Matron*. Kemble's version of the play drew on earlier versions by James Thomson and Thomas Sheridan, from whom he drew the subtitle that highlighted Volumnia/Siddons's central role in the action. On stage, her martial mother overshadowed all, including 240 extras, in the mind of actor Charles Mayne Young: "She came alone, marching and beating time to the music; rolling . . . from side to side, swelling with the triumph of her son. Such was the intoxication of joy which flashed from her eye, and lit up her whole face, that the effect was irresistible. She seemed to me to reap all the glory of that procession to herself. I could not take my eye from her. Coriolanus, banner, and pageant, all went for nothing to me, after she had walked to her place."[91] Evaluating reception of Siddons in the part, scholar Jonathan Bate labels her Volumnia, "the mother of the nation," meaning both Rome in the play and Britain.[92] Here was another role that drew both on Siddons's maternity, and her associations with queenship and nationalism. Drury Lane performed the play seven times in its opening season and sporadically from 1789 to 1796, its popularity occasionally disrupted by both domestic and international events and always subject to Siddons's ability to appear.[93]

Volumnia is a very different kind of mother than Isabella or Andromache, both of whom are driven by a consuming need to protect their sons at all costs. Volumnia is first and foremost a patriot, opposing her daughter-in-law Virgilia's softer nature, which is dominated by love of and fear for her husband. In their first scene, Volumnia mocks Virgilia's fears that Coriolanus will die in action: "Had I a dozen sons, each in my love alike, and none less dear than thine and my good Marcius, I had rather had eleven die nobly for their country, than one voluptuously surfeit out of action."[94] Though Volumnia loves her son, when Coriolanus rebels against Rome, the proud matron refuses to support him, declaiming in the amended version: "A grave in Rome would better please me than a throne at Antium" (43). After pleading in vain for Coriolanus not to march on his own city, Sheridan/Kemble's Volumnia draws a dagger, planning to die by suicide rather than return to Rome in disgrace. Volumnia's unwavering patriotism, exceeding even loyalty to her family, makes her an embodiment of Roman ideals and Rome itself, both Roman Matron and *Roma mater*. In the context of the Regency crisis and heightened nationalistic feeling, performance of these Roman characters by a British author became a patriotic act, and Kemble and Siddons were both warmly applauded. Like all of Siddons's best performances, Volumnia incorporated strength, nobility, and affecting pathos while drawing on her maternal persona.

Volumnia was a powerful maternal figure for a time of uncertainty and crisis. Julie Kipp has argued that as the century drew to a close "the overly sympathetic mother becomes emblematic of the dangers associated with narrow allegiances or highly localized loyalties, and so plays a key role in discussions concerning the fostering of nationalist bonds. An obsessive concern for things local proves a distraction from duty to nation."[95] Volumnia demonstrates the appropriate priorities for such a time: she is fiercely loyal to her son but love of country runs deeper. Joining her celebrity with Volumnia throughout a tumultuous time of uncertainty and war linked Siddons's maternity with the Roman Matron's patriotism. It also reflected the position of the queen, distressed and anxious in her domestic life but steadfast in her duty to country: on January 30, the week before the premiere, Charlotte acknowledged the necessity of a Regency for the "happiness of a great, loyal and affectionate people."[96]

In addition to resonating with the country's political situation, *Coriolanus* contains significant echoes of *Macbeth*, thus allowing Siddons's Scottish queen to resonate with this Roman matron. Volumnia imagines Coriolanus a "thing of blood" in battle (15), recalling the bloody captain's description of Macbeth carving a passage through soldiers' bodies to "unseam" the rebel Macdonwald (1.2.22). She takes pride in her own undaunted mettle, which not only shaped Coriolanus in the womb but also gave him his fighting spirit: "Thy valiantness was mine, thou suck'd it from me" (29). There are only two references to fathers in the play, and both refer to Coriolanus as father to his young son; like the parthogenic fantasy of the child Siddons carried in 1785 or Macbeth's invocation to Lady Macbeth, Volumnia is a woman whose dominance shaped her son in seeming excess or even exclusion of a male contribution. The part is, in considerable ways, a vision of the mother Lady Macbeth might have been.

On April 21, 1789, two months after the *Coriolanus* debut, Siddons participated in celebrations for George III's return to health. In costume as Britannia, Siddons recited a fifteen-minute-long ode to the king. The ode ended with Siddons re-creating Britannia's pose as shown on several denominations of British currency: seated with a shield bearing the Union Flag, a spear, and an olive branch. The event in April was a private one, though crowded and widely reported; Siddons also repeated the Ode publicly at Drury Lane on May 11.[97] Shearer West writes, "The visual slippages between Siddons and the Tragic Muse/Queen and as Britannia, the allegory of a united nation, was particularly powerful at a time of incipient revolution in France. . . . Siddons' pose [as Britannia] was an indexical sign for a queen who was seen to have nursed her husband through a period of crisis."[98] As Siddons finished, the band struck up an appropriately patriotic tune: not, as one might suppose, "God Save the King," but "Rule Britannia." Embodying the nation, Siddons added another layer of association to her existing celebrity body. In the wake of her performances of Katherine, Volumnia, and Britannia, she embodied a martial, dignified, and patriotic maternity, resilient and indomitable; her celebrity body suggested the strength not only of the nation but also of Britain's queen.

At the same time, however, her body natural was ailing. Siddons struggled with a persistent venereal complaint contracted from her husband, which, in combination with her miscarriages and perhaps other illnesses, was debilitating enough to disrupt her performance schedule for nearly two years.[99] Siddons was on tour in the summer of 1789 when French citizens stormed the Bastille; she had a second miscarriage in August while she was acting at Exeter, and it was again reported in the papers.[100] She did not return at all for the 1789–90 season, but she haunts Burke's *Reflections on the Revolution in France*, printed in November 1790. Burke likens the witnessing of the horrors of the Revolution (exaggerated at the time, but prescient considering later violence) to the experience of weeping at Garrick or Siddons's performances. When he imagines Marie Antoinette's separation from her children or pictures her concealing a "sharp antidote" in her bosom to avoid an indignant end, his descriptions echo Siddons's performances of maternal and queenly characters; significant among them is Volumnia, particularly when he calls the French Queen a Roman Matron.[101] Much as Siddons's tragic performances could offer moral instruction through exposure to the sublime, Burke suggested that familiarity with the actress made it easier to envision and sympathize with a real tragic queen.

Shortly after Burke's *Reflections* appeared, Siddons returned to the stage for seven performances between December 1790 and May 1791 but was clearly unwell: "Never did the heroine of the scene [Jane Shore] murmur forth her woes to affect more deeply the heart that can melt as it contemplates the imagery of distress, where it is true to nature's colouring, and while it conveys a lesson to the fairest and best part of creation. We were sorry to remark that a long illness had left the countenance of this admirable actress but too much prepared to picture the dying Shore—little was left for the hand of art to effect in the dressing room."[102] For this reviewer, returning to the stage in poor health made Siddons's physical state too close to the character's condition for comfort. Siddons's ailing body natural in a time of national turmoil could both reinforce and trouble the iconic and nationalistic associations with Siddons's celebrity body, as Lisa Freeman observes: "Etched in memory as an emblem of the nation, Siddons's characteristic dignity both on the stage and off came to function . . . as a surety of the posterity of the nation . . . [but] her body's state revealed that neither her immortality nor that of the nation was assured."[103] In these years, the goddess who would birth a young Roscius or a new Shakespeare was suddenly human; so were kings, as both George III's bout of madness and Louis XVI's execution made clear. Their tragic queens—Charlotte who had fought against her son for a husband who forgot and rejected her in his madness, and Marie Antoinette, who would lose her children and her head—underscored that the frightening vulnerabilities of Siddons's stage performances were real.

Siddons had a third miscarriage in early August 1791; Hester Piozzi details this and Siddons's deep melancholy afterward.[104] As a result, Siddons stayed away from the London theater until January 1792. By the fall of 1793, when she set off on a tour in Ireland, she seemed vastly better in both physical and mental health, and, while in Dublin that winter, she became pregnant for the tenth and final time at thirty-nine. Siddons's extended tour coincided with the long wait for the new theater to reopen, which it finally did on Easter Monday 1794. Audiences enthusiastically greeted Siddons's reappearance after five years of frequent absence and illness. Linda Colley argues that the king's earlier illness—the susceptibility of his body natural—became an important form of what Roach would term charismata, feeding the affective ties between the king and his people and leading to a surge in patriotism after his recovery. Similarly, Siddons's years of ill health followed by a triumphant return, glowingly and fulsomely pregnant, also created an outpouring of support and acclaim. This pregnancy allows us to understand Siddons's personal experiences of pregnancy more fully, to compare her pregnancy repertoire in 1794 with her repertoire in 1785, and to trace the palimpsests of meaning layered into her performances of Lady Macbeth.

"Splendor and Certainty": 1794

Drury Lane reopened in the spring of 1794. One paper declared it a "TRIUMPH for the TASTE and FANCY of the NATION!"[105] The new building expanded seating to 3,611 and was a wonderland of mirrored lights, cut glass chandeliers, and opulent ornamentation. As in 1785, Siddons's pregnancy created urgency around her appearances for audiences were aware of her condition before she began performing. In late February, when she was about nineteen weeks pregnant, it was announced that Siddons would shortly "present another offering at the shrine of Lucina."[106] In March, she attended the opening of the new theater as an audience member at the oratorio performances, where she could both see and be seen. Before her debut, one reporter explained, "Mrs. Siddons performs only a few nights when she retires to act the maternal character upon a private Theatre," characterizing her pregnancy as another Siddonian performance.[107]

Siddons's 1794 pregnancy offers a chance to understand how this experience of pregnancy may have differed from her experiences in 1785. At the end of April, about twelve weeks before giving birth, she mused to Hester Piozzi, "I am sure there must be two I am so frightfully large and heavy."[108] Her size may have contributed to some confusion about her due date, for she appears to have been expecting the birth in early July and Cecilia did not arrive until the twenty-fifth. After recovering, Siddons described the delivery as a "long, laborious time" and affectionally referred to her new baby as "the dear fat little lump;" in contrast, she had given birth so quickly in 1785 that James Ford did not make it to the house before George appeared.[109] Her physical experience of this pregnancy was different, her size and the baby's larger, and her labor more extended. She had hired a male accoucheur again, a Mr. Batty, but without the fanfare that had accompanied James Ford's involvement. As always, however, she expressed anxiety for her family, especially her daughters, in case they were to "lose her."[110] Despite these fears and the perhaps more difficult experience of late pregnancy, she participated wholeheartedly in the opening of the new theater.

Between April 21 and her withdrawal on June 6 Siddons acted twenty nights, far more frequently than she had in 1785. The vast majority of her appearances were as Lady Macbeth (13 times), interspersed with performances of other tragic heroines: Lady Randolph in John Home's *Douglas* (1), Mrs. Beverley in Edward Moore's *The Gamester* (3), Queen Katherine in *Henry VIII* (2)—when Katherine perhaps made especially compelling claims about her fertility—and the virginal princess Hermione in *The Distrest Mother* (1). Lady Macbeth, Lady Randolph, and Mrs. Beverley were roles she had also acted while pregnant in 1785, none of which had provoked anxiety or censure. Queen Katherine, recommended as a pregnancy part in 1785, made 1794 a delayed fulfillment of popular request. The majority of Siddons's repertoire in 1794, then, appears to be a refining of the easy tragic repertoire from 1785 focused on those roles that were most compatible with her condition physically and dramatically. Chief among them was Lady Macbeth, an "easy" tragic part, the hallmark of her celebrity, and the role in which her pregnancy was most tantalizingly evocative in 1785.

Interestingly, despite the vast number of contemporaneous responses to Siddons's 1785 pregnancy, scholars more frequently note her 1794 pregnancy. This is due chiefly to a comment from Hester Piozzi, who expressed concerns about how her pregnancy would be read by audiences that, like Boaden's comments about Henrietta Smith, have come to stand for both general attitudes toward pregnant performers and toward Siddons: "Mrs Siddons is going to act Lady Macbeth on the new Theatre Drury Lane. . . . She is big with Child, & I fear will for that reason scarce be well received: for People have a notion She is covetous, and this unnecessary Exertion to gain Money will confirm it. And yet, says Lord Deerhurst, 'She thinks I suppose to carry all before her.' Lord Deerhurst is very comical."[111] Piozzi is not objecting to Lady Macbeth specifically, but any appearance Siddons might make during pregnancy. Piozzi notes, correctly, that Siddons had a periodically problematic reputation for avarice for demanding high salaries in London and the provinces. In this context, she fears a public response that reads the pregnancy in relation to that stigmatic aspect of Siddons's persona, rather than as a sign of charismatic professional devotion (the reading that dominated in 1785).

Helen Brooks points to similar warnings of the incompatibility of commercial and maternal labor in conduct books and advice manuals in the 1790s. Siddons's contemporary Richard Cumberland, for example, muses on the "divided heart of the actress," whose attempts to fulfill both a professional and maternal role mean neither is done to satisfaction in 1791; and in 1798, philanthropist Priscilla Wakefield charged women with extreme care during pregnancy so as to avoid "puny offspring, inadequate to the noble energies of patriotism and virtue."[112] Thus, Brooks argues, the pregnant performer became "a physical representation of their abnegation of maternal and patriotic duty for commercial gain."[113] Such charges are similar to Hester Piozzi's fears, and perhaps help us explain the logic behind them. But the visibly reproductive body—especially Siddons's—also indexed the health of the nation and signaled exactly the kind of patriotic duty expected of women. Just as her 1785 pregnancy was the apotheosis of her celebrity reputation as the Tragic Muse, so this was her apotheosis as Britannia Mater. After *Macbeth* opened Piozzi wrote to a friend, "Mrs Siddons is very big, yet looks beautifully on the Stage," making no mention of her former concerns, nor was such a reaction recorded in the press.[114] Piozzi's speculative fears have been used to represent a wider and more negative audience response to Siddons's pregnant body than can be supported by contemporaneous evidence.[115]

Rather than objections, in fact, Siddons's pregnant performances prompted expressions of zealous support. Siddons's first appearance was met with "an enthusiastic roar of applause."[116] Her Queen Katherine was "a combination of excellence" that represented "all that the Stage can do;" her last appearance as Lady Randolph, acted only five weeks before giving birth, was "never more irresistible" before a house so overflowing it was "as if it had been Mid-January within, in spite of June without."[117] In Lady Macbeth her "splendour and certainty are both never-failing"; the play was "popular from the *witches* and the *music*, but dear to us for the fine acting of SIDDONS."[118] On the one hand, these assertions of welcomed consistency may suggest Carlson's ghosting effect, the erasure or denial of change for the comfort of familiarity.[119] But on the other hand, like Mary Tickell's response to Siddons's pregnant Lady Macbeth performances in 1785, there is also an assertion that these performances exceed in some way—her Lady Randolph is *better* than normal, her Queen Katherine shows "all that the stage can do," there is certainty *and* splendor to her Lady Macbeth. To explore this, I want to consider what it might mean for audiences to see in Siddons's 1794 Lady Macbeth the layers of meaning her body natural, character body, and celebrity body had developed between 1785 and 1794.

Reviewers affirmed that Siddons was still the best aspect of the production, but they recorded few details of her performance. Instead, newspaper coverage focused on innovations such as Kemble's decision to omit an actor to portray Banquo's ghost and to introduce a large number of children into the apparition scene in act four.[120] Several scholars have connected such innovations, particularly the first, with understandings of Macbeth as a stand-in for Robespierre, a connection encouraged by newspaper references as well as satirical prints.[121] In such a reading, Siddons's associations with the British monarchy or even with Marie Antoinette from Burke's *Reflections* may or may not be relevant. But Siddons's celebrity body, heavy with meaning and with child, also presented challenges to such readings, productively reinforcing themes of ambiguity within the play. When Kemble's Macbeth "bent his eye" on actual vacancy in the banquet scene, for example, it moved the audience closer to experiencing the scene through the eyes of Lady Macbeth and her guests. This aligned them with those who do not see rather than the man who does and showed a king of disturbed mind only five years after the Regency crisis of 1788–89, a connection perhaps encouraged by Siddons's celebrity associations with Queen Charlotte and appearance as Britannia during the 1789 celebrations for the king's recovery. Similarly, Lady Macbeth's ambition could hint at accusations leveled at Queen Charlotte during and after the crisis, including in James Gillray's print "Weird Sisters: Ministers of Darkness; Minions of the Moon" (1791).[122]

As a play, lost children always haunt *Macbeth*.[123] In literalizing them, Kemble's staging underscored the issues of dynasty at the heart of the play, physicalizing the thing that Macbeth cannot have (*will* not have, despite his wife's visible pregnancy) but Macduff has in abundance. The child actors also suggested the many dead or absent children in the play, from Lady Macbeth/Siddons's lost child(ren) to the missing Donalbain and Fleance to the "pretty chickens" Macbeth will murder, and the infants, human and not, from whom the witches derive their power. Through Siddons's body natural, Lady Macbeth's tragic maternal history might also resonate with the loss of Eliza Ann in 1788, Siddons's series of miscarriages, and the similar losses of those in her audiences, including those sending their children to war with France. Siddons's age and recent ill health, moreover, might position this pregnancy as Lady Macbeth's final chance for a child, just as it might be for the actress. Through her celebrity body's associations with royalty, however, questions of dynasty in the play might also resonate with the Duke of York's recently failed marriage, which had started in great hope but ended in miscarriage and a permanent separation. Siddons/Lady Macbeth becomes an ambiguous figure caught between dread and hope: Siddons's presence on stage signals a healthy, functioning body natural that is also an index for the strength and health of the British state, while the character body tells a story of regicide, dynastic failure, and rightful monarchy restored. Once again, Siddons's pregnancy could exquisitely enhance the pleasure and the pain of the sublime.

When Siddons emerged from the darkness for the sleepwalking scene, her fearful mutterings about the murder of the Thane of Fife's wife and children echoed those of women of all classes throughout Britain whose sense of security was shattered by the execution of Marie Antoinette.[124] Perhaps they also resonated with the French nation, whom Wordsworth later thought would "Sleep no more" in the wake of the Terror.[125] The "cry of women" that raised the specter of death in childbirth in 1785 is also altered: Lady Macbeth's reported death by suicide might now recall Siddons's Volumnia, who is willing to die rather than return to Rome in disgrace, and Burke's appropriation of this image for Marie Antoinette. It no longer indicates only the Scottish queen's possible madness, guilt, and death but perhaps the last defiant act of a person—be she a French queen, a Roman matron, or Britannia herself—who would rather kill herself and her unborn child than fall into the hands of her enemies.[126] In short, she represented a particular kind of indomitable and terrible patriotism available only to women.

Siddons was powerfully associated with Lady Macbeth and brought aspects of her celebrity to the role that made it a particularly rich ground for audience imagination during her 1785 pregnancy. In 1794, she stepped on stage in a production that scholars have read as equating Macbeth with Robespierre, and therefore the play as the downfall of those who have murdered a rightful king. It was and is this, of course, but Siddons's celebrity meant this was not only what it was: it was also the story of a woman and eventual queen whose ambition might be mapped—through her affective associations with their tragic lives—onto the stories of both the French queen and the British one, obscuring national difference. Her pitiful disintegration became a result both of the pressures of supporting an increasingly erratic king and her personal guilt, as Siddons's later "Remarks" explained; her strength and resolve were those of Siddons herself, of Volumnia, and of Britannia, and could be deeply admired, but could also lead to an act of regicide, illegitimate rule, and the bloody horrors perpetuated to maintain it.

Despite these evocative possibilities, reviews consistently deferred a specific reading or accounting of her performance in this revival or any mention of her pregnancy, instead emphasizing the stability and supremacy of her excellence in the part. Though Siddons is famous for re-rehearsing and deepening her understanding of a character at each new revival, that work here is largely effaced with comments declaring it beyond the power of language to capture, or so familiar as to need no description.[127] Even the technical modifications she made to translate her work into the larger space—Boaden mentions more erect carriage, a statelier walk, and grander gestures inspired by statuary—go unnoted.[128] There is a resistance to reading the performance anew and, in the midst of a new theater, new production choices, new designs, and new costumes, it is presented as stable and unaffected, unchanged from the triumph of 1785. In 1785 papers celebrated her pregnancy as heralding a new era of excellence for the stage and perhaps the nation; her 1794 pregnancy was, as Siddons put it, "frightfully . . . heavy" weighted with contradictory meaning, fraught as the times in which she lived. Rather than engage with these meanings in print, respondents focused on the woman they admired and the powerful feelings she raised, closing the lapse in time between 1785 and 1794 (an act perhaps aided by her condition) and deferring an engagement with their origin and larger meaning, an act commensurate with the "abstraction" and "displacement" of Romantic responses to the French Revolution.[129] Using the concept of a palimpsestic performance, however, opens up the possibility of rereading pregnancy's impact in the wake of significant cultural and personal change.

Conclusion

Lisa Forman Cody argues that the success and safety of maternal labor became an increasingly powerful political and social symbol as the eighteenth century progressed: "Late eighteenth-century British culture valued motherhood and treated the successfully reproductive body as an aesthetic, cultural, and political ideal."[130] At midcentury, war and an expanding empire prompted the establishment of Foundling and Lying-in Hospitals to support and encourage population growth. As one preacher put it, "War consumes us; and if it were possible, according to the waste should be the growth."[131] In 1785, Siddons was a glowingly pregnant mother of four, soon to be five, with possibly many more reproductive years ahead of her; in 1794, she was pregnant once again at thirty-nine, but she was also a woman in uncertain physical health who had lost four children in three years and was likely nearing the end of her fertility. She powerfully encoded both the maternal ideal, and the potential failure of it at a time of upheaval, war, and uncertainty. Her iconic, celebrity body was associated with the strength and nobility of her country in and beyond the theater, but like the king's was distressingly subject to the vagaries of her body natural. In both cases, however, vulnerability became strength and productively linked stage and actual royalty in a time of crisis.

Throughout her career, Siddons used domestic circumstances to her advantage, encouraging a conflation between her onstage roles as wives and mothers and her offstage life. Through this conflation, Siddons built a celebrity persona that adhered to domestic ideals for women at the time and made her acceptable to a diverse range of social classes while profiting off the public performance of this ostensibly private ideal, a masterful use of charismata. She demonstrates the sustained impact of strategies that Anne Oldfield reportedly used in 1712–13 and that George Anne Bellamy attempted at midcentury. Her affiliation with the figures of the tragic muse and Lady Macbeth existed alongside, and within, the larger framework of Siddons the devoted wife and mother. Instead of the personal tragedies that may have fostered Anne Oldfield and Susanna Mountfort's continued performances during pregnancy at the beginning of the long eighteenth century, Siddons's pregnant performances in

1785 were taken as indicative of a goodwill toward her audience, a genuine desire to please, and a recognition of her professional duties. This apparent change over time may be a function of the archive, or it may suggest that the valuing of domesticity and sensibility, along with notions of "good" motherhood and healthy behavior during pregnancy enabled audiences to read pregnant performances as coming not simply from economic necessity but a reciprocal sentimental relationship between performer and audience. In return for the performer's contributions to the entertainment of the public, the audience took on the role of protector, advocating for or supporting repertory shifts that would protect the woman and her child.

Understanding the conscious ways in which pregnancy shaped Siddons's repertoire in 1785 allows us to look back and see similar patterns elsewhere: after Susannah Cibber completed the initial run of *Zara* at the end of January 1736, for example, she did not appear again in tragedy until her performance as Andromache in *The Distrest Mother* on March 23, undoubtedly an "easy" tragic part. For nearly two months, she had instead performed pathetic parts in comedy, perhaps allowing her to reinforce her abilities in tragedy within the bounds of a safer genre. Siddons's experience also asks us to consider how much agency Anne Oldfield had in determining how long she could safely act in *Cato*, and what barometer she used to gauge that safety. George Anne Bellamy performed up until she went into labor on several occasions, should we consider the roles she played, at least in the final weeks and months, more "easy" parts in tragedy? These are questions for another time but speak to the value of reading women's experiences across the century so we may ask better questions around archival gaps and silences. If we begin to look more closely, we can attend to the ways in which Siddons, so often held up as exceptional, truly was exceptional, and the ways in which she is merely the most visible example of a system that, to limited but tangible degrees, accommodated working mothers.

Siddons's pregnancies did, as others have acknowledged, connect to and enhance her preexisting associations with maternity. But conflating them with this larger, lifelong role obscures the interesting and powerful effect her changing body had on audiences. Siddons's celebrity persona drove a conflation of her body natural with the character body of Lady Macbeth that resulted in fantasies endowing

Siddons with not simply creative, but generative, genius and gave her admirers new ways of conceptualizing her importance as an artistic and national figure. In 1794, responses to Siddons's pregnant body are less pronounced but help us ask valuable questions about the intersection of social, cultural, and political realities with personal history and stage tradition. Our next subject, Dorothy Jordan, will also demonstrate the shifting meaning of the pregnant body as personal and political circumstances changed throughout her career in the 1780s and 1790s. Like her contemporary Sarah Siddons, Dorothy Jordan was a leading lady at Drury Lane at the end of the eighteenth century, and a vital component of the company's economic success. Like Sarah Siddons, she had a close connection to the royal family, though the nature of this connection was quite different: for twenty years, she was the long-time mistress of the Duke of Clarence, and mother to ten of his children. Like Sarah Siddons, Jordan learned to use her maternity to aid her career, but she used her maternity to a very different end. While Sarah Siddons used it to reinforce her personal connection to her characters, becoming in Joseph Roach's terms a "role-icon," Dorothy Jordan used her maternity to enforce a separation between her on- and off-stage life and reappropriate control over public perceptions of her private character and professional identity.

4
PROLIFIC MUSE
Dorothy Jordan

Dorothy Jordan lived what sounds like a fairytale. Born into impoverished circumstances, she used her talents and wit to rise to the heights of celebrity in late eighteenth-century London. As an actress, she became famous, beloved, and applauded. As a private individual, she fell in love with a prince and lived as his wife in all but name for two decades. A mother of three already, she bore him ten children whom they raised together on a large estate. But this is not a fairytale. It is the story of a woman who worked constantly to navigate the often-dangerous waters of fame, fortune, and family to build and maintain a complex celebrity persona that could not be reduced to her stage characters or her status as royal mistress. This chapter traces changing reactions to Jordan's pregnant body from her early career in London (1785–1790) through sexual scandal in 1791 and finally into the stable image of domestic probity she enjoyed at the end of the century. Jordan is a fitting end to this study, for she offers many opportunities to revisit and reconsider the experiences of those who came before her.

Dorothy (also Dorothea or most commonly, Dora) was born in London on November 22, 1761 to Francis Bland, the disinherited son of an Irish judge, and actress Grace Phillips, daughter of a Welsh clergyman. She was one of at least six and perhaps as many as nine. Eventually, her father left the family, then living in Dublin, and Jordan went to work to support her mother and siblings. She appeared as

"Miss Francis" at the Crow Street theater and then at Smock Alley, where she stayed less than a year. At twenty, she left Ireland for England in May 1782 three months pregnant with manager Richard Daly's child.[1] In July she joined Tate Wilkinson's Yorkshire company and began performing as Mrs. Jordan in deference to her visible pregnancy. Her first child, Frances (Fanny) was born in November 1782. Jordan stayed with Wilkinson's company for three years, playing in tragedy, comedy, opera, and farce before moving to Drury Lane in 1785, where she worked until 1812. The London managers initially planned to make her a second to Siddons in tragedy, but Jordan convinced them to allow her to demonstrate a different specialty altogether: that of low comic women. Naive and bumbling country girls, romps, and hoydenish young women became her specialty, along with roles in breeches ranging from Shakespeare's sweet and sentimental Viola to swaggering Sir Harry Wildair in Farquhar's *The Constant Couple* (a triumph for Peg Woffington earlier in the century) and the boy-hero Little Pickle in *The Spoiled Child*.[2] Just as Siddons's towering, majestic form suited her to tragedy, Jordan's was an asset to her in comedy. She was small of stature with "a certain roundness & embonpoint that is very pretty and Graceful," legs that inspired rapture and masses of irrepressible brown curls.[3]

During her London career Jordan had two long-term monogamous relationships: the first with lawyer Richard Ford, which produced two surviving daughters and four pregnancies between 1786 and 1791; the second and more famous was with William, Duke of Clarence, which lasted from 1791 to 1811 and resulted in ten surviving children and thirteen pregnancies (see Table A.1 in the appendix). If, as was rumored, she was also pregnant in the fall of 1791, then she was pregnant at least nineteen times in her adult life, and eighteen times in twenty-two years of her London career. As with Siddons, Jordan's substantial though largely undated correspondence offers us insight into her embodied experiences with pregnancy. Early pregnancy brought nausea, which could make travel unpleasant. She consistently found that carriages, especially closed carriages, worsened her symptoms: "Dear love have the goodness to fetch me in the Curicle, as I have been rather unwell . . . and am afraid of the motion of the little carriage."[4] This nausea could escalate into more persistent or severe trouble at times, which was worrisome in later pregnancy for its weakening effects. Fainting or feeling faint was another symptom she experienced at various points in her pregnancies, sometimes at night or when performing, when it may have been difficult to conceal from audiences. Headaches and the need to avoid exertion also crop up; she writes several letters from a bed, couch, or sofa as she rests herself. She writes of lethargy and bouts of insomnia, especially in the final weeks of pregnancy. In 1807, just prior to the birth of her last child, she confessed: "I am very sleepy and (if *possible*) more *stupid* than usual, forever sleeping or waking."[5] Throughout her long and varied career Jordan battled through these symptoms and more while playing to packed houses, encountering crowds outside her homes and the theater waiting to catch a glimpse of her, and being painted by the era's most famous artists. She also managed her ever-growing family, took care of her mother and siblings, and worked through illness, miscarriage, and sexual scandal to maintain her career.

The Child of Nature: Jordan's Celebrity

Shortly after her London debut, Jordan posed for a full-length, nearly life-sized painting by John Hoppner (1758–1810) (Figure 4.1). Hoppner exhibited it at the Royal Academy in May 1786, the end of her first London season. It shows Jordan as Thalia, the comic muse, in spangled white garments and gold sandals amidst a forested mountain landscape. Jordan, hair and clothing caught by the wind, embraces Euphrosyne, the goddess of mirth and good cheer. Euphrosyne holds out a hand to protect her from the advances of a satyr leering from behind a nearby tree.[6] Jordan—perhaps unaware of the danger—looks out at the viewer, head tilted and smiling slightly. The painting evokes her emerging celebrity persona: she embraces mirth and good cheer while being untouched by the lascivious attention she may inspire. Her appeal is unconscious, and a higher power protects her from its effects. Even so, it is not to this protector that she turns. Instead, she looks toward the viewer, returning the gaze of an adoring public, acknowledging us as we acknowledge her. The light that illuminates Jordan's face separates her from the other figures, while her awareness of us moves her to our plane, out of their world and into ours. Siddons's grand painting frames her as inaccessible to the

Figure 4.1. John Hoppner, *Mrs. Jordan as the Comic Muse (1785/6)*. Buckingham Palace, Royal Collection Trust © Her Majesty Queen Elizabeth II 2020

viewer, Jordan's as tantalizingly close. It is a powerful, seductive example of Jordan's particular flavor of public intimacy—the illusion of availability—that creates a desire for more in the spectator.

Evaluations of Jordan's performance style reveal the yearning this public intimacy created in audiences. On stage, she was hailed as entirely natural, with no detectable artifice to her performances: "It was not as an actress, but as herself, that she charmed everyone. . . . She was all gaiety, openness, and good-nature."[7] Throughout her life, this was the explanation people returned to again and again for her "bewitching" presence: that it was not any particular gift of physical beauty, polished manner, or refined sentiment, but her ability to "irresistibly gain your affection" by being her fascinating self.[8] In short, Jordan possessed "It"—that undeniable but unconscious magnetism of the abnormally interesting person.[9] She seemed to always be speaking spontaneously and from the heart, allowing tears and laughter to flow as naturally as breathing. This gave her a kind of magic: "Her childlike spirit shook off the load of years from her spectators; she seemed one whom care could not come near; a privileged being sent to teach mankind what he most wants—joyousness."[10] The power of Jordan's palpable physical presence acted on audiences both physically (making them young again) and metaphysically (teaching them joy). If Siddons's role-icon status was a dominant aspect of her charismata, blending private and public into a seamless whole, fundamental to Jordan's charismata was her ability to radiate sincerity and joy.

Jordan's apparent sincerity onstage could be a double-edged sword. Helen Brooks, building on Lionel Trilling, uses Siddons and Jordan to explore a shift in the last decades of the century: a "new cultural moment which sought to align internal and external presentation."[11] In this context, seeming to show the authentic self on the stage and off signaled adherence to wider social values. Jordan's celebrity power therefore lent credence to her stage performances while lessening the threat of artificiality and deception (especially in women) that could plague stage performers. Brooks identifies various elements of Jordan's celebrity, such as her acting style and her laugh, as "techniques of sincerity."[12] I suggest the candidness with which she revealed her private life, sometimes explicitly and deliberately, and other times by simply not disguising it, is another. Despite clear advantages, however, Jordan's ability to seem entirely the thing she played was not without its challenges. Fanny Burney, novelist and member of court, found herself defending Mrs. Jordan to a friend:

> Observing the silence of Colonel Wellbred, we called upon him to explain it.
>
> "I have seen [Mrs. Jordan]," he answered quietly, "but in one part."
>
> "Whatever it was," cried Mr. Fairly, "it must have been well done."
>
> "Yes . . . and so well that it seemed to be her real character; and I disliked her for that very reason, for it was a character that, off the stage or on, is equally distasteful to me—a hoyden."
>
> I had a little of this feeling myself when I saw her in "The Romp," . . . but afterwards she displayed such uncommon humour that it brought me to pardon her assumed vulgarity, in favour of a representation of nature.[13]

Jordan's style of playing was compelling but could invite a conflation of her stage and private characters, as Wellbred's criticism shows. Unlike Siddons's or Cibber's admirable tragic heroines, for Jordan this conflation could be damaging, for many of her comic heroines reveled in transgressive behavior.[14] In the foregoing story, it is only Burney's more extensive contact with the actress that has given her the ability to read this "assumed vulgarity" as a carefully crafted performance. As with Susanna Mountfort Verbruggen, another way to balance onstage transgressions was through offstage virtuous behaviors, including marriage and childbearing. Jordan's frequent and highly visible pregnancies with monogamous partners, therefore, became a form of sincerity—a seemingly unvarnished and total sharing of self—and appeared to place the actress within the bounds of normative femininity offstage.

Jordan was an "it" girl, demonstrating the "apparently effortless embodiment of contradictory qualities" that Roach articulates as inherent and necessary to celebrity appeal.[15] She was both the naive country girl and an experienced professional, both the romp and a mother, both the rakishly masculine Sir Harry Wildair and undeniably feminine, both a flirt and the loyal companion to first Richard Ford and later the Duke of Clarence. In large part, Jordan succeeded in creating a symbiotic relationship between these facets of her identity, as we will see during her relationship with Richard Ford. To embody the contradictions necessary for celebrity, however, almost always leads to moments of failure, when balance is lost and the public persona endangered. For Roach, these are moments when a celebrity's charismata is outweighed by stigmata, or when behavior that goes against the celebrity's established "brand" makes the public question the truthfulness of the previously accepted image; this is exactly the challenge Jordan faced during the 1791 scandal when she became mistress to the Duke of Clarence. The next decade finds Jordan successfully reconstituting her image as a devoted partner, professional, and mother to a growing family.

London: 1785–1791

In the fall of 1785, Jordan joined Drury Lane on a salary of £4 a week, placing her in the third rank of female performers.[16] Her first London role was the sweet and comically simple Peggy in David Garrick's *The Country Girl* (a sanitized adaptation of Wycherley's *The Country Wife*) on October 18, 1785. Though not hailed as a great beauty, reviewers considered her pleasing, with an excellent figure and a delightful voice. Mary Tickell saw her on October 21 and wrote enthusiastically to her sister the next day: "I can assure you . . . she is the most valuable Acquisition Drury L. has ever had, except Mrs. S."[17] Her next role was Viola in *Twelfth Night* on November 11, when a puffing supporter declared, "The great powers of Mrs Jordan cannot be better displayed than in the wonderful contrast of her *Country Girl* and *Viola*. In one all archness and vivacity; in the other serious, gentle, tender, and sentimental."[18] Within weeks of her first appearance, newspapers were congratulating not simply Drury Lane, but the entire theater-going population of London, on their new "acquisition," emphasizing Jordan's position as a public object whose value has been sanctioned by a paying audience.[19]

Her rise in London was aided by the birth of Sarah Siddons's sixth child, another important illustration of the wider influence of celebrity pregnancy on the century's theater history. When Siddons left the stage, tragedy went with her, leaving the theater bereft of more than half its repertory. In consequence, Jordan's value became readily apparent: "Mrs Siddons' accouchement . . . is a very unfavourable visitation of time and chance. Notwithstanding the pantomime, and the Jordon rage, her presence must be necessary."[20] The pantomime was a flop, but Jordan stayed the rage. These circumstances gave Jordan leverage. On December 16, less than two months after arriving in London, she signed a four-year contract with the theater at £8 per week, double her starting salary.[21] By the end of the season, she had also taken in £200 at her benefit and received £300 in gifts from the members of Brook's Club, which included the Prince of Wales.

"Mrs. Ford": Concealing Illegitimacy

In her first season, Jordan met Richard Ford, a lawyer and the son of Drury Lane co-owner and royal accoucheur Dr. James Ford, whom we met in George Anne Bellamy's *Apology* and who attended Sarah Siddons during pregnancy in 1785. Ford and Jordan moved into a house just north of Bedford Square together in the fall of 1786, and Jordan almost immediately became pregnant. Dorothea Maria (Dodee) was born in Edinburgh in late July 1787 while Jordan was on a summer tour, and Lucy arrived on January 2, 1790 in London. She also had miscarriages in the fall of 1788 and the winter or early spring of 1790–91. Neither the relationship nor Jordan's frequent pregnancies were cause for censure, however, because Jordan and Ford were presenting themselves as a married couple: "It was given out by both parties, and universally believed, that if they were not actually married, yet they were bound together equally strong, but that Mr. F could not declare her his wife, as his father's resentment might deprive him of an ample fortune. The lady and even the public were satisfied with this story, nor was she ever classed among the easy dames of the theatre."[22] Ford called Jordan "Mrs. Ford" in letters and presented her as his wife to his friends; moreover, like Bellamy and Calcraft, they lived together openly and had children. This behavior meant observers did not construe Jordan's pregnancies as a source of shame or condemnation. On the contrary, supporters touted her continued performances during pregnancy as a sign of her dedication to her public. Audiences had an understanding and appreciation of the emotional and physical exertion required to perform during pregnancy, either because of their own experiences with the condition, or because they were intimate witnesses to it within their families and social circles, and this knowledge could translate into gratitude. Jordan's pregnancies during her relationship with Ford are almost entirely unexamined in biography and contemporary scholarship.[23] A closer look offers helpful evidence about her early career in London and her increasing value to the theater, and provides important context to later events. Like Siddons's 1785 pregnancy, these early experiences also afford us a look at various accommodations for pregnancy Jordan received from her managers.

By 1788, Jordan was earning £12 a week; in 1789, she arranged instead a flat fee of £10 per performance, generally amounting to £20–30 a week.[24] When in London and on contract for a weekly sum, Jordan continued to receive her full salary throughout absences associated with miscarriages and births. During her pregnancies she also enjoyed physical accommodations particular to leading comic actresses: an exemption from appearing twice in the same evening from about the end of her fourth month onward, and the temporary suspension of particularly strenuous roles from her repertoire.[25] Between March 3 and May 1, 1787, for example, Jordan appeared twice in one evening on only two occasions, one of which was her benefit night. In fact, over half of her appearances were in the shorter afterpieces, further reducing the strain of each evening of performance. She also ended her London season early that year, beginning her summer tour at the start of her seventh month of pregnancy. Though the pace of her schedule in London slowed in deference to her physical safety, the variety of parts she played did not alter. Even on tour in the summer of 1787, she continued to play her popular breeches roles late into the pregnancy. Jordan and her managers established that pregnancy would neither prevent her continued performances nor prevent the display of her famous figure in breeches, altered as it may have been. Such practices, which neither hid the body nor treated it as a source of shame, aligned well with Jordan's charismatic sincerity and perceived status as Ford's wife.

To receive these accommodations, Jordan would have at some point informed the managers of her condition. We do not know when this happened, but Mary Tickell tells us that her mother Mary Linley, wardrobe mistress and wife and mother-in-law to two of the theater's managers, learned of it in late January: "My Mother whisper'd as the greatest of all possible secrets—that Mrs. Mills (Mrs Jordan's Dresser) had made some curious *female* observations on that Lady for these last 10 or 12 Weeks—which certainly (if they are true) portend something or the other of consequence to the Ford Family but *everything* at present as my M. says is *under the Rose*."[26] Mills's intimate access to Jordan's body enabled her to read signs not yet publicly visible, probably when lacing her stays or costumes or by observing the amenorrhea, nausea, or faintness of early pregnancy. Tickell's letter draws our attention to the powerful networks of communication that might exist within theatrical spaces while rarely leaving direct archival traces. It also suggests ways in which these private observations might become public, for Tickell continued, "When Miss Rein [another wardrobe employee] makes any Discovery, the secret will be no longer worth keeping." Once the news was out, papers commented on Jordan's condition regularly. When she was nearing six months pregnant at the end of March a notice about Jordan's summer travels read: "The *Jordan* . . . will escape—travels by land and by water—and so forth."[27] The allusion comes from the litany from the *Book of Common Prayer*, which continues, "all women laboring of child."[28] A more explicit reference appeared in May: "Mrs. Jordan, who is generally stiled the daughter of *Thalia*, will soon make the muse a *grand-mother*."[29] Jordan made her way north to Edinburgh, where she performed before giving birth and lying in. When Dodee's birth was announced in late July, London papers offered, "our hearty wishes, and the prayers of the Litany to assist her—all those travelling by sea and land, *all women*."[30] A month later, they reported her recovery progress using references to aristocratic rituals, something papers had also done with Siddons's 1785 pregnancy: "Mrs. Jordan's knocker is completely *muffled*, the lady of the mansion being at this moment in the *straw* but has so perfectly timed this her second offering at the shrine of Lucina, that she will be enabled to take her post again in the ranks of Thalia on the Boards of Old Drury."[31] The *Public Advertiser* cast Jordan as a woman of quality ("the lady of the mansion") and complimented her work–life balance: so good to her public that she has arranged the birth of her child to cause *them* the least possible inconvenience. The lighthearted, open, yet respectful discussion of Jordan's condition and summer travels in 1787 echoes reporting on Siddons's 1785 pregnancy, reinforcing the belief that Ford and Jordan were married.

About fifteen months later, in the fall of 1788, Jordan lost a pregnancy and missed two weeks of the season (October 30 to November 13). The reason for her absence seemed to underscore her commitment to her profession: "The last time [Mrs. Jordan] played, she and her mother went to the Theatre in her carriage. Near the house they were stopt by a parish funeral, when the coffin slipped from off the shoulders of the bearers, and burst open in the sight of Mrs. J. She got the better of the fright or emotion this occasioned, and played: went home, relapsed, and brought forth an abortion."[32] Despite receiving a shock on the way to the theater, an incident that would have been clearly understood as dangerous to a pregnant woman, Jordan is represented as determinedly fulfilling her professional duties, disciplining her body and mind successfully for the duration of the performance and falling prey to her sensibility only later. She seems to have recovered from this miscarriage quickly, in body at least, even debuting two new parts shortly after her return: Corinna, a gauche but innocent young girl in Vanbrugh's *The City Wives' Confederacy* on November 19, and Beatrice in the new afterpiece *The Panel* on November 28, at least the first of which may have been rehearsed during her absence. Jordan maintained a busy schedule for the rest of the season, where her labor in service of the theater and the public despite the challenges to her health was conspicuous.

Before the end of the 1788–89 season, Jordan became pregnant once again, for her daughter Lucy was born in early January 1790. Jordan spent much of this pregnancy out of the public eye. The summer of 1789 was a difficult one. She ran into problems on tour in Leeds, where her popular travesty role of Sir Harry Wildair was met with censure; she also had a conflict with the Scottish manager John Jackson that he took to the papers, claiming he had lost money on her visit.[33] Her mother, who accompanied her on summer tours to help with the children, grew suddenly ill and died in Edinburgh. Rather than return to London after her final touring engagements in

September, Jordan took several months off in the country before Lucy's birth.

Perhaps because she spent so much time out of London, confusion around the date of Lucy's birth abounds. The *Biographical Dictionary of Actors* (*BDA*) lists it only as sometime in 1789. Claire Tomalin suggests the fall after an engagement at Chester. There was confusion at the time too. A report that she had given birth to twins in late September (the basis for Tomalin's date) was not corrected until mid-November: "The report of Mrs. Jordan having been 'brought to bed of *twins*,' is premature, although, from the present rotundity of the *little* favourite of Thalia, such an event will, in all probabily [*sic*], occur at no very distant period."[34] By early December she was back in town and preparing for the birth. On Christmas day, however, there was still no news, and the *Public Advertiser* declared, "Mrs. Jordan, though *expecting* every hour, is not as yet in the *straw:—twins*, at least, are looked for to stock the *farm:—*"Think of that, Master Brooke!"[35] To those without access to Jordan's person, the papers depicted an impossibly elongated process of gestation—a constant and never-ending swelling that made the little actress ever more spherical before she was finally relieved. Recent memories of Jordan's pregnant body would help to shape audience imaginings; her publicized miscarriage the previous year, meanwhile, might explain her reluctance to perform until after the birth. The anticipated twins either did not arrive or only one survived: Lucy Hester Rachel Ford was born on January 2. Jordan lay in a little over a month and returned to Drury Lane on February 8.

Jordan's extended absence had a significant impact on Drury Lane's 1789–90 repertory, letting us briefly consider celebrity pregnancy's impact on other performers. Without her, many of the plays in which she usually appeared were left out of the season, among them *The Country Girl*, *Twelfth Night*, *A Trip to Scarborough*, *She Wou'd and She Wou'd Not*, *The Confederacy*, and the afterpieces *The Sultan*, *The Devil to Pay*, and *The Romp*. Other plays continued with substitutes: Anna Maria Crouch played Matilda in the afterpiece *Richard Coeur de Lion*, Elizabeth Farren appeared as the Comic Muse in *The Jubilee*, Miss Romanzini (later Jordan's sister-in-law) took Lucy in *The Virgin Unmasked*, and a new performer, Miss

Prideaux, acted Miss Prue in *Love for Love*. Charlotte Goodall played Rosalind in *As You Like It* once in September, and Sir Harry Wildair in *The Constant Couple* twice, both major Jordan roles. The latter may have been a response to provocation from the other company: Covent Garden's Catherine Achmet was trying her hand at Sir Harry that year, the first time a woman appeared in the part at that theater in many years. With Jordan absent, it was an ideal time for Covent Garden to test Achmet's success in one of Jordan's signature parts; it was also an important opportunity for Charlotte Goodall, usually a comic third to Farren and Jordan, to demonstrate her worth to the theater. Account books show that Goodall was given a small raise in recognition of her contributions.[36] Jordan's absence gave members of the Drury Lane company, and those of the rival house, potentially lucrative opportunities to raise their status with audiences and managers.

Almost a year after Lucy's birth, in the winter of 1790–91, another pregnancy caused Jordan to miss almost two weeks in December: "Mrs. Jordan is at present very much indisposed, in consequence of a premature labour."[37] Whatever symptoms she experienced, perhaps pain or bleeding, caused alarm; she was probably put on bed rest and may have been bled and treated, internally and externally, with astringents meant to close the womb.[38] She would have been advised to maintain quiet and perhaps darkness, to avoid straining her eyes, and eschew all activities or thoughts that would create agitation and anxiety. Perhaps these measures worked, for she was on stage again by December, and in late January the *Public Advertiser* suggested that Jordan was still pregnant: "Mrs. Jordan's late turn-over in her carriage, was fortunately productive of nothing more than alarm:—considering that Lady's situation, either *two deaths*—or an *additional* life might naturally have been the consequence of the disaster!"[39] This is the last mention of this pregnancy I have found in the papers.

Lacking such sources, however, we can turn to repertory records for evidence of the kinds of accommodations she received in 1787. Between her absence in December and February 2, Jordan performed only once an evening and often only in the afterpiece; from February 2 to her benefit on March 22, she played twice a night on only three occasions, one of which was by Royal Command. This schedule suggests the theater was responding to health concerns, though we cannot be sure if they were specifically related to a continuing pregnancy or to the loss of one, and there are other references to other, unrelated illnesses that year. Jordan's commitment to her profession in the face of health crises in the fall of 1788 and again in 1790–91 signaled her value as a professional. In the spring of 1791 one writer commented, "Mrs. Jordan will close her London dramatic season with the fame of having struggled more with disorder to gratify a delighted public, than any Actress perhaps ever did."[40] Jordan's repertoire remained comic, but the presence and subsequent absence of her pregnant and/or ailing body drew attention to the effort and sacrifice her career involved, as well as the value she held as an asset to the theater and audience.

The treatment of Jordan and her condition throughout these four pregnancies suggests a stable persona that avoided associations with illicit sexuality and illegitimacy. Performing while pregnant was indicative of her openness, professionalism, and adherence to expected and acceptable female behavior, perhaps mitigating any alarm or censure her enthusiastic portrayals of non-normative behavior onstage might inspire. In this way, Jordan echoes Mountfort Verbruggen's on- and offstage balance. Throughout the relationship with Richard Ford, Jordan's pregnancies are discussed in the papers with relatively little innuendo or moral criticism, reinforcing her appearance of married respectability. Meanwhile, she was building a steadily more lucrative career in London and on tour. Like Siddons, she was also becoming a favorite of the king and queen, who had in addition to her London performances seen her at Cheltenham Spa in the summer of 1788. The anonymous author of an early biography of the actress wrote, "In private as well as public life, she evinces the best claims on our praise, since to a sweetness of temper she unites a pliability and benevolence of disposition, that insures domestic tranquility, and yields comfort and happiness to her family."[41] Two years after this biography appeared, satirists and the press called these same virtues into question when Jordan became royal mistress to the Duke of Clarence, then third in line to the British throne. Charismatic readings of Jordan's body and private life gave way to stigmatic, grotesque speculation.

Pregnancy, Suspicion, and Scandal: 1791

Back on tour in the summer of 1791, Jordan and Ford were outside London when papers began noting the interest William, Duke of Clarence was showing in the actress. Clarence was twenty-six and had returned to England two years before from a tour to Canada and the Caribbean as a member of the royal navy. He met Jordan in the winter of 1790–91, perhaps during her pregnancy, and by July was traveling to see her perform. The publicity surrounding his interest proved problematic, and papers began publishing contradictory information about Jordan and Ford's relationship. In August the *Evening Mail* announced, "It is generally understood, that Mrs. Jordan makes her first appearance next season, in the character of Mrs. FORD!" suggesting they were married; two weeks later, an account from York claimed that Jordan, "performed no character in public, because she could not play Mrs. *Ford* in private," implying the opposite.[42] Jordan's identity as Ford's wife was crumbling, and by early October all of London knew she had left Ford for the Duke. As rumors gave way to open scandal, the coincidence of the names and professions of these parties would lead to endless punning on a sailor (or "tar") "Fording" the "River Jordan."

Confusion about the couple's marital status was pervasive. In a letter dated October 13, 1791, Clarence wrote joyfully to his brother, the Prince of Wales, "You may safely congratulate me on my success . . . they were never married: I have all proofs requisite and even legal ones."[43] While Clarence's letter was all joy and excitement, Jordan was steeling herself for coming attacks, writing to Clarence, "I must prepare myself for a thousand cruel stories, both against you and me, and learn to treat them with the contempt they deserve."[44] As discussed in the introduction to this book, Jordan encountered scandal and ridicule in her early career on the Yorkshire circuit, and it prepared her for some of what was coming. She knew, for example, that those who could not "find fault with me as a performer" would "catch at every opportunity of endeavoring to injure me as a woman."[45] She was correct; just as attacks on Anne Oldfield in 1712–13 focused not on her professional abilities but her sexual health and continence, Jordan's changed circumstances fueled sexualized bon mots and innuendo, gossipy pamphlets and magazines, and devastatingly funny and disturbing satirical prints—at least nineteen by four different artists—for several months. Beneath the mockery were serious questions that threatened the foundations of her success and fame: if Jordan had duped the audience into believing she was one thing (a wife), while all the while being something else (a promiscuous mistress), what else might she be concealing? The scandal was dangerous because it called into question the sincerity that had held her on- and offstage lives in balance, undermining her persona as a devoted mother, a respectable wife, and a trustworthy professional. Concurrent rumors that Jordan was pregnant exacerbated the situation, suggesting that Jordan and her body were continuing to hide secrets from the audience.

In the wake of cultural shifts that emphasized the vital importance of being authentic, Helen Brooks notes, "A desire to see the body as being a clear and uncomplicated signifier of internal emotions and truth."[46] Pregnancy, however, is overdetermined: it marries sex and sensibility within a singular body, and is capable of being read in myriad, conflicting ways that can at any moment privilege one set of associations over another. Particularly at this moment in Jordan's life, her body could no longer be an "uncomplicated signifier"—instead, it became a metaphor for the uncertainty and instability Jordan's public felt after learning that the woman who always purported to be transparently herself had concealed a monumental secret. Long charismatic and sentimental, in 1791–92 critics used the change in Jordan's domestic circumstances to render her fertile body sexualized, stigmatic, and suspicious; in short, grotesque. Thus, what Sharon Marcus calls the "suspenseful, interactive, serial drama" of celebrity kicked into overdrive: the country girl had undoubtedly metamorphosed, but into what was now the question the newspapers, the print shops, and Jordan all competed to answer for the public.[47]

During the scandal, reported gossip and visual caricature created what Joseph Roach and Vic Gattrell have called "effigies" of the actress that could compete with Jordan's own performances of self for superiority in the minds of audiences.[48] As Roach indicates, the harm of such satire comes to fruition "when the caricature substitutes itself for the public image of the original" in audiences' minds.[49] During this scandal, and much like Anne Oldfield in 1712–13, Jordan had to assert the validity of her own performances of self or risk allowing textual, and in this case visual, effigies to supersede that performance in the public imagination. To understand the range of attacks to which Jordan was subjected, her responses, and the role her suspected pregnancy played in each, I will explore the scandal in the three phases in which it unfolded. During the first, Jordan remained on stage while weathering attacks on her intelligence, sexual morality, and identity as a mother. In the second phase, an illness that kept Jordan from the stage for two weeks brought audience anger and anxiety to a head, resulting in a climax to the crisis that Jordan managed by returning to the stage, offering up her body for monitoring and evaluation. In the third phase, textual sources show continued surveillance of Jordan's body for signs of pregnancy, while two prints by Isaac Cruikshank linger on the events of November/December, connecting them to earlier pregnancy rumors and using these rumors to foment continued mistrust of Jordan's integrity. Just as reactions to Jordan's pregnant body during her relationship with Richard Ford demonstrate the symbiosis between her stage performance and offstage reputation, Jordan's rumored pregnancy in 1791 reveals the instability of her persona of authenticity in light of her new relationship.

Phase One: "Nell of Clarence"

When Jordan left Ford for the duke, papers and prints responded by offering reconfigurations of Jordan's persona that relied on collapsing her offstage identity with her stage characters—effacing the crucial distinction between stage transgression and private domesticity she had created in the first years of her London career. On October 11, one paper crowed: "The comic Syren of the Old Drury has abandoned her quondam mate, for the superior attractions of a Royal Lodge, to which little Pickle was long invited! She has in return, all the solace which a new and elevated lover can bestow, with the added hope that history will record her attractions, and that she may be looked on as the NELL GWYN of a future day."[50] The notice offers several identities for Jordan, none particularly flattering. "Little Pickle" was the lead character in *The Spoil'd Child* (1790), a popular farce written for (and perhaps by) Jordan about an uncontrollable, destructive young boy who disguises himself as a sailor. This sobriquet was a favorite to use when making cutting comments about the actress during this crisis. Evoking the image of a siren, meanwhile, suggested Jordan was the possessor of an irresistible yet dangerous sexuality who intentionally lures sailors (like Clarence) to their doom. Aligning Jordan with Nell Gwyn, meanwhile, cast her in the specific role of the low-born actress who becomes a royal mistress.

The name "Nell" also suggested one of Jordan's popular stage roles: Nell from Charles Coffey's ballad opera *The Devil to Pay: or, the Wives Metamorphosed*, performed for the first time that season on September 24.[51] Coffey's Nell is the wide-eyed, innocent wife of an abusive, drunken cobbler. One day, a magician attempts to relieve her undeserved fate by temporarily changing her place with that of Lady Lovemore, the abusive wife to a local lord; when Nell's husband and Lady Lovemore have learned to appreciate their respective spouses, the magic is reversed. Satirical prints such as James Gillray's "The Devil to Pay" used the role to mock Jordan's supposed belief that her new connection would result in marriage, when in fact it was a temporary change (Figure 4.2). The only lasting effect for the actress was to make her a "public" woman, as Gillray put it on the chamber pot beneath the bed, "open to all parties." The valances of meaning in portraying Jordan as "Nell of Clarence" allowed readers and viewers to apply a constellation of potential truths to the actress, from venal sexuality to social and moral ineptitude.[52] Press and print shop used these tropes—of mercenary femininity, deception, and excessive sexuality—to discredit the persona of the respectable woman, good mother, and devoted professional she had previously enjoyed. Jordan may have been a well-known figure who acted frequently during pregnancy, but it was not until the 1791 crisis that her body and sexuality were conflated with excess and shame.

Jordan's reputation for prolific fertility makes it unsurprising that her maternity shortly entered the conversation. The day after news of their relationship became public the papers began to envision the future of Jordan's family: "*Little Pickle's* family will present a curious assemblage of infants. *Irish*, *Scotch*, and *English*, and probably Princes and Princesses."[53] Quickly, however, the relationship began to be construed as incompatible with maternal feeling: "To be mistress to the King's son Little Pickle thinks it respectable, and so away go all tender ties to children."[54] There are two ways to

Figure 4.2. James Gillray, *The Devil to Pay: The Wife Metamorphos'd, or, Neptune Reposing after Fording the Jordan* (London: Hannah Humphrey, October 24, 1791). Courtesy of The Lewis Walpole Library, Yale University

understand this comment. The first is that it references the possibility that Richard Ford would bar her from her existing children (as she had no legal rights to them), and this was a consequence of her actions she was willing to accept. The other is that being a royal mistress was incompatible with good motherhood to her existing children—the sexual demands and financial allure of the former overriding the latter. As one paper put it, "The exact price at which Little Pickle sold her maternal feelings, and sent her children to their father, was, according to report, £3000 down, and £1000 per annum."[55] As a performer whose public persona was partially predicated on charismatic sincerity and stable domesticity, the accusation targeted both her professional integrity and her private identity—in Jordan's words, they attacked the performer *by* attacking the woman.

In response to accusations that she had abandoned her children—a charge she confessed to Clarence had "hurt me extremely"—Jordan sent signed letters from Richard Ford to the press, where they appeared in various papers throughout Britain between October 17 and 19.[56] The letters outlined Jordan's generous financial arrangements for the children: she had settled £600 per year on her daughters, £50 of which went directly to her sister, Hester, who lived with the children in a separate household where both parents could visit. Ford's letters also confirmed that Jordan still had access to the girls "provided her visits are not attended by any circumstances which may be improper to them or unpleasant to me."[57] Legally, their father could have kept her from them, so their ongoing visits suggested Jordan's fit maternity. Further, in materially providing for her children Jordan demonstrated good, responsible motherhood while her desire to see and be with her daughters showed affection and sentiment. By printing the actual letters and not her own words, moreover, she gave the impression of revealing the unvarnished truth from the source least likely to be generous to her; it was a decision that recalled the open sincerity on which she had built her career. In response to these letters, the editor of the *Morning Chronicle* wrote, "It is but justice to her, to shew, that whatever opinion may be entertained of her discretion, she has never been deficient in the duties of a mother."[58] Jordan's actions disrupted insinuations that she was an irresponsible mother to her existing children, and no further attacks of this kind appeared in the papers or the printshop windows that fall.

Ford's letters stopped claims about Jordan abandoning her existing children and prevented such rumors from making the leap from textual to visual sources. The same was not true for a rumored pregnancy, which became a locus for visual satirists aiming to expose the actress's secrets. The pregnancy rumors began only four days after papers broke the news of the relationship, and *Bon Ton*'s November 1791 issue mockingly suggested such an event must indicate divine approval: "The Ford that formerly ran into this bright prolific river, which like that of Babylon fertilized and improved in all its progressions, will no doubt always lament the parting from its current; but every thing seems to prove and approve its present course, and to avow that it was intended by nature for the ploughing of a bolder and more exalted prow."[59] With four pregnancies in the last five years, Jordan was undeniably both prolific and fertile, as this paragraph calls audiences to remember. Now "nature" signals approval of the duke's "ploughing"—an activity whose purpose is to maximize the fertility of a piece of land—by, it is implied, yielding crops.

Other bon mots mocked the supposed worth of her pregnant body: "The Little Pickle Frigate will prove an invaluable acquisition to her new Commander, as she had taken in a cargo immediately previous to the late contract."[60] There was open speculation about who the father might be: "Little Pickle is again pregnant, but whether the child is to be an *Admiral* [Clarence] or a *Lawyer* [Ford] time only can discover."[61] Such comments suggested Jordan maintained relationships with both men simultaneously or in such quick succession that the father of the child might be unclear until the birth. The phrase "again pregnant" evoked earlier images of Jordan's pregnant body to lend credence to claims audiences cannot yet verify for themselves by allowing the image of her past pregnancies to haunt her body in the present. The anxieties of the opaque pregnant body were brought to bear on Jordan and her imagined sexual exploits: Was she pregnant? Who was responsible, and could paternity ever be certain? As the fall progressed, these questions began to shape visual depictions of the actress.

VISUALIZING THE JORDAN Lampoons in textual sources fed visual satires, but these satires did much more than simply replicate and illustrate printed gossip. Visual satire was able to capture and fix impressions, feelings, and truths about a person that went beyond words.[62] They also had access to an entirely different, image-based vocabulary for this work and were, crucially, not subject to libel laws. While the papers identified Jordan using references to her stage characters ("Little Pickle" or "Nell"), visual satire purported to show the woman herself. In caricature, she ran roughshod over taxpayers in an expensive new coach, wore a ducal coronet, and lounged in bedroom scenes with the duke. As satirists built on each other's work that fall, they established a visual pun for Jordan: the use of a chamber pot, colloquially called a "jordan," to indicate both her (im)morality and her sexual organs. As this pun developed, it also offered satirists a way to further explore the pregnancy rumors begun in the daily papers.

Initially, satirists depicted the chamber pot as separate from Jordan's body and used it to indicate the condition of her sexual morality and private character. James Gillray's first print, for example, labeled the chamber pot "public" and "open to all parties." By early November, the meaning of "jordan" shifted from a symbol of

Figure 4.3. James Gillray, *Lubber's Hole, alias, The Crack'd Jordan* (London: Hannah Humphrey, November 1, 1791). Yale Center for British Art

moral character to a synecdoche of Jordan's physical body, specifically her sexual organs. Gillray made the synthesis brilliantly clear in "The Lubber's Hole, alias, the Crack'd Jordan" (Figure 4.3).[63] In this image, Gillray replaces nearly Jordan's entire body with a large, cracked chamber pot whose curving lines suggest both a vulva and visible pregnancy. A vaginal opening runs nearly the pot's entire length, into which the duke is diving, face-first, while calling "Yeo Yee Yeo," a

Figure 4.4. William Dent, *Fording the Jordan* (London: W. Aitken, November 8, 1791), © The Trustees of the British Museum

sailor's call and the chorus to "What Girl But Loves a Merry Tar," Jordan's popular stage song from *The Spoil'd Child*. Tiny feet and a hint of skirt are the only signs of Jordan's human body; everything else about her is subsumed to her oversized sex organs.

William Dent's "Fording the Jordan," one of a number of prints he made during the scandal, shows the actress reclining as though painted on the side of another abnormally large pot (Figure 4.4). The cracked pot is filled with liquid and labeled with the supposed price of Jordan's annuity as royal mistress. In the pot, the duke bobs, waist-deep, crying "I shall be lost in Thee JORDAN"; she avers, "Where should a wounded Tar [sailor] be but in the Cockpit?"[64] Jordan is again dwarfed by her larger-than-life sex organs—the chamber pot/cockpit into which the duke fears he will be "lost." Her bared breasts are visible while the chamber pot stands in for the part of her body covered by the flowing skirt. The focus of Dent's print is on Jordan and her sexuality as a corrupting force, manifested in the image of the liquid-filled pot that threatens to drown the duke. But the duke's presence in the liquid filling the chamber pot also calls to mind images of doctors examining a patient's urine to determine pregnancy, in which the artist indicated a positive result with the presence of a homunculus floating in the liquid. Among its potential readings, then, Dent's design suggested that Jordan's "jordan" might contain a tiny duke: that the actress was pregnant.

In "Fording the Jordan" and "The Lubber's Hole" the duke's bodily engagement with the jordan/Jordan, particularly a damaged one, suggests a grotesque and contaminating sexuality in addition to the rumored pregnancy. Representing Jordan's sex organs as oversized chamber pots into which Clarence disappears implies a dangerous excess to their relationship while dehumanizing and fetishizing Jordan. Like the figures of insatiable lust or hunger that populate Rabelais's writings, Jordan's grotesque body consumes.[65] Both visual and textual sources in the fall of 1791 showed an abiding belief that Jordan's body—long a source of pleasure and attraction to her audience while sustaining visible and regular evidence of her respectable life offstage—was now suspect, wanton, and in need of monitoring and exposure. Representations of the actress that fall suggested that time would tell if Jordan was pregnant or not, and this, in turn, would reveal her true character.

STAGING RESISTANCE Throughout the attacks in October and November, Jordan remained a steady presence on the stage, understanding the importance of business as usual: "I am strongly advised to play in the farce tomorrow, it is thought and I think very properly that withdrawing myself *just now* for a couple of nights might have a very bad effect on the minds of the audience, who received me very kindly the other night."[66] Jordan's performances—the person and persona she offered onstage in contrast to these effigies—remained popular, but this balance could be lost if she withdrew even temporarily. In consequence, she pushed through emotional and physical turmoil to continue her public appearances, using her enchanting stage presence to charm audiences. The charismata of her actual presence, as well as the professional devotion it seemed to display, worked to counteract the stigmata of visual and textual effigy that cast Jordan as immoral and unworthy of support. Though she did not directly address her attackers, Jordan's repertory could place her new relationship in a more sentimental than sexual light. She acted many of her usual characters that fall, including (perhaps surprisingly) those being employed in the press to reference her new relationship: Nell in *The Devil to Pay* and Little Pickle in *The Spoil'd Child*. She also played Rosalind, Viola, and Hippolyta, all breeches roles that involved some degree of bodily display, and sang Matilda in *Richard Coeur de Lion*, another breeches role in which a queen disguises herself as a blind minstrel to rescue her husband. She did not, however, play the pugilistic Priscilla Tomboy after October 23, perhaps because her song "How I Long to Get Married"–which mentioned her yearning for a baby and a carriage—was too topical. There was also no Sir Harry Wildair; though the part was always popular in London, Sir Harry's rakish behavior and lax sexual mores might, again, have created unwanted associations between actress and character.[67]

Other roles contained the potential to tacitly comment on her private situation favorably. Just before the news of the relationship broke on October 11, for example, Jordan appeared as Peggy in *The Country Girl* on October 6, the role with which she had begun her London career. When Garrick overhauled Wycherley's play in the 1760s, he reverted to a setup similar to that in Moliere's *School for Wives*, changing Peggy from a married woman into an unmarried woman who has been deceived by her guardian/fiancé Moody into believing herself legally married. Instead of an unrepentant rake seducing her, Peggy finds love and manages to marry her preferred partner, Bellville. Having realized the extent of the deception practiced upon her, Peggy shames Moody in the final scene: "How dare you look me in the face, Bud? Have you not given me to another, when you ought to have married me yourself? Have you not pretended to be married to me, when you knew in your conscience you was not?—And have you not been shilly shally for a long time? So if I had not married dear Mr. Bellville, I should not have married at all—so I should not."[68] One can hardly imagine a more topical reference to Jordan's five-year wait for marriage and Richard Ford's "shilly shally" pretense in calling her Mrs. Ford, though Garrick wrote the play a quarter century earlier. The epilogue, which Jordan performed on October 22 in the thick of initial responses to the relationship, offered a similar opportunity. Like all epilogues, it existed in a liminal space that encouraged slippage between actress and character:

> Great Folk, I know, will call me simple Slut,
> "Marry for love!" They cry, the Country Put,
> Marriage for them's a Fashion—soon grows cool:
> But I'm for loving always, like a Fool.
> For half my Fortune, I would rather part,
> Than be all Finery, with an aching Heart:
> For these strange awkward notions don't abuse me,
> And, as I know no better, pray excuse me.[69]

The epilogue frames the relationship with the duke as a love match and more genuine, perhaps, than fashionable marriage. When Jordan referenced parting with "half [her] fortune" to marry for love, moreover, the audience knew that Jordan had done this and more to provide for her children. Jordan/Peggy's professed innocence and request not to be abused for her actions, moreover, resonated strongly in the context of public attacks on the actress. Other roles, including Lydia Languish in *The Rivals*, also emphasized the heroine's desire to marry for love while rejecting pecuniary advantage. Just as audiences may have tacitly accepted Desdemona's innocence on behalf of Susannah Cibber or read Anne Oldfield's losses into Andromache's grief, the texts of *The Country Girl* and *The Rivals* offered Jordan a way to frame a controversial decision, and even to ask for pardon, without having to address the scandal directly.

The necessity of minimizing attention to the financial benefits of her relationship was twofold. First, prints and press had used the settlements to equate Jordan with prostitution and suggest a lack of maternal feeling. Second, her new income—particularly coupled with a pregnancy—raised the possibility that she would retire: "Every

Actress in Drury-lane Theatre has of late been studying some of Mrs. Jordan's characters, in hopes that little Pickle will retire from the stage."[70] This was the larger and more specific tension between actress and audience: Mrs. Jordan was considered a public employee; audiences paid money to see her, she became rich, but owed her success to their indulgence. Any lover who granted her a generous annuity compromised the power dynamic between audience and actress by making her less dependent on her theatrical salary and, therefore, more likely to retire or become negligent in her professional duties. Clarence, however, was a prince. He received his entire income from public tax money. If she left the stage permanently (as Nell Gwyn did during her second pregnancy by Charles II), the public would essentially be funding Jordan's private sexual performances for the duke without any benefit to themselves in public access to her person. *The Caledonian Mercury*, who had labeled Jordan "the *prostitute-actress*" suggested, "If the public money is to be thus applied to support the dignity of Princes, new *Ways and Means* must be devised for levying it, that the people may not suppose themselves the subscribing abettors of *dignified immorality!*"[71] Behind these complaints lay not only larger questions of monarchy and taxation, but a real anxiety that Jordan would leave the profession entirely. Initially, Jordan's continued appearances and the audience's goodwill suggested that she would remain. This all changed when Jordan withdrew from the stage for two weeks, provoking a violent outcry from the audience that, for the first time, truly threatened her career.

Phase Two: Crisis

On November 26, Jordan was scheduled to appear in *Richard Coeur de Lion*, but sent word "*a few instants before the curtain drew up*" that she would be unable to perform because she was ill.[72] When the management explained and proposed substituting another afterpiece the audience nearly rioted. They demanded the managers return their money or that the play continue with another actress. Some called for the management to immediately fire Mrs. Jordan. Eventually, Anna Maria Crouch took Jordan's part and *Richard Coeur de Lion* continued. Whereas in the past the papers often printed information about Jordan's illnesses, especially her pregnancies and miscarriages, without questioning their validity and even used them to highlight her professional devotion, now her indisposition played into wider anxieties about her duplicity, wanton sexuality, and unprofessionalism. One commentator warned, "The public are indulgent and generous, but they are not to be trifled with."[73]

Jordan was away for almost two weeks and under the care of royal physicians, including Dr. Richard Warren. The complaint was reported to be a "violent spitting of blood," a problem she also had over the summer that seemed to be exacerbated by singing.[74] The relapse was, according to the duke's letters, precipitated by a particularly vicious attack printed in the *Morning Herald* on the day she was to perform.[75] The tide Jordan's continued presence had kept at bay finally spilled over into the theatrical space in her absence. In the ensuing days, a debate started in the papers about what right the public had to examine or condemn the private lives of public figures. Some claimed that audiences deserved to know the moral character of those whom their ticket money supported, else "excellence will extenuate ENORMITY, and those who *polish* life, may at the same time *deprave* it."[76] Others suggested that as long as her career continued the audience should "suspend their morality in their pleasure," a phrase rife with innuendo.[77] Now, instead of attacking the performer by attacking the woman, attacks on Jordan questioned her fitness as a working professional directly.

On December 1, still recovering, Jordan responded with a letter to the press. She called the abuses heaped upon her in the public papers "unprovoked and unmanly." While she felt it right to remain silent on "subjects about which the public could not be interested," it was her "duty to reply" to attacks on her professional conduct. In this framing, Jordan asserted a clear line between public (her profession) and private (her relationship with the duke). Her identity as a mother, however, existed somewhere in between. Her profession was the means by which she supported her children, so those who attacked her as a professional compromised her ability to fulfill her maternal obligations; if her detractors succeeded in "driv[ing] me from that profession, they would take from me the only income I have or mean to possess, the whole earnings of which upon the past, and one half for the future, I have already settled upon my children."[78] Jordan reiterated the information about her theatrical income going to the children's maintenance, and informed the audience that she had also pledged her entire savings to their use. In such circumstances, she assured the public that she would continue to perform to fulfill her duties as a good mother and would do nothing so foolish as pretending illness when it might endanger her career and her children's security. Jordan's letter was an attempt to force audiences to confront her as a known individual rather than an abstracted, stereotyped figure about whom rumor and innuendo could circulate with impunity.

Jordan returned to the stage on December 10, playing Roxalana in the farce *The Sultan*. Roxalana is an enslaved Englishwoman in the sultan's harem whose witty high spirits win his affection, convert him to monogamy, and make her a queen. The sultan gives Roxalana political power and control over the empire, which she vows to remodel along principles of British freedom. In performing this honorable, nationalistic Christian character upon her return to the stage, perhaps Jordan was suggesting that the audience might find those same virtues in herself. She was also, of course, acting the part of a woman whose attractions gain her political power over a male ruler, perhaps offering the audience a chance to confront and laugh at a situation far more politically dire than her own.

The audience variously cheered and hissed Jordan from the moment she took the stage. When it became clear the audience would not desist if she ignored them, she addressed them directly: "I should consider myself as totally unworthy of the distinguished favour and approbation I have ever received from you, if the smallest mark of your displeasure did not sensibly afflict me. . . . I never absented myself from the Theatre, but when compelled to it by real indisposition . . . it has been my pride, my unremitting study, to endeavor to entertain and amuse you; and I trust I may, while so employed, consider myself as under your protection."[79] Dropping entirely her stage persona of joyful, riotous humor, Jordan instead presented herself as a serious professional who worked, and worked hard, for the position she enjoyed. She offered her vulnerable self in this moment, making it clear that she relied on the audience for support on stage and emotional well-being offstage, acknowledging the power dynamic critics had been attempting to assert since they felt wronged by her nonappearance. In raising the specter of herself as a private individual truly and closely tied to her audience's wishes and feelings, Jordan reasserted her identity as a woman sensible of her obligations to the audience and distinct from the characters she played on stage. She also displaced the callous, hypersexual caricatures of visual satires and appealed to her audience's sentimentality: in this speech, she suggested it was not the duke who was her true her protector, but the paying public.

Phase Three: Aftermath

Jordan had effectively refocused the public debate on her professional integrity, which she explicitly tied to her maternal persona while refusing to acknowledge the question of her sexual morality or rumored pregnancy in any direct way. Still, returning to the stage offered her body up for continued public scrutiny, allowing audiences to judge for themselves the degree of her transgression (Would she prove to be pregnant? If so, how far along? Would the pregnancy's progress prove she had maintained sexual relationships with both men simultaneously?). And monitored her body most certainly was: on January 4 *The Star* noted "Mrs. Jordan has of late grown thin; but there is great prospect that in the Spring, she may get *round* a little." A satirical print in March suggested a miscarriage, while in June, Clarence was seen about town in a new carriage, the color of which (yellow) sparked yet more pregnancy speculation: "From the *colour* of the Duke of Clarence's new carriages, it is not at all improbable that Mrs. Jordan will very shortly be in the *straw!*"[80] So long as she continued to appear regularly, which she did for the remainder of the season, Jordan kept attacks at bay within the theatrical space. In visual satire, however, the crisis was not over. Two caricatures by Isaac Cruikshank persistently suggested duplicity on the part of Jordan around her absence in the fall, using the rumored pregnancy to question her right to audience acceptance and support.

In the first, "The Humbug"—a term indicating deliberate deceit—he painstakingly re-created the scene in the theater immediately before Jordan gave her address, with two important changes (Figure 4.5). The first was to have the Prince of Wales in the royal box telling Clarence he would "clap" Jordan, with its double meaning of applaud and infect with venereal disease. The second change

Figure 4.5. Isaac Cruikshank, *The Humbug or an Attempt at Tragedy, with the Joram Upsett* (London: S.W. Fores, December 20, 1791). Yale Center for British Art

was to substitute the Duke of Clarence for her costar William Barrymore. Clarence holds Jordan on his knee and offers her a glass of gin (not water, as reported). He rails against the ungrateful audience, while Jordan protests, "I ~~was~~ am indisposed," a term for any illness but also a euphemism for pregnancy. Across the stage, a large container of gin is rolling, spilling its contents. In this image, the container associated with Jordan is once again a leaking vessel, though not a chamber pot. That the vessel is filled with gin has two possible connotations: the more general is the vice and drunkenness associated with the drink, which was blamed for moral dissipation, prostitution, and disease. Another association for gin, however, is with unfit motherhood and infanticide, as in Hogarth's moralizing print *Gin Lane* (1751).[81] Juniper or savin, from which gin was derived, was also a widely known and used abortifacient, perhaps furthering the associations between the drink and unfit motherhood and providing a particularly vicious possible reading of Jordan's absence and Clarence's offer of a glass in the print.[82] While Cruikshank's exact meaning is ambiguous, it is clear he means to suggest that the public's acceptance of Jordan's apology may have come too easily. He aligns her at the least with grotesque drunkenness, immorality, bad motherhood, and sexual disease, and possibly suggests that she has procured an abortion to facilitate her return to the stage.

Cruikshank again took up the idea of concealed pregnancy in March, this time purporting to answer the questions raised by pregnancy rumors in the fall around the supposed child's paternity. Dated March 15, 1791, but actually printed in 1792, the print is titled, "Mrs. Pickle's mistake or the new Papa Disappointed by Justice Shallow's attempts to Charm the Brutes"[83] (Figure 4.6). It shows Clarence dressed as a midwife standing on the balcony of Jordan's house in Somerset Street. Below him is a man, presumably Richard Ford, onto whom he is dumping the contents of a chamber pot labeled "DC" (Duke of Clarence). Ford leads a pair of convicts in a "charivari," a censorious procession used to shame participants in an unusual or objectionable relationship.[84] Next to Clarence is Richard Warren, then one of the physicians in ordinary attending on the royal family.[85] Warren holds a variety of lethal-looking instruments while dangling a male child in a pair of forceps over the balcony. He admonishes the noisemakers, saying "Mrs. Pickle has just made a faux Couche" (had a miscarriage) of a "young Sea Gull" (Clarence). A woman on the street comments on how much the "slink," a premature or stillborn baby (also implying illegitimacy), looks like its father. Both this testimony, the star that appears on the child's chest and echoes the Garter star on the sleeve of his nurse's uniform, and the "DC" on the chamber pot (signaling his ownership of Jordan's body) seem to verify the child's paternity; Richard Ford, however, also wears a star, leaving continued doubt. Though the print is related to the pregnancy rumors that circulated in October, its setting and characters (particularly Dr. Warren) suggest it is attempting to expose the truth behind her two-week absence in late November and early December. When Jordan's actual body failed to affirm the validity of the pregnancy rumors, visual satire allowed those rumors to gestate, develop, and eventually culminate in an imagined birth scene that rewrote recent history.

Was Jordan pregnant in the fall of 1791? We do not know, for her surviving letters are undated. When the public confronted Jordan's new relationship, rumors of a pregnancy may have simply

Figure 4.6. Isaac Cruikshank, *Mrs. Pickle's Mistake, or the New Papa Disappointed by Justice Shallow's Attempts to Charm the Brutes* (London: S.W. Fores, March 15, 1791). Yale Center for British Art

been a useful shorthand for expressing the suspicion and uncertainty that now surrounded her public image, for she had grown to fame on the appearance of sincerity and professional devotion. It seemed for a time that she could not be what she had always appeared, and both textual and visual sources capitalized on this anxiety to purport to show the public a more authentic version of the actress than she herself was offering. There was little Jordan could do to refute such rumors. Going into hiding, as Susannah Cibber did in the wake of her scandal, would only create anger. Continuing to perform—the tactic Anne Oldfield used in 1712–13—allowed audiences to judge her behavior and monitor her body directly while enabling Jordan to leverage her popularity and charm to dispel the hypersexual, negative images of her that circulated outside the theater. Against visual and textual effigy, she offered actual, bewitching presence, and at least the appearance of transparency and accessibility over subterfuge and deceit. While the crisis was not entirely over, as Cruikshank's cartoons show, attacks decreased significantly after her reappearance, and audiences received her performances without further incidents.[86]

Pregnancy and Patriotism: 1792–1800

Despite its sensational beginnings, critics eventually either accepted or ignored Jordan and Clarence's relationship as they settled into an almost mundane domesticity during a decade of international turmoil. There were hard lines around what was acceptable—Jordan would never be received at Court, and Clarence's periodic tendency to treat her as his wife in social settings caused confusion and embarrassment.[87] But Clarence was to all appearances a doting partner, and several of his brothers socialized with Jordan as though she were his wife. Even the king grew tolerant enough to affectionately "tease Clarence about Mrs. J."[88] In this decade, reactions to Jordan's many pregnancies again serve to mark changing perceptions of the actress.

Not long after the tumultuous 1791–92 season, Jordan suffered a life-threatening miscarriage in August 1792, the same month the French monarchs were arrested. Echoing the mocking tone of the previous year, some papers made light of the loss, but the seriousness of the situation was made clear when Jordan stayed home until the end of February 1793. She returned to the stage just over a month after news of Louis XVI's execution reached London and with Britain now at war. Perhaps these circumstances discouraged criticism in some way, even of a royal mistress, or perhaps Jordan was an especially welcome presence during such a grim time. For two months after her return, *Bon Ton Magazine* ran a remarkably sympathetic two-part biography of Jordan. Far from the lampoons and critiques of 1791, she was praised for being "a woman of so rare a natural genius . . . who, instead of forcing [Clarence] into dissipation and folly, leads him to domestic life, to study, and improvement; who, if she may be somewhat expensive, prevents prodigality to a dangerous extent."[89] The rag that ridiculed Jordan as unfeeling and corrupt in 1791 now positioned her as a moral force for good. Her positive domestic influence was underscored by Clarence's ready acceptance of her other children as part of his life: "The Duke of Clarence enjoys domestic happiness with all its charms at Petersham; Mrs. Jordan's daughters are with him, and live in such easy state of familiarity that when speaking to or of his Royal Highness, they call him papa, and papa Clarence."[90] Though they could never marry, one author claimed, "she lives as the nature of her connection will allow; and it may be said of her what of many ladies legally connected cannot be said: 'Tho' she boasts not the *name*, she's the *truth* of a wife.'"[91] As the decade unfolded, this would increasingly be the perception of their relationship.

Between 1794 and 1807, Jordan and Clarence had ten surviving children, five boys and five girls in neat alteration. Their first four were born on January 29, 1794 (George); March 4, 1795 (Sophia); March 8, 1797 (Henry Edward), and December 19, 1798 (Mary) while Jordan was still appearing regularly in London.[92] After Mary's birth Jordan preferred acting outside London during her pregnancies—especially in Richmond near the home they established at Bushy Park in 1797—confessing at one point that she felt a growing "repugnance" toward her profession.[93] She rarely stopped working completely, however, for her family needed the income. Not only was Clarence rarely flush himself (she once loaned him £2400, and smaller but also significant amounts on other occasions), but she had three illegitimate daughters to support whose fathers could not be relied on.[94] This decade of Jordan's life was shaped by her royal relationship and the many pregnancies which attended it, both of which impacted her theatrical work and public reputation. Larger events, including the war with France, meanwhile, coupled with her associations with the royal family, brought changes to her onstage repertoire. In the middle of this busy decade, a publicized miscarriage in January 1796 followed by another pregnancy before the end of the year appear to show a clear turn in representations of their relationship away from the sexual or cynical and back toward the sentimental. This turn shaped reception of Jordan's performances, and illustrates the strategies she used to frame her personal and professional obligations.

Jordan's pregnancy with George, their eldest surviving child, took place largely out of the public eye. Instead, she was content to stay home throughout the pregnancy and after the birth, nursing her first son herself. As with Lucy's birth in 1790 following her 1788 miscarriage, the experience of miscarriage in 1792 may have encouraged Jordan to approach her professional obligations with an abundance of caution. Despite her absence from the stage, press sources noted the pregnancy, and she, as was the fashion, had a London birth at her home on Somerset Street. The birth inspired bon mots and some grumbling took place over the supposed £1,000 cost of Jordan's confinement, but the birth was not the target of satirical prints. In light of the war with France and her relationship with Clarence, in fact, George's arrival was more the subject of gallows humor than censure: "Mrs. JORDAN's new-born boy is to be immediately entered a Midshipman. If we are not to have a Peace until France is conquered, it is probable that before the conclusion of the War he will be made an *Admiral*."[95] Her first appearance back on stage, a benefit for naval widows and orphans in July 1794, further emphasized her new associations. It was a patriotic cause easily read as close to her heart as a woman whose partner and son might be called for naval service. Clarence, sidelined from actual naval duty, assisted in the planning and execution of the displays for the performance.[96] Jordan's continued and increasingly frequent appearances while pregnant, while in a relationship with a member of the royal family, and while being a British subject during a war with France suggested that the pregnancies too were part of her nationalistic fervor. A bon mot anticipating the birth of their third child in the midst of fears of a French invasion in 1796/97 thought the country should be consoled that, "Little Pickle . . . though she keeps one tar *at home*, is willing enough to produce others to supply his place *abroad*!"[97] The tone is mocking, but it also resonated with the emphasis on British women's roles in populating an expanding empire and creating soldiers to defend it, which had been a preoccupation since at least the middle of the century and took on new urgency in this decade.

Despite the disruptions to her performance schedule between 1792–94, Jordan remained at the top of her profession. In September 1794, when George was nearing eight months old and she was already three months pregnant with Sophy, Jordan signed a new contract with Sheridan for the ensuing five seasons. It guaranteed her an income of £31.10 a week each year between November and the end of May, and additional payments of £10.10 a night when she appeared outside these dates or performed more than three times a week. She was dressed at the expense of the theater and received a yearly benefit, usually free of house charges. Additionally, each April 30 she was to receive an additional £210 for incidental expenses. If Jordan or the theater did not adhere to these terms, the penalty was set at £1,000.[98] The contract made clear Jordan's value as a performer and tied compensation to her appearances, meaning both Jordan and the theater had more flexibility in the event she was unable or unwilling to perform.

During the five years this contract was valid she had three children, missing at least three months of the season each time. These extended absences were perhaps out of an abundance of caution, because continual childbearing was taking a physical toll, or simply because Jordan wished to perform less often in an advanced state of pregnancy. As we saw in the Siddons chapter, advice manuals in this decade were also increasingly critical of overwork during pregnancy, meaning that even as Jordan engaged in behavior that could be read as indulgently privileged, it was also possible to read her extended absences as a form of patriotism and good motherhood. The additional time off always came before the births, not after; Jordan consistently lay in no longer than six weeks, never taking more time than social norms suggested women should after a birth. This was difficult and tiring, for she was almost continuously pregnant and always caring for several infants as well. Indeed, the two years between Sophia and Henry's births—the longest birth interval between her first four surviving children by Clarence—also saw two miscarriages, one in July 1795 and another in January 1796. By early 1796, it was difficult to deny that Jordan's attempts to fulfill both personal and professional obligations in this relationship, just as in the relationship with Ford, were both real and sometimes dangerous. Her visible labor on behalf of her public despite these challenges suggested Jordan was much as she had always been despite her change in private circumstances.

Jordan's many pregnancies during the 1790s affected her and the theater's repertoire through her extended absences, of course, but there were also changes to what she performed when she was present. Some of these changes appear to be about the relationship in general. Jordan and her managers were fully aware that her career would be seen in light of her personal connection and made permanent changes to her repertoire after the relationship began. Gone was Sir Harry Wildair, for example, the part that had so thrilled London audiences with the character's outrageous behavior and lax morals.[99] A less expected loss was Matilda in *Richard Coeur de Lion*. In this case, it was not the play itself but its associations with the 1791 scandal that made the change permanent. After the outrage directed at Jordan by her audience in November 1791 bestowed the part on Anna Maria Crouch, it remained in the other actress's repertoire permanently. Changes related specifically to pregnancy were fewer, but a notable one is that once with Clarence Jordan appeared less frequently in breeches roles during pregnancy, though she often played them after lying in.[100] Thus, while her pregnancies during the relationship with Richard Ford had little if any impact on her breeches roles repertoire, her pregnancies during the relationship with Clarence certainly did. Whether this was out of a sense of decorum or because of the bodily changes that accompanied aging and near-constant pregnancy is unclear.

Jordan's relationship also brought her new roles. In the context of war and her relationship with a member of the royal family, Jordan's pregnancies and her children were inextricably bound up in ideas of nationalism and monarchy. One effect of this was that Jordan's evolving repertoire took on patriotic overtones linked to her partner's naval service, in both existing roles like Little

Pickle, who disguises himself as a sailor, and new ones like Albina in *The Will* (1797), a young woman who assumes the identity of a naval lieutenant. Early in her pregnancy with Frederick (born in December 1799), Jordan took on a different kind of patriotic role. She acted Cora, mother to an imperiled infant (perhaps played by five-month-old Mary) in Sheridan's nationalistic melodrama *Pizarro* in May and June 1799.[101] The play aimed to redeem Sheridan and Drury Lane in the eyes of the king and to stave off bankruptcy. Both were successful, and the king and queen attended a performance at Drury Lane for the first time in five years to see a double bill featuring their son's lover and one of their illegitimate grandchildren. *Pizarro* was one culmination of the shifts in her repertoire post-Clarence, for beginning in 1796 she started appearing, selectively, in tragedy.

The season of 1796–97 was a crucial time for Jordan and seems to mark a turning point—or returning point—in her public persona, from the royal mistress back to a near-wife and faithful mother. This turn is illustrated in reception of both familiar roles and new ones. Jordan acted steadily from October 1 to December 17, 1796, and again from April 19 to June 14, 1797 after Henry's birth in March. In the fall, she played a series of familiar parts in mainpieces and afterpieces (such as Peggy in *The Country* Girl and Nell in *The Devil to Pay*), but her newest and most exciting role was Ophelia in *Hamlet* opposite John Philip Kemble. They first played the parts in the spring of 1796, shortly after her January 1796 miscarriage, and theatergoers eagerly anticipated a more extended run in the fall. When the time came, however, the performance had to be delayed: "The expectation of the Public are very much baulked of the expected treat of HAMLET at Drury-lane this evening. The cause, we understand, to be the sudden indisposition of a *Royal Infant* under inoculation."[102] Sophy had fallen ill after receiving her smallpox inoculation in October, and Jordan—whom the audience were reminded was "far gone in her pregnancy"—nursed her through the illness herself.[103] Once Sophy recovered Jordan returned and acted Ophelia five times before leaving the stage around the start of her seventh month of pregnancy.

Jordan's appearances as Ophelia were the greatest success she had in a tragic role. Leigh Hunt suggested this was because Ophelia is not a tragic character, but a character made tragic by circumstance.

Jordan's cheerfulness in Ophelia's mad scenes, then, was the more heartbreaking for the lack of awareness she displayed of her fallen condition. In her incisive re-evaluation of Jordan's place in the history of Shakespearean performance, however, Fiona Ritchie urges our attention to the way Jordan's traditional associations with comedy have led us to devalue her skills with pathos, when this was precisely what made roles like Viola so compelling. Ritchie writes that these Shakespeare heroines "offered Jordan a particular opportunity . . . because they were commonly melancholy in nature, requiring a mixture of both comedy and tragedy that Jordan was uniquely able to render on the stage."[104] Ophelia was a character that capitalized on this aspect of her identity; it was also a singing role, and this contributed greatly to her success. Of all Jordan's roles to this point in her career, moreover, Ophelia—beloved but abandoned by a prince, insensible of her own distress—was one both by content and genre that facilitated audience desire to meld Jordan's public and private lives, her body natural with her character body. Appearing in the role while pregnant might, as with Siddons in Lady Macbeth or other women in Andromache, add to the pathos and its biographical resonance: in this case, the consequence of consummated love without hope of marriage to a royal prince.

When Sophia's illness delayed the first performance of *Hamlet* that season, the full details of Jordan's absence appeared in the initial notification to the audience and were directly tied to her private identity as a responsible and affectionate mother. This was a deliberate strategy, and one that may have been connected with reactions to her miscarriage in January 1796. After this miscarriage, Jordan missed two weeks of the season to recover. Initially, the papers had not named the cause of her absence, leading to accusations of caprice that echoed the angry response to her absence in 1791. Defending her, the new Tory paper the *Tomahawk or Censor General* wrote that she was "very well known" to have "often attended her duty at the theatre, to the very risk of her life, rather than disappoint the amusement of her best friends, the public."[105] Ten days later, a detailed description of her sudden illness and miscarriage appeared in a short news article that emphasized the "acute pain in her side" and her "nervous head-ache" along with Dr. Warren's advice that she continue to rest.[106] Foregrounding her bodily suffering and devotion to the public recalled the strategies she employed in 1791, strategies that were increasingly effective as public acceptance of her relationship grew.

Nine months later, when she had to defer her appearance as Ophelia, there was no delay in the dissemination of information around the cause of her absence. Notices about Sophy's illness emphasized that, despite her privileged status and her physical condition, Jordan tended her daughter herself, an action signaling her participation in natural and sentimental constructions of affectionate parenthood. While the public was disappointed there was no widespread outcry against Jordan for neglecting her professional duties as in the fall of 1791 or even the previous winter. Indeed, the reminder of her pregnancy placed added weight and value on her willingness to continue performing at all. As her relationship with Clarence progressed, the decision to keep working during pregnancy and the explicit sharing of personal and familial information when conflicts might arise between her maternal and theatrical duties helped Jordan maintain her persona of sincere devotion first to her children, and then to her public.

Jordan's changed domestic circumstances and visible pregnancies also affected audience reception of existing roles in her repertoire. In late November 1796, perhaps influenced by her tragic performances as Ophelia and the twin devotion she showed to Sophy and to her public, an audience member had an unexpected response to Jordan's Nell in *The Devil to Pay*. They reported, "Mrs. JORDAN performed *Nell* with her accustomed excellence and was encored in some songs. Her appearance on the stage in *her situation* is a strong proof of her wishes to please the Public. The audience felt this; and they were equally filled with admiration, gratitude, and pity."[107] In 1791, satirists used the similitude between Nell's fictional life and Jordan's situation prominently, mocking Jordan's perceived naivete in entering into an association with Clarence and suggesting she would soon return to her rightful place. By 1796, however, and despite having played the role consistently over the previous five years, Jordan's pregnancy gave the part an entirely different meaning for at least one supporter. Rather than the sexualized stigmatic force pregnancy had been in the fall of 1791, this notice made Jordan's 1796–97 pregnancy a powerful charismatic force once again, one that enhanced

Figure 4.7. James Gillray, *La Promenade en Famille, a Sketch from Life* (London: Hannah Humphrey, April 23, 1797). Yale Center for British Art

the performance and allowed the body natural and celebrity bodies to supersede the character body.

Around this same time, a striking act of generosity from the king suggested a further change in attitude toward Jordan and Clarence. After Jordan withdrew from the stage in 1797 but before Henry's birth, George III bestowed on Clarence the rangership at Bushy Park, a country estate near Hampton Court, which relieved many difficulties for the growing family. James Gillray, the cartoonist who had made several biting prints in 1791, released "La Promenade en Famillie: A Sketch from Life" in April 1797 (Figure 4.7). It depicts the duke and Jordan moving George, Sophy, and baby Henry to Bushy Park. Jordan walks with script in hand, while Clarence pulls the children in a small cart emblazoned with a ducal coronet surmounting a chamber pot. Unlike earlier prints, this one contains no overt moral judgment about Jordan or her relationship, nor is she depicted in the *dishabille* common in earlier prints. While Gillray caricatures the duke and appears to poke fun at him for taking care of the children while Jordan works, Jordan is not the grotesque siren of earlier satires, but a working mother and professional actress. Gillray even draws the chamber pot, so crucial to understanding Jordan's moral and physical integrity in 1791, healed of its cracked and leaking appearance.

This representation of Jordan aligned closely with the persona she projected from the stage: a hardworking professional whose honest labor supported a growing family. That that family was royal made her labor more visible, but no less real. Linda Colley sees criticism of the monarchy after the end of the American Revolution as that which, "sought to provoke ridicule not hatred . . . laughter takes the sting out of criticism. And laughing at royal individuals led in practice very easily to amused tolerance for royalty itself."[108] Clarence, like his royal father "farmer George" was presented as solidly and stolidly British and domestic. Jordan, like the Queen, was prolific in her fertility but no less dedicated to her public role. After tumult and rupture, Jordan's transparent exposure of her private life onstage during pregnancy and in the papers when the children's health prevented her appearances helped her re-establish the stability and support she enjoyed in the 1780s.

Conclusion

Reactions to Jordan's pregnancies show that her fertile body was both a symptom and a cause of changing audience responses to the woman and her private circumstances. They also echo many of the responses to pregnancy we saw in earlier performers. Like Susanna Mountfort Verbruggen, she specialized in comedy, including breeches roles and low comic women, and frequently performed throughout pregnancy, where her perceived marital status might offset transgressive performances onstage. Like Anne Oldfield, she had two long-term monogamous relationships without marrying; the wide-spread belief that she was married during the first, however—partly because of cohabitation and frequent childbearing—echoes George Anne Bellamy's experiences in the mid-1750s. While imagined to be the wife of Richard Ford, papers suggest that audiences accepted her pregnancies and lauded her continued performances during pregnancy and illness as they did Sarah Siddons's. That relationship ended, like Susannah Cibber's marriage, in a spectacular fashion that challenged audience perceptions of their stage favorite in 1791 amid rumors of pregnancy. Her affair with Clarence prompted prints and press notices that cast her as a fallen woman and excessively sexual. Within these, the rumored pregnancy was a powerful stigmatic force used to express fears and doubts about her seemingly false nature and render her body grotesque. Unlike Susannah Cibber and like Anne Oldfield, Jordan managed this crisis by remaining on stage, providing access to her "real" self in the theater to counteract stigmatic and grotesque readings of her body in newspapers and visual sources. After this crisis, and like Sarah Siddons, Jordan used her maternity to reconstitute the sympathetic power of her visibly pregnant body in a time of national upheaval.

Jordan's "art" as an actress was based on her ability to appear completely natural and sincere on stage. She used this sincerity offstage by intervening when enemies appropriated her image, actions, and behaviors for satiric or harmful ends. In sharing personal information about her children in the press and performing while visibly pregnant, she reminded audiences of the realities of her offstage life that could become invisible when she performed her carefree comic parts. By 1796, her domestic life had once again begun to diffuse the stigmatic associations with her position as royal mistress, as was clear in reactions to her pregnant performances of Shakespeare's Ophelia and Nell in *The Devil to Pay*. Jordan's resistance to hiding her private life—most visibly by performing while pregnant—and open acknowledgment of the conflicts that sometimes arose in professional and maternal duty asserted a subject position, an autonomous identity that existed beyond the stage even if it was still bounded by larger social notions of gender and motherhood.[109] Far from damaging her career, Jordan received steadily more lucrative contracts in and beyond London as her family and prominence grew. Her changing repertory and frequent absences, moreover, gave important opportunities to those around her to raise their own celebrity.

In Siddons and Jordan we appear to have two archetypal visions of actresses and women in society—with Siddons we might look forward to a domestic ideal of womanhood that flourished into the nineteenth century (at least in didactic literature); with Jordan, we could turn back to the archetype of the actress as royal mistress, casting her as another Nell Gwyn. However, Jordan's use of her domestic circumstances to deflect charges of amoral or unprofessional behavior while asserting her rights to a continued career complicates this simple distinction. Jordan was much more than a woman of pleasure and idleness in the public mind; she was, as one writer put it, "the truth of a wife," bearing children, taking care of her partner, and contributing to the family's maintenance.[110] Linda Colley argues that the female figures of the British monarchy (Queen Charlotte, Queen Caroline, and Princess Charlotte) "made . . . the wrongs and rites of passage of ordinary women's lives seem important and valuable in a way that no other aspect of British political life could or can do."[111] Public expressions of gratitude to Queen Charlotte after the 1789 Regency Crisis, public mourning after Princess Charlotte's death in 1817, and petitioning by tens of thousands of middle-class women protesting George IV's attempts to put his wife on trial for adultery in 1820 are just some evidence of the way these prominent women's lives were seen to reflect and amplify the lives of all women. Something similar happened with Jordan. By the time her relationship with Clarence ended in 1811, her supporters denounced the duke for his cruel ingratitude for leaving

> [His] faithful friend for twenty years
> As much your wife in honor's eye,
> As if fast bound in wedlock's tie.[112]

Even ten years later, five years after Jordan died alone in France, her ghost haunted and shamed Clarence for disloyal behavior in a satirical print.[113] Jordan's steady and highly visible maternal and professional labor, like any faithful wife, should have earned her more consideration.

Dora Jordan was neither a queen nor a princess; apart from occasional stage roles, nor did she ever try to act like one. She had no official status in the monarchy, but she was also a real, tangible, woman visibly living an ordinary life in extraordinary circumstances. As William Hazlitt put it, "She was Cleopatra turned into an oyster-wench without knowing she was Cleopatra or caring that she was an oyster-wench."[114] When her pregnancies, the childhood illnesses she tended, and the physical efforts she made were discussed and disseminated in a national press, these everyday realities of womanhood and motherhood were also acknowledged and even celebrated.

She also toured the whole length and breadth of the island, seeing and being seen by thousands of citizens; she was proximate to royalty but far more accessible, fostering an earthly and unvarnished public intimacy that endeared her to many. Her regular appearances while pregnant allowed her to share this portion of her life with audiences, cultivating a reciprocal sentimental relationship. It was not by erasing private associations but by seeming to display them with frankness and honesty—an echo with a difference of both Susannah Cibber's tenebrism and Sarah Siddons's iconicity—that Jordan gained acceptance as "a wife in all but name" not once, but twice in the course of her career.

CONCLUSION

Celebrity Pregnancy, Then and Now

In February 2017, Beyoncé Knowles Carter created a sensation with a lush, richly symbolic, body-baring pregnancy photoshoot. The photoshoot was a celebration, but also a response to those who had questioned the validity of her embodied experience during her first pregnancy in 2011. Beyoncé had revealed that pregnancy at the MTV Video Music Awards to the delight of fans, but her later reserve in sharing pictures of herself with a growing bump were used to suggest she had faked the pregnancy for attention and had a surrogate carry her daughter to preserve her valuable figure. When she failed to continue embodying and gesticulating in culturally ascribed ways, Beyoncé's body became suspicious and prompted increasing surveillance.[1] In 1688, immediately before this study begins (with Susanna Mountfort Verbruggen's 1689–90 pregnancy), Mary of Modena, Queen to James II was similarly judged and found wanting in a performance of pregnancy.

In 1689, there were few visual sources for what the evolution of a "normal" pregnancy looked like and how it progressed, and only a handful of widely available textual ones; instead, those around the queen gauged the veracity of her pregnancy by comparing her experiences to their own and those of other women they had observed. Attempting to determine if she was truly pregnant, ladies in waiting compared the size and growth of her belly to theirs and suggested it grew faster and therefore was simply padding. Poignantly, Princess

Anne (later queen), wrote to her sister Mary (also later queen) that she did not believe the queen could be pregnant because she seemed too happy and healthy.[2] Anne had had five pregnancies in five years of marriage resulting in two stillborn children and one miscarriage. She had also lost her two surviving infant daughters to smallpox. Anne would go on to lose all but one of at least twelve additional pregnancies. When Anne thought that Mary of Modena was too happy and healthy to be pregnant, she did so because her own sad history was her primary point of reference. Mary of Modena's labor and the birth of the child were eventually witnessed by forty people, but the political expediency of believing the "warming pan" scandal so James (a Catholic) could be removed in favor of William and Mary meant the physical labor of her body during pregnancy and in childbirth was denied; the performance was insistently reviewed as false. Mary of Modena went into exile and her son the "Old Pretender" sought, uselessly, to regain his throne and assert the validity of her pregnancy and his birth for his entire life. Nearly three hundred and fifty years later, critics tried to deny Beyoncé ownership of her experience of pregnancy and childbirth. She used the massive public platform of her celebrity to not simply reveal and claim embodied experience in her second pregnancy, but to position herself as a secular and sacred icon.

Between these two stories are many years, many celebrities, and many social, cultural, and medical changes around pregnancy. Eighteenth-century actresses were a crucial part of these changes. Pregnant actresses on stage in Britain during the Restoration and long eighteenth century were the first generations of publicly known, pregnant working women available for sustained scrutiny by a diverse cross-section of society; among many other effects, their presence expanded the visual vocabulary of pregnancy. In December 1784, in fact, a writer for *Rambler's Magazine* declared Covent Garden theater "the most prolific place in England" because six of its female performers were pregnant or lying in; in a single season, audiences might compare the relative sizes, health, symptoms, and fashions of half a dozen women just on stage, let alone in the audience. Neither familial nor royal, neither anonymous nor abstracted, the power of public intimacy, the feeling that they were known and knowable to their audiences, made these celebrity women unique.

Actresses appeared on stage several nights a week, many throughout the duration of their pregnancies. As celebrities, their individual bodies were also social bodies; their pregnancies, then, were social pregnancies. The pregnant body denoted a private, domestic, sexual act made public. Over the century, changing understandings of pregnancy from a medical and social perspective—from a rite of passage to the start of lifelong motherhood, for example—altered the semiotic and affective meanings of the pregnant body. In this context, visible pregnancy could be read along a continuum from the sexual, signaling base appetites fulfilled, to a locus for sensibility, a marker of normative womanhood and the fulfillment of domestic ideals. Celebrity actresses, I have argued, already adept at creating and maintaining public personas through on- and offstage performances, turned these meanings to their advantage, using both familiar stage roles and new ones, print sources, epilogues and addresses, and artistic representations. This project has expanded the archive of material at our disposal for understanding and incorporating women's pregnancies into the history of the century's theater and provided a method for doing so. Having drawn many specific parallels between the women in this study within the individual chapters, here, after a brief review, I want to expand on the implications of this study beyond the eighteenth century.

The introduction suggested a project looking in two directions, considering how pregnancy mattered to theatrical celebrity, and how celebrity pregnancy mattered to theater. To the first point, we have seen pregnancy align with women's self-fashioning productively, from the enhancements it offered to Susanna Mountfort Verbruggen's grotesques in the 1690s to the total synthesis of body natural, celebrity body, and character body Siddons's pregnancies created around her performances of Lady Macbeth and the Tragic Muse at the end of the century. Both Anne Oldfield and Susannah Cibber made major, successful career shifts during pregnancy. Even when pregnancy presented challenges, women used celebrity power to overcome them: Susannah Cibber by absenting her body temporarily, Dorothy Jordan by remaining on stage and recommitting to a persona of total transparency. Pregnancy was a tool for validating offstage extramarital partnerships, as in the cases of Anne Oldfield, George Anne Bellamy, and Dorothy Jordan. Pregnancy also facilitated performances of status. Papers discussed both Sarah Siddons's and Dorothy Jordan's pregnancies as though they were aristocratic women of quality, and both women used expensive royal accoucheurs. The queen's fears for Siddons's health and the £1,000 Jordan and Clarence spent for their first child's lying-in also reinforced social status and economic value. By securing prominent members of society for her children's godparents, meanwhile, George Anne Bellamy reinforced her social value and perceptions that she was legally married. And when Susannah Cibber left the stage in 1749–50 she went to Bath, the spa town Queen Anne made famous when she declared its waters healthful for pregnant women.

Throughout this study, we have also consistently seen the way that pregnancy can both create and feed on the "compelling contradictions" that Joseph Roach articulates at the heart of celebrity power. Jordan and Mountfort Verbruggen balanced domesticity off-stage with lively and sometimes carnivalesque performances on stage; Anne Oldfield countered stigmatic sexual attacks outside the theater with a classically contained, disciplined pregnant body inside it; Sarah Siddons's visible, maternal vulnerability, especially during pregnancy, helped balance potentially frightening and masculine sublimity. Bellamy's pregnancies and cohabitation with John Calcraft helped steady the impetuous reputation of her earlier days. And while Susannah Cibber's later pregnancies may have been difficult to navigate, her early pregnancies were public proof of her victimhood in the breakdown of her marriage, of her efforts to be a good wife to a man who did not deserve her.

In performance, celebrity pregnancy appears to have prompted an array of responses. Audiences were able to separate the body natural from the character body when a woman played virginal ingenues or male roles, accepting that safety was a more important consideration than verisimilitude for performing women and their managers. Especially as birth neared, however, pregnancy could provoke anxiety or discomfort in audiences that distracted from stage fiction, as we saw in responses to Siddons's performance of Jane Shore in 1785, and as was also the case for Isabella Mattocks in 1773. Importantly and less often acknowledged is the fact that pregnancy could enhance stage fiction. This was true, perhaps surprisingly, less often in roles that were themselves explicitly written as pregnant (though George Anne Bellamy played Imoinda in *Oroonoko* and Janey Cibber Celia in *The Perjured Lover*) than in roles in which pregnancy could increase either comedy (Mountfort Verbruggen's grotesques) or pathos by adding something new to a part without triggering fears around safety. Andromache in *The Distrest Mother* is a dominant example, played by four heavily pregnant women in this study alone. Lady Macbeth, too, was one for Sarah Siddons and, earlier in the century, Hannah Pritchard.

Celebrity pregnancy mattered to the professional theater in an array of ways, most obviously by impacting repertory planning and profitability. Handling pregnancy was both individual and case specific and appears to have operated within a consistent set of parameters. We have seen, for example, managers both elect to leave pregnant women out of new play premieres (sometimes Susanna Mountfort Verbruggen), and to include them, despite looming due dates (Oldfield in 1713, George Anne Bellamy in 1754). Managers used reductions in performance schedules, narrowing of repertoires, and even temporary changes of genre as tactics to keep women on stage safely for as long as possible, for celebrity performers were integral to the financial health of their institutions. Here, this was most visible in the chapter on Sarah Siddons and in Dorothy Jordan's increasingly lucrative contracts. This may be in large part, however, simply the vagaries of the archive: financial records are more complete and consistent after 1760. Before this, for example, we know that George Anne Bellamy secured backpay from John Rich during a half-season absence in 1749–50 for the birth of her first child.

Celebrity pregnancy's impact on planning means that it can function methodologically for our analysis of other questions about the professional theater. Attending to which plays managers suspended during a performer's absence versus which plays continued with substitute performers can offer insight into where the popularity of a piece lay. Substitutes, meanwhile, offer a window into career trajectory and perhaps formal or informal systems of mentoring younger performers, such as with Charlotte Goodall in the 1790s. Looking at parts performed late in a pregnancy can also suggest which were considered easier to perform and which harder. Analyzing casting during a celebrity's time away, meanwhile, offers insight into how such absences enabled other women in the company to gain useful exposure and rise either within the same company, or in a different one (as George Anne Bellamy did when she went to Drury Lane in 1750). Remembering the constant state of competition between houses, celebrity lying-ins around pregnancy and birth show performers and managers at other theaters attempting to take advantage of actresses' absences, such as when Catherine Achmet attempted Sir Harry Wildair during Jordan's extended absence in 1789, or tragedienne Harriet Brunton made her London debut at Covent Garden just before Sarah Siddons left Drury Lane for two months in 1785. The stable but highly flexible repertory system of the eighteenth-century commercial theater accommodated women's reproductive lives in a variety of ways, for women's continued careers were a benefit to all.

Studying the pregnancies of these first generations of celebrity actresses asks us to be both precise with our focus and expansive in our creation of context, to remain "in the moment" with our analyses and resist deploying historical hindsight to cover, explain away, or soften nuance and disruption in individual careers. Celebrity actresses, indeed all actresses, are also valuable figures for testing out many of the metanarratives that tacitly or overtly underlie historical writing. For example, scholars like Ruth Perry and Felicity Nussbaum have articulated a growing disconnect between sexuality and maternity as the century, and the empire, grew.[3] Women's maternal labor (pregnancy, birth, breastfeeding, childrearing), they argue, was harnessed for the sake of global expansion, and to this end the sanitized, desexualized mother was held up as an ideal: a private woman at home with a baby at the breast, neither politically nor sexually ambitious. Sexual desire was displaced onto "torrid zones" consisting of disenfranchised women at home and exoticized "others" abroad. Where does this leave female performers, whose physical attractiveness was undeniably relevant to their stage careers, but who might also wield great economic power? Is the category "actress" necessarily always other, and therefore a location for displaced sexuality? Perhaps, though many were also recognized and respected wives. When pregnant, did performing women remain objects of desire, or did they illustrate this turn from the sexual to the maternal? Throughout the 1780s, Dorothy Jordan continued to display her famous legs in breeches regardless of pregnancy. Though she changed this practice during her relationship with the Duke of Clarence, she often still acted in breeches at or shortly after her return to the stage, suggesting that offering audiences a view of her returning figure was important.

Dror Wahrman, in fact, uses Jordan to illustrate what he sees as lag between the "gender panic" of ca. 1780 and the practices of the commercial theater, pointing to her giving up the role of Sir Harry Wildair as proof of gender's sudden immutability.[4] But if Jordan gave up the role because of her new relationship, and it was not given to another woman in the company out of deference to Jordan or because her ghosting of the role would stymie another actress's efforts to be successful—in short, if it was a change partially or wholly driven by the workings of commercial and celebrity systems, how might this matter to the argument? More saliently for this study, what role did Jordan's obvious femininity and regular pregnancies in breeches have in mitigating a "gender panic" or delaying its effects? I pose these questions not to dismantle what are complex and insightful arguments in this brief conclusion, but to suggest how the public position and power celebrity performers held—and the visibility of their reproductive labor—offers ground to further interrogate and explore larger ideas, bringing us back to Amanda Vickery's championing of the case study in bolstering, exploring, and subverting large-scale historical narratives.

Eighteenth-century actresses expanded the role models available for public consumption for what pregnancy looked like, how women moved, how and how long one worked during pregnancy, how safe or not this was, and when and how to navigate a return to working life. Moreover, they worked during a century that saw tremendous changes in the management of childbirth, and vast publication of tracts advising pregnant women and new mothers on behavior. Women's diaries and correspondence show a constant interest in the reproductive lives of those around them. It was also the century during which the importance of the strong and successfully reproductive body took on nationalistic importance, first as Britain expanded its Empire post-1750, and later during times of war, particularly with France. Social and political historians like Toni Bowers and Lisa

Forman Cody have advocated for maternity's central place in public discourse of the time, as well as the century's increasing attachment to the ideal of the full-time mother.[5] But neither specifically considers how actresses intersected with such ideals and discourses. I have provided ample evidence to help us do so.

Having looked both from the stage to the audience and from the audience to the stage in the eighteenth century, the question at hand now is what do these historical women and their pregnancies mean to us? Celebrity pregnancy did not end in the English-speaking world with the close of the eighteenth century. It is a phenomenon we are intimately familiar with today. Past and present sit together oddly yet productively in this topic—the biological processes of human reproduction have changed little in the ensuing centuries, but our understanding and management of these processes are vastly different. Professional theater is both the same and different—live bodies and (usually) live audiences perpetuate—but its practices vary widely across company, town, city, nation, and world, including in its protections and accommodations for pregnant artists. Celebrity, too, operates in sometimes surprisingly similar ways in both time periods, yet the technologies (and speed) by which we receive information have altered drastically; the content, too, is arguably different and more insistently personal. A satirical print, no matter how gauche, is not a sex tape.

To close this study, then, it is worth laying out stories from women's experiences with pregnancy, then and now, that seem to parallel, echo, or otherwise illuminate each other, asking, What can the present teach us to ask of, or perhaps even understand about, the past? What can the past help us to imagine or see anew in the present? In conversation, the present offers the past helpful ways of imagining embodied and lived experience, and of course (as noted throughout the book, but particularly in relationship to Susannah Cibber) medical insights; the past offers the present a set of challenges to reconceive our understanding of the intersections of reproductive and commercial labor. To order these examples, I return to the contexts introduced in the introduction: repertory studies and managerial practice, celebrity studies and stage performance, and performances of maternity beyond the theater.

Behind the Scenes

In a recent essay for HowlRound, "Working Like a Mother" playwright Rachel Bonds wrote, "It feels very scary to be a mother in this business. . . . To suddenly have a whole new set of physical and financial needs, and to feel like your career is at stake if you ask for these needs to be met."[6] Bonds's essay illuminates the tensions between the professional activities artists need and want to participate in, and the systems that exclude and discourage those who parent. Her experiences also resonate powerfully with those we can only glimpse in historical records.

When Sarah Siddons received an offer from David Garrick to join the company at Drury Lane for the 1775–76 season, she was six and a half months pregnant. Garrick expressed his willingness to let the young mother recover for as long as was necessary before taking up her post and he advanced the family £20, the equivalent of a month's salary, to support them during the weeks she would be unable to work.[7] Siddons debuted on the London stage six weeks after the birth of her second child. In those weeks she had moved her young family to the capital, established a new household (including finding household staff and help with childcare), and begun rehearsals with the company. She was the primary (often only) financial support for her family; although Garrick might offer her as much time as she wanted, that did not mean she could afford to take it. While there were many reasons Siddons's first attempt on the capital failed, it is reasonable to wonder if, like Bonds, she needed more accommodation than was offered, but did not ask for help, fearing she too might be "seen as weak or a pain in the ass."[8] Bonds's powerful accounts of exhaustion and infection—embodied experiences of new motherhood that transcend time but do not necessarily mark our archives—remind us of the physical cost women might be paying to keep their professional obligations when a performance calendar or playbill simply records their presence. If these experiences are too often invisible to us now, what hope do we have of recovering them across the span of hundreds of years? Awakening our own awareness of such potentialities may not fill archival gaps in ways sanctioned by the traditional methodologies of theater history, but they might help us better imagine the nuances and materiality of experience.

Ten years after her first London debut, Siddons was pregnant with her sixth child in the fall of 1785. She had returned to London three years earlier and was the most successful actress in Britain. She was also clearly more comfortable making her needs known to managers. Siddons outlined the parts she would and would not play in late pregnancy, and informed the theater that she would be bringing her new baby to the theater on the nights she performed so she might breastfeed as needed between scenes.[9] Unlike Bonds, and unlike her younger self, Siddons was now able to shape her career to accommodate the way *she* wanted to mother within the boundaries of her professional obligations. She could do so, in part, because she was an invaluable commodity—she could not simply be replaced; she had the singularity of widely recognized celebrity derived from her visible stage presence.

Such singularity, then and now, offers access to accommodation. In 2018, Pippa Nixon starred in a production of *The Importance of Being Earnest* while breastfeeding her four-month-old. The theater provided childcare support, space in the theater to set up a nursery for the baby, and scheduling assistance that let Nixon be home early most nights of the week during rehearsals, and let her put her daughter to bed in the green room before getting into her wig each night during the run.[10] Her costumes and corsets were made—as women's clothing was for centuries—to enable her to breastfeed as needed backstage between scenes without undressing.[11] In 1785, Siddons was given two lavish new gowns by the theater while she was heavily pregnant; Mary Linley's staff would make and fit them to accommodate Siddons's pregnancy, then alter them afterward so she could continue to use them. Did those alterations, or others Siddons made herself, enable breastfeeding? Siddons's insistence that she would nurse the child herself between scenes backstage would suggest it. The essential needs of the reproducing body—space, access, rest—have not changed, and embodied experience today can inform our sense of its history.

Intimacy on Stage

In August 2011, Beyoncé was performing live at MTV's VMA awards. After singing her hit, "Love on Top" in stilettos and a sparkling pink blazer, stomping energetically around the stage, once even dropping to the floor, Beyoncé tossed her mic, unbuttoned her jacket, and, looking straight into the camera, broke into a knowing grin and began rubbing her belly. At first taken aback, the audience quickly realized—reading the cultural meaning of her gesture correctly—that Beyoncé was announcing a pregnancy. Her daughter, Blue Ivy, was born the following January. Officially entering the realm of working mother, Carter picked her moment carefully, showing us her healthy, happy working body before she revealed that it was also a pregnant body.[12]

In chapter 1, I suggested something similar regarding the epilogue to John Dryden's *Don Sebastian*, in which Susanna and William Mountfort joked about the consequences of a one-night stand while Susanna was four months pregnant, speculating on whether or not this served as a kind of public announcement of her pregnancy. It is difficult to tell in that case, but Dorothy Jordan is credited with something similar in the fall of 1790. At the time, Jordan was living with lawyer Richard Ford. They had two children, and Jordan was pregnant again. After a performance, one reviewer wrote, "Mrs. JORDAN was delightful in the Romp on Saturday evening, both in action and voice. She gave 'A sweet little Baby' with such archness, that the house called for it again; upon which she sweetly said in French behind the scenes—*Je ne puis donner au jour la meme enfants, mais ils aurant les jumeaux*, adding in English, 'Dr. F—always told me I should have *twins*.'"[13] The "Dr. F" was Richard Ford's father, the royal accoucheur who had delivered Queen Charlotte's last child in 1783 and, for a time, one of Drury Lane's owners. Was the attention to the "archness" with which she performed a song in which her character longed to have "a sweet little baby" intended to gesture toward her own pregnancy, and her children's grandfather? Was it accompanied with a recognizable gesture or pose, a knowing twinkle in the eye?

In this source—which may have no relationship to truth, of course—we can imagine such a look, such a gesture, because we have seen it before. Even if the anecdote is untrue, its presence suggests a desire for the kind of intimate connection between performer and audience such a gesture would signal. The fan wants to believe they know the celebrity and are privy to their intimate self and secrets, even if the fan is only one of several thousand (or million) in a crowded audience. It is why Beyoncé looked at the camera; it is why Jordan might joke about pregnancy, sharing intimacy in public. That both revelations occur in the context of their professional labor while clearly radiating health and joy, positions their bodies as cherished, valued, and valuable, neither shameful nor debilitating nor excluding them from a market economy, a synthesis of the personal and the professional. Indeed, the positive affective response to each suggests that pregnancy might make one more valuable, more "abnormally interesting."[14]

Social Bodies and Shared Experience

On September 30, 2020, model and social media star Chrissy Teigen shared the news of a placental abruption that resulted in the loss of her third child, a baby boy she and husband John Legend had named Jack. Teigen was about halfway through her pregnancy and had been on bed rest for several weeks.[15] In the days that followed, others began to share their own stories of pregnancy loss publicly, often identifying this as the first time they had shared the information beyond partners or immediate family. Multiple layers of grief and pain marked these stories. In addition to the losses themselves, people who had lost pregnancies named the social stigma around miscarriage that had kept them silent and either discouraged from or unable to take leaves of absence, ask for lenience or compassion, or even tell coworkers or friends what had happened. Coupled to this was widespread ignorance of the statistics around miscarriage, stillbirth, and other fatal or potentially fatal complications among childbearers until they experienced such an event; doctors, too, seemed to suffer from stigmas or ignorance that kept them from warning patients, or sharing complete medical information about miscarriage management.

Reading these physically and psychologically painful experiences, the fear and rage that people only now felt they could express, calls attention anew to an important function of celebrity. "Celebrity" can appear little more than a frippery in our culture. The phrase "celebrity pregnancy" conjures a kind of false veneer: a glossy magazine cover, a perfect but perfectly casual Instagram shot, an impeccably dressed and impossibly "cute" bump on a red carpet. We make fun of fans (usually women) for investing in the lives of people they do not know and who could not possibly care for them. We mock too-overt attempts to model oneself on these shiny, unreal people. But one real power and true importance of celebrity is this: bringing lived experiences, especially those we never discuss, into the light. The personal is political; celebrity magnifies and individualizes this fact, bringing it home for some in ways statistics or strangers never will. When Susannah Cibber, a wronged wife who managed to escape an abusive marriage, railed against the position of married women on stage, she gave vent to real frustrations and represented some hope of escape. When Teigen shared her story and elicited public sharing, support, and collective mourning, it altered my understanding of Sarah Siddons's 1788 miscarriage.

Siddons miscarried during the run of a new play, *The Regent*, a fact announced in the papers to excuse the disrupted run. While absent, her six-year-old daughter Eliza Ann also passed suddenly of an illness, and the papers reported this too. When Siddons returned on April 26 to play her maternal character in *The Regent*, the papers suggested her recent losses made her performance even more moving for audiences. I had felt indignant at this: how callous to emphasize the audience's heightened response in such circumstances, to derive additional pleasure from fiction because of real tragedy? But reading responses to Teigen's story, and the connections it was making between strangers, I realized I had missed another thread in this response.

Siddons confided to a friend later in life that she missed her profession for the outlet it gave her to exorcise feelings she could not express in private life. The causes of those feelings were often unknown to audiences, but in 1788 responding strongly to Siddons's performance was a way of sharing her grief through the reciprocal bonds of sentiment, to feel what she felt and reflect it back to her, and thus to validate her grief. Through this, those in the audience who had experienced similar losses also had the opportunity to see the great Siddons manifest their private griefs, and to see those griefs held and expressed by fellow audience members. Siddons, perhaps, because her grief was not silenced or hidden, could use stage performance as an outlet for her own grief and, by performing that grief in public, make space for others to share and alleviate their own. Sometimes, celebrity is a conduit that better connects us to each other. We should not underestimate how the relationship between stage and audience around pregnancy and parenthood might matter to our understanding of the time period; we have ample evidence for how it matters in our own.

Legal scholar Renee Ann Cramer articulates the role of celebrity pregnancy in crafting often unattainable "ideals" of how to be pregnant: "good" pregnant celebrities are slim, have small, stylishly dressed bumps, are always happy and healthy, and return to their pre-baby bodies with alacrity. Bodies that do not behave (gain too much weight, for example) according to these ideals are openly censured, while the less glamorous aspects of pregnancy are frequently hidden behind an Instagram-worthy facade.[16] In short, media representations of pregnancy often continue to suggest a binary between grotesque overabundance and classical containment. Pregnant women watching these celebrities absorb this idealization and can suffer severe anxiety and depression when their own bodies fail to perform to the impossible standards staring at them from the racks at the grocery store and on social media.[17] Yet such performances can also open up *how* one can see and perform pregnancy, what is "normal," and what is acceptable.

Then and now, this is also a question of genre: Ali Wong (*Baby Cobra* and *Hard Knock Wife*) and Amy Schumer's (*Growing*) stand-up specials during pregnancy capitalized on just these grotesque aspects of the experience to heighten comedy and to draw attention to the vast physical labor required of incipient and new mothers. And Anne Helen Petersen has written of the importance of Kim Kardashian's first pregnancy in 2013; as she struggled with illness, weight gain, and eventually pre-eclampsia, Kardashian made visible the experiences of many women whose pregnancies do not fit our most visible cultural narratives.[18] Celebrity pregnancy can challenge, to some degree, social taboos and stereotypes as well. Women like Dorothy Jordan and Anne Oldfield, for example, could challenge ideas that unmarried, sexually active women were necessarily immoral or bad mothers; and George Anne Bellamy rewrote her 1749 birth story to position herself as an authoritative subject rather than a helpless object of medical intervention. Beyoncé's

2017 Grammys performance while pregnant with twins drew on iconography of goddesses and queens from African, Indian, and Christian traditions to cast her in the role of mother of the world, a figure of abundance and grace. In the context of audience awareness of her personal life, the pregnancy was symbolic of forgiveness and new beginnings with her husband, Jay-Z, after a rumored affair. And it was far removed from the persistent trope of the "hot sexy mamas" that plague celebrity women of color during pregnancy, or a long history of treating Black women's bodies as subhuman instead of glorious.[19]

Imaginative connections running from the present to the past spark fruitful questions about embodied experience. How might the conditions under which eighteenth-century women performed during pregnancy impact how we think about economic and reproductive labor now? First, we must acknowledge a tendency to position pregnancy today as—ideally—a controlled, planned event. It is not, but workplace policies, social expectations, and medical interventions often create the idea it should be. In the eighteenth century, there were few effective options for planning or controlling reproduction if one engaged in sexual activity and was fertile. Theaters did not start from the question of *if* they should accommodate working mothers (at all levels of employment), only *how* they would do so. Our theaters today would benefit from such a shift. In the eighteenth century, actresses and managers found ways to arrange performance schedules that allowed women shorter days and evenings of work. Actresses might stop performing particularly long or strenuous roles, and they were given the ability to take paid absences before and after birth without losing job security, something few if any performers (few if any child-bearers in any field, in fact) in the U.S. can claim. Currently, one in four childbearers in the United States return to work within two weeks of giving birth because they cannot afford to take further time off, a situation exacerbated by soaring health care costs and limited access to insurance.[20] In the professional theater, these issues are both extant and exacerbated by short-term contracts, lack of union support, and loopholes that allow "artistic integrity" to supersede discrimination laws.

In the UK, in contrast, West End stars have used maternity covers as they would in any other industry. Charlene Ford (*42nd Street*) even worked out a job share arrangement with her cover Jenny Legg that allowed her to come back to work part time after her leave ended.[21] The arrangement allowed Legg to keep the job she held for eight months while giving Ford a less demanding schedule that nonetheless demonstrated her continued ability and willingness to pursue her profession. In an all or nothing world and an all or nothing profession, Ford leveraged her celebrity power to find a middle ground. It is not impossible to accommodate pregnant performers in professional theater if we are motivated to do so. Historical research suggests, in fact, that we might be surprised by the power of watching pregnancy onstage—the power of reflecting life experience back to audiences not only when it is a prop that can be controlled but also in its unruly and uncontained realness.

In some cases, as I have shown throughout this book, in fact, pregnancy created new meaning and new interest in familiar material for audiences. Moreover, I believe we can safely say, looking back, that biological and artistic creation are not mutually exclusive: Sarah Siddons became, arguably, the greatest tragic actress of all time while birthing and raising seven children; Dorothy Jordan enjoyed nearly thirty years as the most popular, bankable, and beloved woman of the London theater—she also brought up thirteen children and was pregnant at least eighteen times in twenty-two years. These women raised their children, sometimes quite literally, in the theater, alongside many other company members' children; the theater was a space in which parental and theatrical labor were neither mutually exclusive nor necessarily contentious. Perhaps this is the most significant offering of history: what Rachel Bonds asks, what Pippa Nixon secured, what Beyoncé does, has been done before; the systems we need to overturn are not, in fact, products of "the way it has always been." Finding better paths forward is, in part at least, an excavation of certain historical practices, not the reinvention of the wheel. Resurrecting this past shows both a past and a potential future in which pregnant performers can carry all before them.

APPENDIX

Table A.1. Birth and Christening Dates

Mother	Child Name	Birth Date	Christening
Susanna Mountfort Verbruggen	Susanna (Susan) Mountfort	April 27, 1690	May 11, 1690
	Edward Mountfort	April 1, 1691	
	Elizabeth Mountfort	March 22, 1692	
	Mary Mountfort		April 27, 1693
	Lewis Verbruggen	May 16, 1703	May 27, 1703
Anne Oldfield	Arthur Maynwaring	ca. July 19, 1709	
	Unknown	May 1713	
	Charles Churchill	Fall 1720	
Susannah Cibber	Susannah Cibber	February 1735	
	Caius Gabriel Cibber	April 5, 1736	
	Molly Cibber (Sloper)	February 26, 1739	
	Charles (Sloper)	Fall 1749	
George Anne Bellamy	George Metham	December 17, 1749	
	Unknown	Winter 1752–1753	
	Caroline Calcraft	February 27, 1754	
	Henry Fox Calcraft	ca. September 1756	
Sarah Siddons	Henry	October 4, 1774	
	Sally (Sarah Martha)	November 5, 1775	
	Maria	July 1, 1779	
	Frances Emelia		April 26, 1781
	Eliza Ann	June 2, 1782	

(*cont.*)

Table A.1. Birth and Christening Dates (*cont.*)

Mother	Child Name	Birth Date	Christening
	George	December 27, 1785	
	Cecilia	July 25, 1794	
Dorothy Jordan	Frances (Fanny) Daly	November 1782	
	Dorothy (Dodee) Ford	July/August 1787	
	Lucy Hester Ford	January 2, 1791	
	George FitzClarence[1]	January 29, 1794	
	Sophia FitzClarence	March 4, 1795	
	Henry FitzClarence	March 8, 1797	
	Mary FitzClarence	December 19, 1798	
	Frederick FitzClarence	December 9, 1799	
	Elizabeth FitzClarence	January 17, 1801	
	Adolphus FitzClarence	February 17, 1802	
	Augusta FitzClarence	November 3, 1803	
	Augustus FitzClarence	March 1, 1805	
	Amelia FitzClarence	March 21, 1807	

[1]The surname eventually given to the children of Dorothy Jordan and the Duke of Clarence.

NOTES

Introduction

1. Audra McDonald, Twitter post, May 10, 2016, 12:54 P.M., https://twitter.com/AudraEqualityMc/status/730078509926854656.

2. Michael Paulson, "'Shuffle Along' Decides It Can't Go on Without Audra McDonald," *New York Times*, June 23, 2016, https://www.nytimes.com/2016/06/24/theater/shuffle-along-decides-it-cant-go-on-without-audra-mcdonald.html.

3. Michael Paulson, "'Shuffle Along' and Insurer Drop Pregnancy-Prompted Lawsuit," *New York Times*, October 21, 2020, https://www.nytimes.com/2020/10/21/theater/shuffle-along-audra-mcdonald-insurer-pregnancy-lawsuit.html.

4. One commentator (username MC0325) emphasized the pregnancy as more proof of McDonald's talents and ability to "have it all": "It's almost unfair to the rest of us that a women [*sic*] so stunningly talented is reproducing. What about the rest of us Audra???" Jackson McHenry, "Audra McDonald Is Pregnant, Postponing West End Debut of *Lady Day* and Return to *Shuffle Along*," Vulture.com, May 10, 2016, https://www.vulture.com/2016/05/audra-mcdonald-pregnant-shuffle-along-lady-day-leave.html#comments.

5. See Linda Fitzsimmons and Arthur W. McDonald, *The Yorkshire Stage, 1766–1803: A Calendar of Plays, Together with Cast Lists for Tate Wilkinson's Circuit of Theatres (Doncaster, Hull, Leeds, Pontefract, Wakefield, and York) and the Yorkshire Company's Engagements in Beverley, Halifax, Newcastle, Sheffield, and Edinburgh* (Metuchen, NJ: Scarecrow Press, 1989), 411–415.

6. James Boaden, *The Life of Mrs, Jordan*, 2 vols. (London: Edward Bull, Holles Street, 1831), 1:40–41.

7. See, for example, Shearer West's "Beauty, Aging, and the Body Politic," in *The First Actresses: Nell Gwyn to Sarah Siddons*, ed. Gill Perry, Joseph Roach, and Shearer West (Ann Arbor: University of Michigan Press, 2011), 114.

8. In August, the pregnancy prompted her to change her stage name from "Miss Francis" to "Mrs. Jordan."

9. As Jacky Bratton demonstrates, Boaden's historiography is deeply inflected by his immediate context, the 1820s and 1830s, when cultural change and social reform encouraged the idolizing of male artistic genius at the expense of women's contributions. See Jacky Bratton, *New Readings in Theatre History* (Cambridge: Cambridge University Press, 2003).

10. For Wilkinson's account, see Tate Wilkinson, *The Wandering Patentee: Or, a History of the York Stage from 1770 to the Present Time*, 4 vols. (York: Wilson, Spence and Mawman, 1795), 2:170–173.

11. Judith Schneid Lewis, *In the Family Way: Childbearing in the British Aristocracy, 1760–1830* (New Brunswick, NJ: Rutgers University Press, 1986), 123; Leonore Davidoff and Catharine Hall, *Family Fortunes: Men and Women of the English Middle Class 1780–1850* (London: Hutchinson Education, 1987), 222–223. Both of the rates cited here are taken from specific studies of a limited number of families. More general birth rates are quite hard to calculate, so I offer these only as guides. See Peter Razzell, "The Growth of Population in Eighteenth-Century England: A Critical Reappraisal," *Journal of Economic History* 53, no. 4 (December 1993): 743–771.

12. Susanna Mountfort Verbruggen (1666–1703) had at least five children, Anne Oldfield (1683–1730) three, Susannah Cibber (1714–1766) four, George Anne Bellamy (ca. 1731–1788) four, Sarah Siddons (1755–1831) seven, and Dorothy Jordan (1761–1816) thirteen.

13. This claim comes from a survey of repertory records and financial documents at both London patent theaters. For examples of the belief that pregnancy endangered some women's jobs, see Joanne Lafler, *The Celebrated Mrs. Oldfield: The Life and Art of an Augustan Actress* (Carbondale: Southern Illinois University Press, 1989), 70 and 138; and Felicity Nussbaum, *Rival Queens: Actresses, Performance, and the Eighteenth-Century British Theatre* (Philadelphia: University of Pennsylvania Press, 2010), 49.

14. Ellen Donkin, "Mrs. Siddons Looks Back in Anger," in *Critical Theory and Performance*, ed. Janelle G. Reinalt and Joseph R. Roach, rev. ed. (Ann Arbor: University of Michigan Press, 2007), 317–333 (330); Helen E. M. Brooks, "The Divided Heart of the Actress: Late Eighteenth-Century Actresses and the 'Cult of Maternity,'" in *Stage Mothers: Women, Work, and the Theatre, 1660–1830*, ed. Laura Engel and Elaine M. McGirr (Lewisburg, PA: Bucknell University Press, 2014), 19–42 (20).

15. For Bellamy's labor, see George Anne Bellamy, *An Apology for the Life of George Anne Bellamy, Late of Covent Garden Theatre*, 3rd ed., 5 vols. (London: J. Bell, 1785), 2:67–69. For more on the consequences of these absences, see Chelsea Phillips, "Bodies in Play: Maternity, Repertory, and the Rival *Romeo and Juliets*, 1748–51," *Theatre Survey* 60, no. 2 (May 2019): 205–236.

16. Rhetorician Lindal Buchanan is one exception, emphasizing the widespread presence of both married and unmarried pregnant women on the seventeenth- and eighteenth-century stage as a prelude to her discussion of nineteenth-century performers. See Lindal Buchanan, "Angels in the (Theatrical) House: Pregnancy,

Rhetorical Access, and the London Stage," *Rhetorica* 30, no. 3 (Summer 2012): 277–305.

17. Donkin, "Mrs. Siddons Looks Back," 329.

18. I borrow the phrase from Heather Nathans, *Hideous Creatures and Beautiful Pagans: Performing Jewish Identity on the Antebellum American Stage* (Ann Arbor: University of Michigan Press, 2017), 4.

19. Imogen Tyler, "Skin-Tight: Celebrity, Pregnancy, and Subjectivity," in *Thinking Through the Skin*, ed. Sara Ahmed and Jackie Stacey (London: Routledge, 2001), 69–83 (78).

20. For example, Dror Wahrman has theorized a "gender panic" around 1780 that sharply and thoroughly reversed decades of a more playful and fluid relationship to gender, rapidly solidified binaries, and essentialized behaviors, in *The Making of the Modern Self: Identity and Culture in Eighteenth-Century England* (New Haven, CT: Yale University Press, 2004). Wahrman connects this crisis to the American Revolution, while Gillian Russell ties these changes to the feminization of culture in the 1760s and 1770s in *Women, Sociability, and the Theatre in Georgian England* (Cambridge: Cambridge University Press, 2007). Thomas Laqueur traces the evolution of conceptions of sexual difference over the course of the century from a one-sex model (in which the female body was seen as the exact inverse of the male, and capable of spontaneously changing) to a two-sex model that saw male and female as fundamentally different and in alignment with gendered categories of men and women. See Thomas Laqueur, *Making Sex: Body and Gender from the Greeks to Freud* (Cambridge, MA: Harvard University Press, 1990). For a productive response to Laqueur's theories that emphasizes the porousness and fluidity of the body, see Gail Kern Paster, *The Body Embarrassed: Drama and Disciplines of Shame in Early Modern England* (Ithaca, NY: Cornell University Press, 1993). Judith Schneid Lewis starts her study of aristocratic women's experiences with pregnancy in 1760 because this is around when "motherhood came to be perceived as a lifelong pursuit" (*In the Family Way*, 59). Linda Colley identifies a "cult of prolific maternity" that arose in the second half of the century, and Lisa Forman Cody argues that men's growing presence in the birthing chamber as professionals during these decades elevated reproduction to a national concern. See Linda Colley, *Britons: Forging the Nation, 1707–1837* (New Haven, CT: Yale University Press, 1992), 240; Lisa Forman Cody, *Birthing the Nation: Sex, Science, and the Conception of Eighteenth-Century Britons* (Oxford: Oxford University Press, 2005).

21. By 1689, the duopoly of the King's and Duke's Companies established in 1660 had collapsed into the United Company, established in 1682, who used the newer Drury Lane theater (1674) for performances. The United Company would survive until 1695, when Thomas Betterton, Elizabeth Barry, and Anne Bracegirdle led a rival faction to the theater at Lincoln's Inn Fields in protest of Christopher Rich, where they remained until 1705. A complicated series of years followed, culminating in the silencing of Drury Lane (and Christopher Rich) by the Lord Chamberlain in 1709, which only lasted until the following November when the theater reopened under William Collier. From 1710 to the early 1730s, Drury Lane was in the hands of a triumvirate of actor-managers. A few

years later, Rich was back and planning to operate a new company at Lincoln's Inn Fields, but he died before it opened, at which point his son, John Rich, began one of the longest managerial tenures of the century: forty-eight years. Following the success of *The Beggar's Opera* in 1728, John Rich began construction on a new theater; Covent Garden opened in 1732.

22. Donkin, "Mrs. Siddons Looks Back," argues that assuming the subject position in this moment prompted audience members to see Siddons as a creative agent in her interpretation and performance of stage characters, which had long-ranging positive consequences for her career.

23. Donkin, "Mrs. Siddons Looks Back," 329. Part of the difficulty in this case was that the birth date was incorrect in Donkin's source, Siddons's entry in the *Biographical Dictionary of Actors.*

24. Ibid, 330.

25. Ibid.

26. As Donkin put it elsewhere, in the absence of information it is easy to "reflexively [construct] . . . a history of defeat," Ellen Donkin, *Getting Into the Act: Women Playwrights in London, 1776–1829* (London: Routledge, 1995), 1.

27. Thomas Postlewait, "The Criteria for Evidence: Anecdotes in Shakespearean Biography, 1709–2000," in *Theorizing Practice: Redefining Theatre History*, ed. W. B. Worthen with Peter Holland (New York: Palgrave Macmillan, 2003), 65.

28. Susan Bennett, "Theatre History, Historiography, and Women's Dramatic Writing," in *Women, Theatre and Performance, New Histories, New Historiographies*, ed. Maggie B. Gale and Viv Gardner (Manchester: Manchester University Press, 2000), 56. Tracy C. Davis, "Questions for a Feminist Methodology in Theatre History," in *Interpreting the Theatrical Past: Essays in the Historiography of Performance*, ed. Thomas Postlewait and Bruce McConachie (Iowa City: University of Iowa Press, 1989), 59–81.

29. Bennett, "Theatre History," 53.

30. Amanda Vickery, "Golden Age to Separate Spheres? A Review of the Categories and Chronology of English Women's History," *Historical Journal* 36, no. 2 (June 1993): 383–414.

31. Peter Burke, *Varieties of Cultural History* (Ithaca, NY: Cornell University Press, 1997), 2.

32. For the "deep" eighteenth century, see Joseph Roach, *It* (Ann Arbor: University of Michigan Press, 2007), 13.

33. Felicity Nussbaum, *Rival Queens*, 6, modifying Allardyce Nicoll.

34. See Laura Engel, *Fashioning Celebrity: Eighteenth-Century British Actresses and Strategies for Image-Making* (Columbus: Ohio State University Press, 2011); Roach, *It*; and Helen E. M. Brooks, *Actresses, Gender, and the Eighteenth-Century Stage: Playing Women* (New York: Palgrave Macmillan, 2015). For Engel's coining of the term "actress studies," see Laura Engel, "Stage Beauties: Actresses and Celebrity Culture in the Long Eighteenth Century," *Literature Compass* 13/12 (2016): 749–761.

35. See, for example, Kimberly Crouch, "The Public Life of Actresses: Prostitutes or Ladies?" in *Gender in Eighteenth Century: Roles, Representations, and*

Responsibilities, ed. Hannah Barker and Elaine Chalus (New York: Longman, 1997), 58–78.

36. Laura Engel and Elaine M. McGirr, eds., *Stage Mothers: Women, Work, and the Theatre 1660–1830* (Lewisburg, PA: Bucknell University Press, 2014), 2. Hereafter *Stage Mothers*. For other discussions of motherhood and theater, see Engel's *Fashioning Celebrity*; and Chapter Five in Brooks's *Actresses, Gender, and the Eighteenth-Century Stage*.

37. Roach, *It*, 3.

38. The multimodal nature of celebrity is also a feature in Engel's *Fashioning Celebrity* and previously cited work of Shearer West, as well as Heather McPherson, *Art and Celebrity in the Age of Garrick and Reynolds* (University Park: Penn State University Press, 2017), and Robin Aselon, "'She Was Tragedy Personified': Crafting the Siddons Legend in Art and Life," in *A Passion for Performance: Sarah Siddons and Her Portraitists* (Los Angeles: J. Paul Getty Museum, 1999), 41–96.

39. Leslie Ritchie, *David Garrick and the Mediation of Celebrity* (Cambridge: Cambridge University Press, 2019), 16.

40. Shearer West calls it the "iconic" body. See Shearer West, "Siddons, Celebrity and Regality: Portraiture and the Aging Actress," in *Theatre and Celebrity in Britain 1660–2000*, ed. Mary Luckhurst and Jane Moody (New York: Palgrave Macmillan, 2005), 191–213, esp. 192.

41. On actor and character bodies colliding, see Karen Gaylord's concept of "double consciousness" in the audience in "Theatrical Performances: Structure and Process, Tradition and Revolt," in *Performers and Performances: The Social Organization of Artistic Work*, ed. Jack B. Kamerman, and Rosanne Martorella (New York: Praeger, 1983), 135–150; Susan Bennett places this idea in a broader context in *Theatre Audiences: A Theory of Interpretation and Reception*, 2nd ed. (New York: Routledge, 1997). On celebrity and character bodies, see Felicity Nussbaum's concept of the "interiority effect" (*Rival Queens*, 19).

42. Marvin Carlson, *The Haunted Stage: The Theatre as Memory Machine* (Ann Arbor: University of Michigan Press, 2001).

43. Lisa A. Freeman, "Mourning the Dignity of the Siddonian Form," *Eighteenth Century Fiction* 27, no. 3–4 (Spring-Summer 2015): 597–629. Shearer West, "Beauty, Aging, and the Body Politic," 117, also points to the problems of disconnect between the body natural and the character body.

44. In the early production history of the play, the role belonged to Mrs. Barry, notorious for sexual affairs with the Earl of Rochester—with whom she had a daughter—and others.

45. Wilkinson, *Wandering Patentee*, 2:149.

46. Ibid.

47. Brian Fothergill, *Dorothy Jordan: Portrait of an Actress* (London: Faber and Faber, 1965), 95.

48. Kristina Straub, *Sexual Suspects: Eighteenth-Century Players and Sexual Ideology* (Princeton, NJ: Princeton University Press, 1992), 90.

49. See Roach, *It*, 37. Roach argues that potential sources of stigmata, if in correct proportion to charismata, actually make the celebrity all the more

fascinating to watch; it is only when potentially stigmatic elements of person or performance style overwhelm charismatic elements that they become a source of true aversion.

50. Such as Judith Milhous and Robert D. Hume, eds., "*The London Stage, 1660–1800*: A New Version of Part 2, 1700–1729," last updated 2001, http://www.personal.psu.edu/hb1/London%20Stage%202001/. Another important resource is the open access, open source *London Stage Database*, created from an early attempt at digitizing *The London Stage* by Mattie Burkert and her team, https://londonstagedatabase.uoregon.edu/.

51. See the *London Stage Database* mentioned in the previous note. Michael Burden, Jonathan Hicks, and their team are currently at work on *The London Stage 1800–1900* with Oxford University.

52. Sandra Richards, *The Rise of the English Actress* (New York: St. Martin's Press, 1993), 62.

53. *Morning Chronicle and London Advertiser*, London, September 30, 1773, Seventeenth and Eighteenth Century Burney Collection Newspapers. British Library. Gale Digital Collections.

54. The patent theaters competed with other venues for audiences. Companies performed at nonpatent theaters, musical entertainments were held at the Royal Academy, opera arose as a popular (and expensive) entertainment with its own dedicated theater, and private events were curated and attended by the theater's wealthiest patrons.

55. These shifts are most visible in the careers of Sarah Siddons, Susannah Cibber, and Dorothy Jordan and will be discussed in their chapters. The actress Hannah Pritchard (1711–1768), who played in both comedy and tragedy, showed similar accommodations earlier in the century, even when she was still an up-and-coming performer in 1738 and 1739.

56. Wilkinson, *The Wandering Patentee*, 2:163. "In the straw" was a common euphemism for childbed, drawing on the Nativity story in the Bible.

57. For Mattocks, see *Ledger of Covent Garden Theatre* (1773–1774), Egerton MS 2278, British Library, London.

58. Sandra Richards, for example, writes that "a rising actress could seldom afford to be away from the boards even during pregnancies." Richards, *Rise of the English Actress*, 36.

59. Cody, *Birthing the Nation*, 306.

60. Colley, *Britons*, 240.

61. Toni Bowers, *The Politics of Motherhood: British Writing and Culture 1660–1760* (Cambridge: Cambridge University Press, 1996).

62. Understandings of marriage in the eighteenth century have undergone a number of important revolutions, from Lawrence Stone's persistent if tenuous claims to the rise and dominance of "companionate marriage" by the end of the eighteenth century to correctives from scholars like Eve Tavor Bannet, Ruth Perry, and Rebecca Probert. See Lawrence Stone, *The Family, Sex, and Marriage in England 1500–1800* (New York: Harper & Row, 1977); Eve Tavor Bannet, *The Domestic Revolution: Enlightenment Feminisms and the Novel* (Baltimore:

Johns Hopkins University Press, 2000); Ruth Perry, *Novel Relations: The Transformation of Kinship in English Literature and Culture, 1748–1818* (Cambridge: Cambridge University Press, 2004); and Rebecca Probert, *Marriage Law and Practice in the Long Eighteenth Century: A Reassessment* (Cambridge: Cambridge University Press, 2009).

63. Helen E. M. Brooks, "Negotiating Marriage and Professional Autonomy in the Careers of Eighteenth-Century Actresses," *Eighteenth-Century Life* 35, no. 2 (2011): 39–75, doi:10.1215/00982601-1214090.

64. Joanne Bailey, *Unquiet Lives: Marriage and Marriage Breakdown in England, 1660–1800* (Cambridge: Cambridge University Press, 2003). Bailey focuses on evidence from fourteen hundred families of the "middling sort" and wage laborer classes between 1660 and 1800 to reconstruct "a set of national expectations about married life [and show] how these altered in a period of great social, economic and cultural change" (2). One of Bailey's aims is to interrogate the gap between law and lived experience in the lives of married couples, focusing on how social expectations might impact power imbalances. This author now publishes as Joanne Begiato.

65. Ibid., 75.

66. Ibid., 195.

67. In addition to these social barriers, the Royal Marriages Act prevented members of the royal family from marrying without permission.

68. Both Oldfield in her later relationship and Dorothy Jordan in her first cultivated an ambiguity about their marital state that may have offered some advantages of both single and married states; in Jordan's case, childbearing and cohabitation helped create the illusion of lawful partnership. See Brooks, "Negotiating Marriage." The various forms that Bailey suggests women's honor might take align closely with Nussbaum's concept of "exceptional virtue," which enabled unmarried female performers to use charitable acts, care of their family, and devotion to their profession to create an aura of virtue that did not rely on sexual integrity. See Nussbaum, *Rival Queens*, 112.

69. Hunter had gathered these images over more than twenty years, completing dissections at his anatomy school in Covent Garden. The images, like many since, remove the body of the mother from the equation as far as possible, depicting the fetus in utero inside a torso whose limbs and head have been removed. For more, see Barbara Duden, *Disembodying Women: Perspectives on Pregnancy and the Unborn* (Cambridge, MA: Harvard University Press, 1993).

70. Sarah Jennings Churchill, Duchess of Marlborough, *Letters of a Grandmother 1732–1735: Being Correspondence of Sarah, Duchess of Marlborough with Her Granddaughter Diana, Duchess of Bedford*, ed. Gladys Scott Thomson (London: Jonathan Cape, 1943), 30 (24 June 1732).

71. Ibid., 164.

72. Lady Sarah Napier to Lady Susan O'Brien Lennox, August 8, 1782, in *The Life and Letters of Lady Sarah Lennox, 1745–1826*, ed. the Countess of Ilchester and Lord Stavordale, 2 vols. (London: J. Murray, 1902), 2:21.

73. This was fairly common advice; for one example, see Henry Bracken, *The Midwife's Companion* (London, 1737), 46.

74. Emma O'Toole, "Dressing the Expectant Mother: Maternity Fashion in Eighteenth and Nineteenth-Century Ireland," *Women's History* 5, (Spring 2016): 26–33. Over the course of the century, clothing styles evolved drastically, and there was rarely a decade when women were not using stays, hoops, panniers, and/or cork or cloth padding alone or in combination to create a fashionable shape. The century began with a silhouette of relatively narrow skirts and a cone-shaped torso, which expanded drastically in the 1740s with the use of hoops and panniers to create width at the hips. After 1780, an "s-shaped" figure emphasized the breasts, a narrow waist, and a padded derriere. By 1795, neoclassical styles and columnar or natural shapes predominated. Some women stopped wearing long stays, and fabrics became thinner and lighter.

75. Quoted in Joanne Begiato, "'Breeding' a 'Little Stranger': Managing Uncertainty in Pregnancy in Georgian England," in *Perceptions of Pregnancy from the Seventeenth to the Twentieth Centuries*, ed. Jennifer Evans and Ciara Meehan (London: Palgrave Macmillan, 2017), 19.

76. Quoted in Linda Baumgarten, "Dressing for Pregnancy: A Maternity Gown of 1780–1795," *Dress* 23, no. 1 (1996): 17.

77. O'Toole, "Dressing the Expectant Mother," 26.

78. J. D. Phillipson, "The Inconveniences of the Female Condition: Anne Oldfield's Pregnancies," in *Stage Mothers: Women, Work, and the Theatre 1660–1830*, ed. Laura Engel and Elaine M. McGirr (Lewisburg, PA: Bucknell University Press, 2014), 50.

79. Amelia Rauser, "Vitalist Statues and the Belly Pad of 1793," *Journal18*, no. 3: *Lifelike* (Spring 2017), doi: 10.30610/3.2017.2.

80. Hume rightfully puts the latter seventeenth century and end of the eighteenth century at extremes of "dearth" and "plentitude" in terms of available archival evidence. See Robert D. Hume, "Theatre History 1660–1800: Aims, Materials, Methodologies," in *Players, Playwrights, Playhouses: Investigating Performance 1660–1800*, ed. Michael Cordner and Peter Holland, (Basingstoke: Palgrave Macmillan, 2007), 9–44, (34).

81. Toni Bowers notes that crediting Rousseau with driving the turn toward sentimental and affective notions of parenting in Britain denies a far longer trend traceable to pre-1740. See Bowers, *The Politics of Motherhood*, 15.

82. "Tenebrism" is a term from art history, a heightened form of chiaroscuro.

1. Inheriting Greatness

1. Gail Kern Paster calls this the "unstable oscillation between shame and celebration [that] constitutes the affective polarities of pregnancy, birth, and infant feeding practices in early modern culture." See Gail Kern Paster, *The Body Embarrassed: Drama and Disciplines of Shame in Early Modern England* (Ithaca, NY: Cornell University Press, 1993), 208.

2. Deirdre E. Heddon, "Verbruggen, Susanna," *Oxford Dictionary of National Biography Online*, Online Edition, January 2008 (Oxford: Oxford University Press, 2004). In archival sources, her first married name is occasionally written as Monfort, Montfort, Mumford, or Munford. Because one of her daughters also

had a stage career and also acted under the name "Mrs. Mountfort," I will refer to Susanna throughout the chapter by both her married last names.

3. Susanna was earning 50 shillings per week, the equivalent of Barry and Bracegirdle. After the split, the Verbruggens initially had a sharing agreement with manager Christopher Rich, though it ultimately seems to have been worthless. See Judith Milhous, *Thomas Betterton and the Management of Lincoln's Inn Fields, 1695–1708* (Carbondale: Southern Illinois University Press, 1979), 69–70.

4. *The London Stage* (hereafter *LS*), the most commonly used source for repertory information of the period, can also be inaccurate, as demonstrated in Judith Milhous and Robert D. Hume, "Dating Play Premières from Publication Data, 1660–1700," *Harvard Library Bulletin* 22, no. 4 (October 1974): 374–405.

5. Thomas Davies, *Dramatic Miscellanies: Consisting of Critical Observations on Several Plays of Shakespeare*, 3 vols. (London: n.p., 1783–84), 3:310. Eighteenth Century Collections Online.

6. Tony Aston, "A Brief Supplement to Colley Cibber, Esq; His Lives of the Famous Actors and Actresses" in Watson Nicholson, *Anthony Aston, Stroller and Adventurer*, 73–98 (South Haven, MI: self-pub, 1920), 92.

7. Colley Cibber, *An Apology for the Life of Mr. Colley Cibber*, 2nd ed., 2 vols. (London: John Watts, 1740), 1:138. Eighteenth Century Collections Online. Cibber's list is meant to illustrate her range in men's roles, from the quoif (coif) worn by a lawyer, to the cocked hat of a soldier, to the man of fashion.

8. See Elizabeth Howe, *The First English Actresses: Women and Drama 1660–1700* (Cambridge: Cambridge University Press, 1992), 82.

9. Cibber, *Apology*, 1:137–138.

10. *A Comparison between the Two Stages, with an Examen of* The Generous Conqueror*; and Some Critical Remarks on* The Funeral, or Grief Alamode, The False Friend, Tamerlane *and Others* (London: [s.n.], 1702), 200, Eighteenth Century Collections Online.

11. Breastfeeding can have a strong, though far from infallible, contraceptive effect.

12. David McKinney, Melissa House, Aimin Chen, Louis Muglia, and Emily Defranco, "The Influence of Interpregnancy Interval on Infant Mortality," *American Journal of Obstetrics and Gynecology* 216, no. 3 (2017): 316.e1-316.e9. doi:10.1016/j.ajog.2016.12.018.

13. See *England, Select Births and Christenings, 1538–1975* (database online) (Provo, UT: Ancestry.com Operations, 2014). Digitized records give baptism dates of May 16 and May 27 from the records of St. Martin-in-the-Fields, where both Susanna and John Verbruggen were buried. I assume May 16 is the birth date.

14. John Dryden, *Don Sebastian: King of Portugal, A Tragedy* (London: 1710), 155–156.

15. As Diana Solomon points out, epilogues had clear, profit-driven motives; thus, the heightening of comedy and creation of intimacy are not simply incidental, but strategies for making the play itself more valuable. See Diana Solomon, *Prologues and Epilogues of Restoration Theatre: Gender and Comedy, Performance and Print* (Newark: University of Delaware Press, 2013), 3–4.

16. Thomas Southerne, "Sir Anthony Love," in *The Works of Thomas Southerne*, edited by Robert Jordan and Harold Love, 2 vols. (Oxford: Oxford University Press, 1988), 1:203–204. Southerne, in particular, delighted in making metatheatrical jokes and created many parts for Mrs. Mountfort, one of his favorite performers. He had her speak the epilogue to *The Fatal Marriage, or the Innocent Adultery* (1694), shortly after her marriage to Jack Verbruggen. In it, she mocks the lead character (played by Mrs. Barry, "a buxom damsel of the playhouse race") for dying by suicide rather than reveling in the "brace" of husbands the play provided. See Southerne, "Fatal Marriage," *Works*, 2:175. Susanna herself was, of course, a "buxom damsel" now enjoying a second husband.

17. While the *LS* dates *Sir Anthony Love* to September 1690, Hume and Milhous suggest November 1690 is more realistic because the play was advertised for publication in late December ("Dating Play Premières," 398). If correct, Mountfort was five months pregnant at the premiere.

18. With Elizabeth Barry and Anne Bracegirdle, she was the highest-paid woman in the company. 50 shillings in 1690 was roughly £300 pounds in 2017 per the *National Archives Currency Converter*, 1270–2017, https://www.nationalarchives.gov.uk/currency-converter/.

19. Aston, *Brief Supplement*, 92.

20. Quoted in "Verbruggen, Mrs. John Baptista, Susanna, née Percival, formerly Mrs. William Mountfort," in *A Biographical Dictionary of Actors, Actresses, Musicians, Dancers, Managers, and Other Stage Personnel in London 1660–1800* (hereafter *BDA*), ed. Philip H. Highfill, Kalman A. Burnim, and Edward A. Langhans, 16 vols. (Carbondale: Southern Illinois University Press, 1973–1993), 15:138.

21. Anne Oldfield's pending labor stopped the run of *Cato* in 1713, the same was true for George Anne Bellamy in 1754, and in 1788 one of Sarah Siddons's miscarriages had a similar effect.

22. The circumstances of William Mountfort's death spawned a variety of poems, odes, songs, and even a short, sensational novella entitled *The Player's Tragedy*. In brief, Mountfort was attacked and stabbed by fifteen-year-old Captain Richard Hill on December 9, 1692. Obsessed with the actress Anne Bracegirdle and having failed in an abduction of her earlier in the evening, Hill was convinced William was Bracegirdle's lover and ran him through on the street outside her home. William survived long enough to write a will leaving everything to his "Deare Wife Susanna," their surviving daughter, and the unborn child. More than a thousand people attended his funeral. See Albert S. Borgman, *Life and Death of William Mountfort* (Cambridge, MA: Harvard University Press, 1935), 140.

23. *Gentleman's Journal* (December 1692); quoted in *The London Stage 1660–1800*, Part 1 of 5, ed. William Van Lennep (Carbondale: Southern Illinois University Press, 1960), 1:417. Tony Leigh's wife, Elinor, was also an actress with several children to support. Her salary was raised after his death, probably in recognition of this ("Leigh, Mrs Anthony, Elinor, née Dixon," *BDA*, 9:228).

24. Gilli Bush-Bailey, *Treading the Bawds: Actresses and Playwrights on the Late-Stuart Stage* (New York: Palgrave, 2005), 93.

25. Peter Holland sees only practicalities in the casting of this play, and notes the company's dearth of older actresses. See Peter Holland, *The Ornament of Action: Text and Performance in Restoration Comedy* (Cambridge: Cambridge University Press, 1979), 153–161.

26. Some of these assumptions come from contemporaneous complaints about pregnant actresses. But married performers Anne Shadwell, Elinor Leigh, and Elizabeth Willis, Mountfort Verbruggen's rough contemporaries, maintained careers throughout their childbearing years without censure. For more on Restoration attitudes toward pregnant performers, see Chelsea Phillips, "Pregnancy and the Restoration Stage," in *Theatrical Anecdotes*, ed. Heather Ladd and Leslie Ritchie (Newark, DE: University of Delaware Press, 2022).

27. Mikhail Bakhtin, *Rabelais and His World*, trans. Hélène Iswolsky (Bloomington: Indiana University Press, 1984), 317. Paster's humoral body, particularly her assertion of its subjectivity and materiality as a corrective and supplement to Rabelais, also shades my use of the grotesque. See Paster, *Body Embarrassed*, 14–17.

28. Thomas Southerne, "The Maid's Last Prayer," in *Works*, 1:373–74 (1.1.70–71). Subsequent citations in text.

29. Bush-Bailey suggests a metatheatrical reference to Mountfort's gait in late pregnancy; it is also an inside joke, as Abigail was another of her roles.

30. William Congreve, *The Dramatic Works of William Congreve*, 2 vols. (Glasgow: Robert Urie, 1752), 1:22.

31. Congreve began the play in 1689 but extensively revised it in consultation with Southerne and Dryden while enjoying free access to the playhouse for six months prior to the play's premiere See Holland, *Ornament of Action*, 205.

32. See Judith Milhous and Robert D. Hume, eds. "*The London Stage, 1660–1800*: A New Version of Part 2, 1700–1729," last updated 2001, http://www.personal.psu.edu/hb1/London%20Stage%202001/. Hereafter "New Version."

33. *The London Stage* suggests a revival in 1690–91 based on a printing of the play, but the casting is not clear. Abigail was a Katherine Corey role for many years, and it passed to Susanna either at her retirement in 1692, or earlier, perhaps for this revival. Corey had a very long career, being one of the first women on the London stage. See "Corey, Mrs John, Katherine, née Mitchell," *BDA*, 3:493–495.

34. Beaumont, Francis, and John Fletcher. *The Scornful Lady* (London: W. Freeman, 1691), quotes on 6, 21.

35. Beaumont and Fletcher, *Scornful Lady*, 2.

36. The play closed after the first night, which Southerne attributed to unwarranted audience objections.

37. Southerne, "Wives' Excuse," *Works*, 1:280.

38. Judith Milhous and Robert D. Hume, *Producible Interpretation: Eight English Plays, 1675–1707* (Carbondale: Southern Illinois University Press, 1985), 237–238.

39. Southerne, "Wives' Excuse," *Works*, 1:290 (2.1.48–50).

40. J. Milling, "Oldfield, Anne." *Oxford Dictionary of National Biography Online*, Online Edition, January 2008 (Oxford: Oxford University Press, 2004).

41. Quoted Joanne Lafler, *The Celebrated Mrs. Oldfield: The Life and Art of an Augustan Actress* (Carbondale: Southern Illinois University Press, 1989), 2.

42. See Cibber, *Apology*, 247–248. A lack of casting information in 1703–04 and 1704–05 make it unclear when she began to play these parts, but all were in her repertoire by 1706–07 with the exception of Narcissa, which came in 1707–08.

43. For the significance of Oldfield's Whig ties in her later career see James Peck, "Anne Oldfield's Lady Townly: Consumption, Credit, and the Whig Hegemony of the 1720s" *Theatre Journal* 49 (December 1997), 397–416, quote on 397. For the Whiggish Kit-Cat Club's role in the building of the Haymarket theater—where Oldfield became a company member in 1706—see Robert J. Allen, "The Kit-Cat Club and the Theatre," *Review of English Studies* 7, no. 25 (January 1931), 56–61.

44. "Each of them loved with a Passion, that could hardly have been stronger, had it been both Her and His first Love" (Lafler, *The Celebrated Mrs. Oldfield*, 4). As many men attached to prominent women, he is credited with "making her" to varying degrees—from coaching on the epilogues he wrote her to being credited entirely with her success. For the way Oldfield's ties to Maynwaring may have aided her career, see Helen E. M. Brooks, "Negotiating Marriage and Professional Autonomy in the Careers of Eighteenth-Century Actresses." *Eighteenth-Century Life* 35, no. 2 (Spring 2011): 61–63.

45. In a document filed in 1737, which I believe I am the first to cite, Arthur attests to being born "on or around" July 19, 1709 ("Maynwaring v. Churchill, bill and two answers," 1737, C 11/2455/26, item 1 [June 28, 1737], *National Archives, Kew*). He may actually have been born a few weeks later, as an announcement that "Lady Betty Modish" (Oldfield) was safely delivered the previous week appeared in the August 17–19, 1709 issue of Delarivier Manley's *The Female Tatler; by Mrs. Crackenthorpe a Lady That Knows Everything* (London: B. Baggs, 1709–10), no. 19.

46. Joanne Lafler and J. D. Phillipson both put her absence down to the desire to conceal her pregnancy, which might embarrass Maynwaring. See Lafler, *The Celebrated Mrs. Oldfield*, 103, and J. D. Phillipson, "The Inconveniences of the Female Condition: Anne Oldfield's Pregnancies," in *Stage Mothers: Women, Work, and the Theatre 1660–1830* (Lewisburg, PA: Bucknell University Press, 2014), 43–62, esp. 45–46). It was also a tumultuous year at the theater, however, and disputes with managers led to the silencing of Drury Lane that summer and Oldfield's departure from the company amidst a fight over her benefit earnings from the spring. For more, see Judith Milhous and Robert D. Hume, "The Silencing of Drury Lane 1709," *Theatre Journal* 32, no. 4 (December 1980): 427–447.

47. Cibber, *Apology*, 250.

48. Edmund Curll [William Egerton, pseud.], *Faithful Memoirs of the Life, Amours, and Performances of That Justly Celebrated, and Most Eminent Actress of Her Time, Mrs. Anne Oldfield.* (London: 1731), 3.

49. Felicity Nussbaum, *Rival Queens: Actresses, Performance, and the Eighteenth-Century British Theatre* (Philadelphia: University of Pennsylvania Press, 2010), 112.

50. Ibid., 93–94.

51. The prose is delightfully purple: "Blush, ye rigid virtuous Women! Blush ye sanctify'd Prudes! who . . . for the sake of a Bedfellow . . . waste your Childrens Patrimony" (*Authentick Memoirs of the Life of That Celebrated Actress Mrs. Ann Oldfield*, 4th ed. [London: Booksellers and Pamphlet-Sellers of London and Westminster, 1730], 27, Eighteenth Century Collections Online).

52. Nussbaum notes this in her analysis of Oldfield, particularly regarding the roles of Jane Shore and Calista in *The Fair Penitent*, in which fictional repentance stands in for actual repentance by the actress for sexual transgressions. See Nussbaum, *Rival Queens*, 108–109.

53. She had earlier opportunities that seem to have been successful, including Monimia in *The Orphan* in March 1707 and Semandra in *Mithridates* in 1707–08 ("Oldfield, Mrs. Anne," *BDA*, 11:101–111, esp. 105–106).

54. She received a very lucrative contract that paid her £200 a year and granted her a clear benefit, probably in recompense for Thomas Doggett's barring her a position as joint manager, see Lafler, *The Celebrated Mrs. Oldfield*, 65–66. Between 1710 and 1714, Drury Lane was the only theater authorized to perform spoken drama as Queen's had been restricted to operas.

55. See Manley, *Female Tatler*, no. 29, September 9–12, 1709.

56. Marvin Carlson, *The Haunted Stage: The Theatre as Memory Machine* (Ann Arbor: University of Michigan Press, 2001).

57. This spelling is used in *The London Stage* and in early printed editions. Andromache was originally meant for Jane Rogers, but, as Oldfield's deeply biased biographer wrote, "The Author, as well as his Friends, were soon convinced that Mrs. OLDFIELD was infinitely the more accomplished Person for so Capital a Part" (Curll, *Faithful Memoirs*, 31–32).

58. Budgell, Eustace [Philomeides, pseud.]. *The Spectator: A New Edition*, no. 290 (February 1, 1712), ed. Henry Morley. (London: George Routledge and Sons, 1891).

59. Curll, *Faithful Memoirs*, 153.

60. A review notes the disappointment of "Sir Roger de Coverley" (an invented figure) who would have been "very glad to have seen the little boy" so charmingly described in the play. See Budgell, *Spectator*, March 25, 1712, no. 335.

61. Lafler, *The Celebrated Mrs. Oldfield*, 103; Phillipson, "Inconveniences," 48.

62. Curll, *Faithful Memoirs*, 49.

63. *Authentick Memoirs*, 31.

64. Curll, *Faithful Memoirs*, 35. In 1712–13, the epilogue was explicitly advertised on October 18 and November 25.

65. Solomon notes that this line ("topping the Widow's Part") might remind audiences of Jane Rogers's claim that Oldfield stole the role. See Solomon, *Prologues*, 175.

66. A double entendre referencing both suicide and masturbation, further sexualizing the previously chaste-seeming Andromache (Solomon, *Prologues*, 176).

67. Ambrose Philips, *The Distrest Mother* (London: S. Buckley; J. Tonson, 1712), Eighteenth Century Collections Online, 74–75.

68. Budgell, *Spectator*, London, April 1, 1712, no. 341. The epilogue was probably written by Budgell's cousin Joseph Addison, and this "defense" a rouse since comic epilogues were fairly standard at the end of tragedy.

69. See Lisa A. Freeman, "Mourning the Dignity of the Siddonian Form," *Eighteenth Century Fiction* 27, no. 3–4 (Spring-Summer 2015), 597–629.

70. Nussbaum, *Rival Queens*, 105.

71. Though it had been a long and lingering illness, Maynwaring had recovered remarkably in the latter half of August and into September, probably when the child was conceived.

72. The autopsy was reportedly performed by two surgeons, Mr. Bussiere and Mr. Browne, and observed by Dr. Beeston, Dr. West, and Maynwaring's apothecary Mr. Buckeridge (Curll, *Faithful Memoirs*, 39). Their verdict was consumption, which covered a range of illnesses but did not, as it would later come to indicate, point specifically to tuberculosis. The verdict exonerated Oldfield.

73. Another document, "The Memorial to Jane Rogers," outlined mistreatment at the hands of the Drury Lane managers who seemed determined to prefer Oldfield at Rogers' expense, "for what merit Publick or Private, they best know," transcribed in Judith Milhous and Robert D. Hume, "Theatrical Politics at Drury Lane: New Light on Letitia Cross, Jane Rogers, and Anne Oldfield," *Bulletin of Research in the Humanities* 85 (1982): 412–429, transcription on 415–418, quote on 415.

74. Transcribed in Milhous and Hume, "Theatrical Politics," quote on 421.

75. Pepys records a similar treatment for Prince Rupert in his diary of January 28, 1666–67, Samuel Pepys, *The Diary of Samuel Pepys, M.A., F.R.S.*, ed. Henry B. Wheatley (London: George Bell & Sons, 1893), Project Gutenberg.

76. Quoted in Milhous and Hume, "Theatrical Politics," 421–422.

77. Brooks, "Negotiating Marriage," and Phillipson, "Inconveniences," note the implications of Maynwaring's decision to make Oldfield his executrix and the backlash this provoked.

78. *The Examiner*, February 6–9, 1713, quoted in Lafler, *The Celebrated Mrs. Oldfield*, 105. This and other dates have been amended to the "new style" Gregorian calendar.

79. Both *Ximena* and *Cinna's Conspiracy* were Colley Cibber adaptations of Corneille tragedies (*Le Cid* and *Cinna ou la Clemence d'Auguste*, respectively).

80. "Oldfield wants Damon—when will he be at her? / Oh, not till Oldfield shall be Cato's daughter: / Why then, if I can guess what may ensue, When Cato's clapped, Damon will be so too," quoted in Lafler, *The Celebrated Mrs. Oldfield*, 110. Lafler attributes the poem to Alexander Pope and gives a citation of the 1889 edition of Cibber's *Apology*, but I do not find the poem as cited.

81. Joseph R. Roach, *The Player's Passion: Studies in the Science of Acting* (Newark: University of Delaware Press, 1985), 52.

82. Helen E. M. Brooks, "Early Eighteenth-Century Performance Historiography: Problems and Possibilities," *Studies in Theatre and Performance* 31, no. 1 (2011), 42.

83. Colley Cibber, *Cinna's Conspiracy* (London: Bernard Lintott, 1713), 1. Eighteenth Century Collections Online.

84. In Cibber's version of the *Le Cid* story, Ximena's father recovers and appears in the final act to solve the play's crisis.

85. See, for example, Jane Sharp's explanation that "too frequent coition . . . makes women barren, and therefore Whores have seldom any Children" in *The Midwives Book, or, the Whole Art of Midwifery Discovered* (London: Simon Miller, 1671), 80. Similar beliefs appear in Nicholas Culpeper's earlier work (1651). While Henry Bracken (1737) does not mention sex workers specifically, he too believed frequent coition made it less likely a woman would conceive.

86. In part because the newly exiled Duke of Marlborough could be aligned with either the dictator, Caesar, or Cato, the hero (Lafler, *The Celebrated Mrs. Oldfield*, 109).

87. For an extensive analysis, see Lisa A. Freeman, *Character's Theater: Genre and Identity on the Eighteenth-Century English Stage* (Philadelphia: University of Pennsylvania Press, 2002), 87–144. Freeman has pointed to the critiques of the love scenes as indicative of a belief that English tragedy's ideal and only subject should be masculinity that rejects effeminacy (associated with foreignness, including the form of neoclassical tragedy) in general, and women in particular. Patriotism can and should be the wellspring of all, not love of women that weakens and dilutes the purity of male homosocial bonds. Lucia's unruly love triangle with Portius and Marcus is a particularly egregious error in this context; I would suggest that Marcia, however, comes much closer to the kind of acceptable femininity—which submits to patriarchal control unerringly—Freeman sees as tacitly endorsed in Nicholas Rowe's she-tragedies.

88. Christine Dunn Henderson and Mark E. Yellin, "Those Stubborn Principles: From Stoicism to Sociability in Joseph Addison's *Cato*," *Review of Politics* 76 (2014), 223–241. For an entertaining account of the critiques see Lisa A. Freeman, "What's Love Got to Do with Addison's *Cato*?" *Studies in English Literature 1500–1900* 39, no. 3 (Summer 1999), 463–482.

89. Henderson and Yellin, "Stubborn Principles," 231.

90. Joseph Addison, *Cato. A Tragedy* (London: J. Tonson, 1713), 21.

91. L. Eusden, "Verses to the Author of the Tragedy of Cato" in Joseph Addison, *Cato. A Tragedy*, 7th ed. (London: J. Tonson, 1713), n.p. [Image 9]. Eighteenth Century Collections Online.

92. George Sewell, *Mr. Sewell's Observations on* Cato, a tragedy. *By Mr. Addison. In a Letter to *** To Which Is Added a Comparison between Cato and Caesar, by Mr. Steele*, 3rd. ed. (London: E. Curll, 1714), 14. Eighteenth Century Collections Online.

93. The Damon poem (see n. 91), suggests Oldfield convincingly disappears into Marcia when performing. Jonathan Swift's observations at a rehearsal on April 6, when he referred to Oldfield as "the drab that acts Cato's daughter" similarly reveals unease not explicitly tied to pregnancy, but to the power of her performance contrasted with moments when she breaks character to call for line. See Walter Scott, *The Works of Jonathan Swift, D. D., Dean of St. Patrick's, Dublin; Containing Additional Letters, Tracts, and Poems Not Hitherto Published; with Notes and a Life of the Author*, 19 vols. (Edinburgh: Archibald Constable and Co., 1814) 3:200.

94. Freeman does suggest that some of the vitriol against *Cato*'s love scenes may have been the pregnant body so clearly signaling femininity and woman's uncontained passion onstage. See Freeman, *Character's Theatre*, 124).

95. Benjamin Rand, *Berkeley and Percival: the Correspondence of George Berkeley and Sir John Percival* (Cambridge: Cambridge University Press, 1914), 1:115–116.

96. Phillipson, "Inconveniences," 53.

97. Cibber, *Apology*, 1:137.

98. Aston wrote that she "was very loath to accept of the Part of *Weldon* in *Oroonoko* . . . having thick Legs and Thighs, corpulent and large Posteriours;—but yet the Town (that respected her) compounded, and receiv'd her with Applause" (*Brief Supplement*, 92). It is unlikely that Aston is referring to her premiere of the part in 1695, for he did not know her until at least 1697; there was a revival in 1699, which may be a more likely occasion for his comment.

99. Howe, *The First English Actresses*, 90.

100. She appears on a proposed company list from April 1703 and acted with her step-father's company at Lincoln's Inn Fields in 1703–04. The similarity of the mother and daughter's names has led to significant confusion between them ("Mountfort, Susanna," *BDA*, 10:352–354).

101. See Diana Taylor, *The Archive and the Repertoire: Performing Cultural Memory in the Americas* (Durham, NC: Duke University Press, 2003).

2. *Pregnant Sensibility*

1. G. J. Barker-Benfield, *The Culture of Sensibility: Sex and Society in Eighteenth-Century Britain* (Chicago: Chicago University Press, 1992), xix.

2. Janet Todd, *Sensibility: An Introduction* (New York: Methuen, 1986), 4.

3. David Hume, *Treatise of Human Nature: Being an Attempt to Introduce the Experimental Method of Reasoning into Moral Subjects*, 3 vols. (London: John Noon, 1739–40).

4. The influence of sentimentalism in theater is often dated earlier than the beginnings of a wider culture of sensibility. Spurred in part by the antitheatrical criticisms of Jeremy Collier and his supporters, as well as periodicals like Richard Steele's *Tatler* (1709) and Steele and Joseph Addison's *The Spectator* (1711) so the story goes, the English theater began to reform itself from Restoration libertinism to eighteenth-century sentimentality. The turn was neither so wholesale, so extreme, nor so early, as Robert D. Hume and others have illustrated—particularly in comedy—but certainly debates about the position theater should hold in society impacted what was seen on and written for the stage. See Robert D. Hume, *The Rakish Stage: Studies in English Drama, 1660–1800* (Carbondale: Southern Illinois University Press).

5. Jean I. Marsden, *Theatres of Feeling: Affect, Performance, and the Eighteenth-Century Stage* (Cambridge: Cambridge University Press, 2019). Matthew J. Kinservik, in turn, has suggested that the 1737 Licensing Act encouraged a new, sympathetic approach to satire that intersected with these wider trends. "Sympathetic" satire, "does not single out malefactors for the mass of spectators to scorn; instead, it

encourages a process of sympathetic identification with the wrongdoer that individualizes each spectator as the object of satiric discipline." See Matthew J. Kinservik, *Disciplining Satire: The Censorship of Satiric Comedy on the Eighteenth-Century London Stage* (Lewisburg, PA: Becknell UP, 2002), 126.

6. Kinservik, *Disciplining Satire*, 107.

7. Hill is best known today as a botanist. The 1750 edition of his treatise known as *The Actor* is largely a translation; the 1755 edition contains enough emendations and additions to qualify as an adaptation. See Joseph R. Roach, *The Player's Passion: Studies in the Science of Acting* (Newark: University of Delaware Press, 1985), 100–101.

8. John Hill, *The Actor: A Treatise on the Art of Playing* (London: R. Griffiths, 1755), 192.

9. Marsden, *Theatres of Feeling*, 66.

10. Hill, *The Actor*, 61.

11. As Julia Fawcett puts it, drawing on Barbara Benedict, "Even in a sentimental tradition that purportedly encourages extreme displays of emotion rewards subjectivity and authority not to the sentimental spectacle but to the sentimental spectator, one who feels sympathy on behalf of others but who resists becoming the object of sympathy herself." See Julia Fawcett, *Spectacular Disappearances: Celebrity and Privacy 1696–1801* (Ann Arbor: University of Michigan Press, 2016), 142.

12. Lisa A. Freeman, *Character's Theater: Genre and Identity on the Eighteenth-Century English Stage* (Philadelphia: University of Pennsylvania Press, 2002), 39.

13. Thomas Davies, *Memoirs of the Life of David Garrick, Esq*, 2 vols. (Dublin: Joseph Hill, 1780), 2:109.

14. See Helen Brooks, "Women and Theatrical Management in the Eighteenth Century," in *The Public's Open to Us All*, ed. Laura Engel (Cambridge: Cambridge Scholars, 2009), 73–75.

15. Davies, *Memoirs of the Life of David Garrick*, 2:110.

16. *An Account of the Life of That Celebrated Actress Mrs. Cibber with Interesting and Amusing Anecdotes. Also the Two Remarkable and Romantic Trials between Theophilus Cibber and William Sloper* (London: n.p., 1887), HathiTrust, 18. From a historiographical perspective, it is fascinating to note that several sources give this quotation as "she was the greatest female *player* belonging to my house," obscuring the agency implied in Garrick's statement. See, for example, Lewis Melville, *Stage Favorites of the Eighteenth Century* (Garden City, NY: Doubleday Doran, 1929), 233.

17. Leslie Ritchie, *David Garrick and the Mediation of Celebrity* (Cambridge: Cambridge University Press, 2019).

18. Susannah Cibber to David Garrick (July 18, 1745) in James Boaden, *Private Correspondence of David Garrick with the Most Celebrated Persons of His Time*, 2 vols. (London: Henry Colburn and Richard Bentley, 1831), 1:34.

19. See Helen E. M. Brooks, "'Your Sincere Friend and Humble Servant': Evidence of Managerial Aspirations in Susannah Cibber's Letters," *Studies in Theatre and Performance* 28, no. 2 (April 2008), 147–159.

20. Hill, *The Actor*, 60. Susannah Cibber's detractors complained of a sameness in her vocal delivery that sounded like singsong. There are several sources for this, so it seems valid, but it is also in tension with the great mimic Tate Wilkinson's stated inability to reproduce her performances: "Mrs. Cibber's excellence was of that superior kind that I can only retain her in my mind's eye," *Memoirs of His Own Life*, 4 vols. (York: William, Spence, and Mawman, 1790), 4:164.

21. Charles Churchill, *The Rosciad*, 3rd ed. (London: 1761), 20–21. He is no relation to Anne Oldfield's partner or son.

22. Fawcett, *Spectacular Disappearances*, 175.

23. The technique is particularly associated with Caravaggio. See, for example, "The Calling of St. Matthew" (ca. 1600) or "The Taking of Christ" (ca. 1602). Jusepe de Ribera, Bartolomé Esteban Murillo, Artemisia Gentileschi, El Greco, and Joseph Wright of Derby all use the technique as well. Maria Rzepińska and Krystyna Malcharek, "Tenebrism in Baroque Painting and Its Ideological Background," *Artibus et Historiae* 7, no. 13 (1986), 91–112.

24. Birth dates from *England, Select Births and Christenings, 1538–1975* [database online] (Provo, UT: Ancestry.com Operations, 2014). The *BDA* does not include the first two children, and Jenny's birthdate is incorrectly given as summer 1730. "Cibber, Mrs. Theophilus the first, Jane née Johnson, 1706–1733," in *A Biographical Dictionary of Actors, Actresses, Musicians, Dancers, Managers, and Other Stage Personnel in London 1660–1800* (*BDA*), ed. Philip H. Highfill, Kalman A. Burnim, and Edward A. Langhans, 16 vols. (Carbondale: Southern Illinois University Press, 1973–1993), 3:260–262.

25. "Cibber, Theophilus, 1703–1758," *BDA*, 3:244.

26. Thomas Davies, *Dramatic Miscellanies: Consisting of Critical Observations on Several Plays of Shakespeare: With a Review of His Principal Characters, and Those of Various Eminent Writers, as Represented by Mr. Garrick and Other Celebrated Comedians*, 3 vols. (London: n.p., 1783–85), 1:294.

27. "Cibber, Mrs. Theophilus the First," *BDA*, 3:261.

28. Quoted in Mary Nash, *The Provoked Wife: The Life and Times of Susannah Cibber* (Boston: Little, Brown, 1977), 74. In the event of her death, the trust passed to her children or, failing issue, to her parents.

29. Helen E. M. Brooks, "Negotiating Marriage and Professional Autonomy in the Careers of Eighteenth-Century Actresses," *Eighteenth Century Life* 35, no. 2 (Spring 2011): 39–75.

30. *The Tryal of a Cause for Criminal Conversation between Theophilus Cibber, Gent. Plaintiff and William Sloper, Esq., Defendant* (Dublin, 1749), 8.

31. Nash, *Provoked Wife*, 87–88.

32. Before this, she and Theophilus appeared together in Fielding's farce *The Lottery*. Jack Stocks (Theophilus), thinking Chloe (Susannah) is wealthy, pursues and marries her, but another man pays him to relinquish his rights. The part was usually Kitty Clive's, who did not respond well, a first volley in the later Polly Wars over the part in the *Beggar's Opera*.

33. Aaron Hill's nephew took the role the first night and failed, resigning it rather than continue. The part was read the next night, and the audience asked if they wished performances to be suspended until a replacement was rehearsed,

but "they unanimously declared for the Continuation of the Plays; and 'twas desired the Part might be read, till one of the Players could be studied in it." *London Daily Post and General Advertiser*, January 14, 1736. Unless otherwise noted, all newspaper citations come from the Seventeenth and Eighteenth Century Burney Collection Newspapers, British Library, Gale Digital Collections.

34. Voltaire [Aaron Hill], *The Tragedy of Zara. As It Is Acted at the Theatre Royal in Drury-Lane* (London: J. Watts, 1736), ii. Voltaire is listed as author, but this is Hill's version.

35. Ibid., iii.

36. Ibid., n.p. (image 3).

37. The couple also commanded her first performance after the birth and loss of her son, Amanda in *Love's Last Shift* on July 23, 1736.

38. Ben Wilson, *The Making of Victorian Values: Decency and Dissent in Britain 1789–1837* (New York: Penguin Press, 2007), 150.

39. In addition to single-edition accounts of the trials themselves, they were included in the following collections: *Adultery Anatomized: in a Selection of Trials for Criminal Conversation, Brought Down from the Infant Ages of Cuckoldom in England, to Its Full Growth in the Present Time* (1761), reprinted in 1771 under the name *Cuckoldom Triumphant*; 1780's *A New and Compleat Collection of the Most Remarkable Trials for Adultery &c. from the Time of Henry VIII to the Present Period* included illustrations of Cibber and Sloper in flagrante; *Trials for Adultery, or the History of Divorce* (also 1780) included their story; 1793's *The Cuckold's Chronicle, Being Select Trials for Adultery, Imbecility, Incest, Ravishment, &c.* capped the trials' eighteenth-century printing history.

40. *Tryal of a Cause*, 15.

41. Ibid., 19–20.

42. Francis Truelove, *The Comforts of Matrimony; Exemplified in the Memorable Case and Trial Lately Had Upon an Action Brought by Theo—s C—r against—- S—r, Esq. for Criminal Conversation with the Plaintiff's Wife*, 6th ed. (London: Sam. Baker, 1739), 9.

43. . *Apology for the Life of Mr. T—- C——*, 63. This mock-autobiography, probably by Henry Fielding, would be a suspect source if not corroborated by others. Lady Stafford, for example, wrote to Lord Wentworth that "his old friend Impudence kept him from being either out of countenance or in the least disturb'd at the noise" (quoted in "Cibber, Theophilus," *BDA*, 3:253).

44. Joanne Bailey, *Unquiet Lives: Marriage and Marriage Breakdown in England 1660–1800* (Cambridge: Cambridge University Press, 2009), 109.

45. Literally, "from bed and board." It allowed a woman to legally separate from her husband, though neither party could remarry. See Truelove, *Comforts*, 13–15 and 37.

46. Ibid., 12–13.

47. See Barbara J. Dunlap, "The Problem of Syphilitic Children in Eighteenth-Century France and England," in *The Secret Malady: Venereal Disease in Eighteenth-Century Britain and France*, ed. Linda E. Merians (Lexington: University of Kentucky Press, 1996), 114–127, esp. 117–118.

48. Syphilis is far more likely to pass to a child in utero or at birth during the primary or secondary stage of the disease, both of which occur over about a one to two-year period after infection; after this, the disease enters its latent stage, which can last more than forty years. See Centers for Disease Control and Prevention, "Syphilis During Pregnancy," *2015 Sexually Transmitted Diseases Treatment Guidelines*, https://www.cdc.gov/std/tg2015/syphilis-pregnancy.htm.

49. Neither Susannah nor Sloper showed signs of the disease at their deaths; Theophilus died in a shipwreck in 1758.

50. See Noelle Gallagher, *Itch, Pox, Clap: Venereal Disease in the Eighteenth-Century Imagination* (New Haven: Yale University Press, 2018), esp. 30–45.

51. Quoted in Nash, *Provoked Wife*, 175.

52. *An Account*, 11, "from the information of a person present."

53. Recognition of the relationship and its origins could be a source of extreme embarrassment. Elizabeth Montague recounted her horror at a faux pas she made while viewing Sloper's estate at West Woodhay with friends in 1747: "The Housekeeper came to me, & ask'd if I would walk in I said I should be glad to see the House if *Mr Cibber* was not at home; the Housekeeper look'd as aghast as if she had spoild a custard, or broke a jelly glass; I coloured, Mrs. Donnellan twittered, Dr. Courager sputtered half French half English . . . we were hear [*sic*] a quarter of an hour before we got out of the coach" (Elizabeth Robinson Montague to Margaret Cavendish, July 6, 1747 [MSS MO 422], *Elizabeth Robinson Montague Collection*, Huntington Library, San Marino, California). This is not the only time when someone mistakenly identified Sloper as "Mr. Cibber," suggesting he was very much the trailing spouse of the relationship.

54. Quoted in Nash, *Provoked Wife*, 249.

55. For a more extended discussion of this event, see Chelsea Phillips, "Bodies in Play: Maternity, Repertory, and the Rival *Romeo and Juliet*s, 1748–1751," *Theatre Survey* 60, no. 2 (May 2019), 207–236.

56. *The London Stage 1660–1800*, Part 4, edited by George Winchester Stone, Jr., (Carbondale, IL: Southern Illinois University Press), 4.1:243.

57. Fawcett, *Spectacular Disappearances*, 175.

58. Her most oft-performed maternal role was Andromache in *The Distrest Mother*, a mother whose child never appears on stage.

59. See Elaine M. McGirr, "'Inimitable Sensibility': Susannah Cibber's Performance of Maternity," in *Stage Mothers: Women, Work, and the Theatre, 1660–1830*, ed. Laura Engel and Elaine M. McGirr (Lewisburg, PA: Bucknell University Press, 2014), 63–78 (74). McGirr says Cibber appeared in the part only eleven times in total and not at all after 1751. *LS* also lists her playing the role eight times in a 1754 Drury Lane revival (from January 23), including for her benefit on March 16 which earned her £240 (see *LS* 4:1:405–414). However, McGirr's point still stands as this was four years before Charles's death.

60. McGirr, "'Inimitable Sensibility," 68.

61. George Anne Bellamy, *Apology for the Life of George Anne Bellamy*, 5 vols., 3rd ed. (London: J. Bell, 1785), 2:192.

62. John Doran, *"Their Majesties Servants" or Annals of the English Stage; from Thomas Betterton to Edmund Kean, Actors—Authors—Audiences*, ed. Robert W. Lowe (London: John C. Nimmo, 1897), 321–322.

63. She published a sixth volume later that year containing additional anecdotes and letters, as well as reviews of the memoir and an "entertainment" by Henry Woodward, a longtime companion.

64. Henry Fielding particularly enjoyed riffing on Colley Cibber for his mock autobiographies, producing *An Apology for the Life of Mr. T—- C—-* and *An Apology for the Life of Shamela Andrews* in the 1740s; the same decade saw *An Apology for the Life of Mr. Bampfylde-Moore Carew, Commonly Called The King of the Beggars*.

65. Bellamy, *Apology*, 1:2.

66. Cheryl Wako, *Roles of Authority: Thespian Biography and Celebrity in Eighteenth-Century Britain* (Lubbock: Texas Tech, 2003).

67. Kristina Straub, *Sexual Suspects: Eighteenth-Century Players and Sexual Ideology* (Princeton: Princeton University Press, 1992), 115.

68. Straub, *Sexual Suspects*, 117.

69. Fawcett, *Spectacular Disappearances*, 171.

70. Ibid.

71. Felicity Nussbaum, *Rival Queens: Actresses, Performance, and the Eighteenth-Century British Theatre* (Philadelphia: University of Pennsylvania Press, 2010), 114–118.

72. The story is first given by Bellamy herself in the *Apology*, though she cites "the public papers" (2:59). The quote is from Lady Fanciful's first speech in the play.

73. Ibid., 2:65.

74. Ibid., 2:67–68. The assistance may have included the use of forceps, instruments male doctors were far more likely to own than female midwives.

75. See G. J. Barker-Benfield, *Culture of Sensibility*, 344–347.

76. Bellamy, *Apology*, 2:68.

77. Ibid., 2:70.

78. Since Calcraft and Bellamy were both wealthy and able to financially support their illegitimate children, moreover, they were probably able to evade some of the criticism that a community might normally level at an unmarried couple whose children were likely to become a financial burden on the community. For more on this topic, see Rebecca Probert, ed., *Cohabitation and Non-Marital Births in England and Wales, 1600–2012* (New York: Palgrave Macmillan, 2014). Bellamy testifies to the presumed validity of her marriage by those around her, including a friend of her father's, General Braddock: "He did not doubt my being married to Mr. Calcraft, from his apparent fondness for me; from the alteration in my behavior; and from the preference I had given him before Mr. Metham." See Bellamy, *Apology*, 2:194).

79. Richard Cross and William Hopkins, *Diaries of Drury Lane Theatre Performances Kept by Richard Cross and William Hopkins, 1747–1760, 1762–1764, 1768–1776*, 14 vols. (Folger Shakespeare Library, Washington, DC), W.a.104, v.2.

80. Ibid.

81. Sarah Ward, for example, who had a child while working at Drury Lane in January 1751, does not receive similar attention.

82. I have already mentioned Jane Johnson Cibber, who played a pregnant woman rejected by her lover in *Caelia or the Perjur'd Lover* in December 1732. Jane Rogers, the original Imoinda (first performed 1695), may have played the role during one of her pregnancies in the early 1700s. More common is to find women playing roles that pregnancy will enhance in some way, such as Andromache in *The Distrest Mother*.

83. In the novella Imoinda is a Black woman, and this whitewashing of the part is part of a long history of such practices on the English stage. See, among many, Lynda Boose, "The Getting of a Lawful Race: Racial Discourse and the 'Unrepresentable' Black Woman in Early Modern England" in *Women, "Race," and Writing in the Early Modern Period*, ed. Margo Hendricks and Patricia Parker (London: Routledge, 1994), 35–54; and Joyce Green Macdonald, "The Disappearing African Woman: Imoinda in 'Oroonoko' After Behn," *ELH* 66, no. 1 (Spring 1999), 71–86.

84. *The Fair Penitent*, another role she played that fall, is also a role in which visible pregnancy enhances the story: now Lothario's seduction of Calista has resulted in pregnancy, an egregious violation of patriarchal control (her father betroths her to the worthy Altamont) that perpetuates not Sciolto/Altamont's perfection, but Lothario's degraded and dishonorable masculinity.

85. Interestingly, three days after the Hardwicke Marriage Act went into effect.

86. Tate Wilkinson moralizes on Bellamy's performance of several of these chaste characters during her pregnancy, but at the root of his complaint is Bellamy's continuing to call herself "Miss" Bellamy instead of "Mrs." As much a marker of maturity as marriage at the time, he aims to highlight the ridiculousness of such an affectation to youth when visibly pregnant (see *Memoirs*, 4:185). As we saw in the introduction, Wilkinson had few concerns about casting pregnant women in virginal roles in his own troupe.

87. Ibid., 2:197.

88. Ibid., 2:199.

89. Cross, *Diaries*, v. 2 (Wed 24 Oct, 1753).

90. Bellamy, *Apology*, 2:192.

91. Ibid., 2:199. My thanks to Emily Friedman for pointing out the echo, particularly in the use of "marmoset," between this passage and Richardson's *Sir Charles Grandison*.

92. Ibid., 3:134.

93. *Lloyd's Evening Post and British Chronicle* (London, January 30–February 1, 1758).

94. Bellamy, *Apology*, 5:51. Bellamy would repeat her appearances in Constance in London only occasionally (December 1764, May 1767, September and December 1767, and May 1769). She may have played the role in Dublin and other regional theaters more regularly, as it was one of her professed favorites from her early days in Dublin in the 1740s.

95. Ibid., 3:105. Some suggested Garrick disliked the play because there was no good part for himself. Leslie Ritchie notes his vengeful attitude to Dodsley for

putting it forth, which included bad-mouthing the play in public, and printing tepid reviews that refused to mention Bellamy by name. See Ritchie, *David Garrick and the Mediation of Celebrity*, 84–86).

96. Note on "Cleone," in *Bell's British Theatre. Consisting of the Most Esteemed English Plays*, 34 vols. (London, 1797), 5:n.p. (image 8).

97. Bellamy, *Apology*, 3:105. Her approach to the madness of the character caused anxiety during a rehearsal, the public being "so accustomed to noise and violence in their *mad* stage ladies," including Cibber (*Apology*, 3:106).

98. *Lloyd's Evening Post and British Chronicle*, London, December 4–6, 1758.

99. Edward Thompson, *The Meretriciad*, 2nd ed. (London: C. Moran, 1761), 16–17.

100. Scholars have suggested this important turn to separating the sexual from the maternal was underway at the midcentury in the context of an expanding empire, which needed to harness and encourage women's reproductive labor. See Ruth Perry, "Colonizing the Breast: Sexuality and Maternity in Eighteenth-Century England," *Journal of the History of Sexuality* 2, no. 2 (October 1991), 204–234; and Felicity Nussbaum, *Torrid Zones: Maternity, Sexuality, and Empire in Eighteenth-Century English Narratives* (Baltimore: Johns Hopkins University Press, 1995).

101. Doran, *Their Majesties Servants*, 322.

102. Nussbaum, *Rival Queens*, 18.

103. "My parrot is the wonder of the time! . . . I have taught him to speak tragedy." Susannah Cibber to David Garrick (October 3, 1765) in Boaden, *David Garrick*, 1:200–201.

104. See Brooks, "'Your Sincere Friend."

105. Thomas Davies writes: "Mrs. Cibber, when the [*King John*] was first in rehearsal, could not easily prevail on Winstone to make Austria appear as odious to an audience as he ought . . . [but] It was impossible for any man long to resist the persuasive manner of Mrs. Cibber: Winstone fully answered her idea of Austria's character" (*Dramatic Miscellanies*, 1:38–39).

106. See "Advertisement" to Susannah Cibber, *The Oracle. A Comedy of One Act. As It Is Acted at the Theatre-Royal in Covent-Garden* (London: R. Dodsley, 1752).

107. Mary Nash's compelling and excellently researched biography continually insists upon reading Susannah Cibber as a passive pawn rather than active agent.

108. Churchill, *Rosciad*, 20.

109. I am drawing on Fawcett's distinction between earnest and mimetic performance here. See Fawcett, *Spectacular Disappearances*, 137.

3. *Conceiving Genius*

An early draft of a portion of this chapter initially appeared as "'I Have Given Suck': The Maternal Body in Sarah Siddons' Lady Macbeth," in *Shakespeare Expressed: Page, Stage, and Classroom in Shakespeare and His Contemporaries*, ed. Kathryn M. Moncrief, Kathryn R. McPherson, and Sarah Enloe (Madison, NJ: Fairleigh Dickinson Press, 2013), 19–33.

1. Lisa Forman Cody, *Birthing the Nation: Sex, Science, and the Conception of Eighteenth-Century Britons* (New Haven, CT: Yale University Press, 1992), 306.

2. There is a mention of a pregnancy in one of Anna Seward's letters from March 1783. See Roger Manvell, *Sarah Siddons: Portrait of an Actress* (New York: G.P. Putnam & Sons, 1971), 73. No mentions in newspapers or other traces seem to exist, however, and Siddons missed no time in the theater.

3. The *Biographical Dictionary* incorrectly gives George's birth as February 27, 1785. See "Siddons, Mrs. William, Sarah, née Kemble," in *A Biographical Dictionary of Actors, Actresses, Musicians, Dancers, Managers, and other stage personnel in London 1660–1800* (hereafter *BDA*), ed. Philip H. Highfill, Kalman A. Burnim, and Edward A. Langhans, 16 vols. (Carbondale: Southern Illinois University Press, 1973–1993), 14:33.

4. Henry Bate to David Garrick, August 12, 1775, *Letters Relating to the First Engagement of Mrs. Siddons at Drury Lane*, ADD MS 25383, British Library, London, U.K.; Mary Tickell to Elizabeth Sheridan, "Friday Morning" [October 7, 1785], *Letters from Mary Tickell to Elizabeth Ann Sheridan*, Y.d.35, f. 148, Folger Shakespeare Library, Washington, DC; Hester Piozzi, *The Piozzi Letters: The Correspondence of Hester Lynch Piozzi, 1784–1821 (Formerly Mrs. Thrale)*, ed. Edward A. Bloom and Lillian D. Bloom (Newark: University of Delaware Press, 1989), 2:173.

5. Joanne Begiato, "'Breeding' a 'Little Stranger': Managing Uncertainty in Pregnancy in Georgian England," in *Perceptions of Pregnancy from the Seventeenth to the Twentieth Centuries*, ed. Jennifer Evans and Ciara Meehan (London: Palgrave MacMillan, 2017), 19.

6. Siddons to Mrs. Piozzi (April 30, 1794), quoted in Manvell, *Sarah Siddons*, 189.

7. Begiato, "'Breeding a Little Stranger,'" 19.

8. Sarah Siddons to an unknown recipient. (October 31, 1785) *Letters from Sarah Siddons to Various Recipients [manuscript], 1783–1820*, MS Y.c.432(26), Folger Shakespeare Library, Washington, DC; Sarah Siddons to Elizabeth Barrington, January 5, 1794, *Barrington Papers, Letters from Sarah Siddons to Elizabeth Barrington, née Adair), Dating from Before 1788 to 1794*, ADD MS 73736 (35/28), *British Library*, London, UK.

9. Joseph Roach, *It* (Ann Arbor: University of Michigan Press, 2007), 40. Roach discusses Siddons's maternity as a charismatic force that helped offset the stigmata of her weight gain in later life; he does not address her pregnancies specifically.

10. The portrait measures 239.7 cm × 147.6 cm, nearly 8 × 5 feet. Shearer West points out that this was the same size as Reynolds's portraits of the king and queen. See Shearer West, "Siddons, Celebrity and Regality: Portraiture and the Aging Actress," *Theatre and Celebrity in Britain 1660–2000*, ed. Mary Luckhurst and Jane Moody (New York: Palgrave Macmillan, 2005), 191–213, on 200.

11. On the significance of Siddons's white skin, see Roach, *It*, 146–173.

12. Thomas Campbell, *Life of Mrs. Siddons*, 2 vols. (London: Effingham Wilson, Royal Exchange, 1834), 1:140.

13. Robyn Aselon, "'She Was Tragedy Personified': Crafting the Siddons Legend in Art and Life," in *A Passion for Performance: Sarah Siddons and Her Portraitists*, ed. Robyn Aselon, (Los Angeles: J. Paul Getty Museum, 1999), 41–96.

14. Laura Engel, *Fashioning Celebrity: Eighteenth-Century British Actresses and Strategies for Image-Making* (Columbus: Ohio State University Press, 2011) and Shearer West, "Siddons, Celebrity and Regality."

15. See Thomas Whalley, *Journals and Correspondence of Thomas Sedgewick Whalley*, ed. Hill Wickham, 2 vols. (London: R. Bentley, 1863), 1:445.

16. The Queen remarked on her poise at court, Siddons reported, and then commented, "At any rate, I had frequently personated Queens." See *The Reminiscences of Sarah Kemble Siddons, 1773–1785*, ed. William Van Lennep (Cambridge: Widener Library, 1942), 22.

17. Anthony Todd Thompson, *The Domestic Management of the Sick-room, Necessary, in Aid of Medical Treatment, for the Cure of Diseases* (London: Longman, Orme, Brown, Green, & Longmans, 1841), 64.

18. Quoted in Michael R. Booth, John Stokes, and Susan Bassnett, *Three Tragic Actresses: Siddons, Rachel, Ristori* (Cambridge: Cambridge University Press, 1996), 19.

19. James Sheridan Knowles, *Lectures in Dramatic Literature*, rev. and ed. F. Harvey. (London: James McHenry, 1873), 167–68.

20. Quoted in Gill Perry, *Spectacular Flirtations: Viewing the Actress in British Art and Theatre, 1768–1820* (New Haven, CT: Yale University Press for the Paul Mellon Centre for Studies in British Art, 2007), 6. "Cracked" in this case indicates that Siddons has disturbed her composure and peace of mind, rendering her incapable of controlling either her pen or her thoughts.

21. *The Beauties of Mrs. Siddons: Or, a Review of Her Performance of the Characters of Belvidera, Zara, Isabella, Margaret of Anjou, Jane Shore, and Lady Randolph in Letters of a Lady of Distinction, to Her Friend in the Country* (London: John Strahan, 1786), 3.

22. In Siddons's *Reminiscences*, 20–21, she records an incident when a woman came to her home to look at her because her doctor would not allow her to attend a performance.

23. Joseph R. Roach, *The Player's Passion* (Newark: University of Delaware Press, 1985), 98 and Janet Todd, *Sensibility: An Introduction* (New York: Methuen, 1986), 24.

24. Jean I. Marsden, *Theatres of Feeling: Affect, Performance, and the Eighteenth-Century Stage* (Cambridge: Cambridge University Press, 2019), 66.

25. See Edmund Burke, *A Philosophical Enquiry into the Origins of Our Ideas of the Sublime and the Beautiful* (1757), ed. Adam Phillips, 1990 (Reprint, New York: Oxford University Press, 1998) and David Hume, *A Treatise of Human Nature: Being an Attempt to Introduce the Experimental Method of Reasoning into Moral Subjects*, 3 vols. (London: 1739–40).

26. Lord Archibald Hamilton to Sir Charles Thomson (1784), quoted in Aselon, "She Was Tragedy Personified," 55.

27. Burke's interest was preceded by Longinus's treatise on the sublime and the work of Burke's near-contemporaries on the feeling, among them Joseph Addison and John Dennis.

28. As such, the sublime stands in contrast with the beautiful, which is small, conformable, and compassable.

29. Pat Rogers, "'Towering Beyond Her Sex': Stature and Sublimity in the Achievement of Sarah Siddons," in *Curtain Calls: British and American Women and the Theatre, 1660–1820*, ed. Mary Anne Schofield and Cecilia Macheski, 48–67 (Athens: Ohio University Press, 1991). Heather McPherson, "Masculinity, Femininity and the Tragic Sublime: Reinventing Lady Macbeth," *Studies in Eighteenth Century Culture* 29 (2000), 299–333; Christopher Reid, "Burke's Tragic Muse: Sarah Siddons and the 'Feminization' of the Reflections" in *Burke and the French Revolution: Bicentennial Essays*, ed. Stephen Blakemore (Athens: University of Georgia Press, 1992), 1–27; Laura J. Rosenthal, "The Sublime, the Beautiful, 'the Siddons,'" in *The Clothes That Wear Us: Essays on Dressing and Transgressing in Eighteenth-Century Culture*, ed. Jessica Munns and Penny Richards (Cranbury, NJ: Associated University Presses, 1999), 56–79.

30. James Boaden, *Memoirs of Mrs. Siddons, Interspersed with Anecdotes of Authors and Actors*, 2 vols. (London: H. Colburn, 1827), 1:15.

31. "Her death-scene in *Jane Shore* would have baffled the power of the pencil, for it was a succession of astonishing changes. Her eagle eye, obedient to her will, at times parted with its lustre, and, though open, looked sightless and bewildered; but resumed its fire as wonderfully, when . . . she turned to her husband" (Thomas Campbell, *Life of Mrs. Siddons*, 1:174).

32. Rosenthal, "The Sublime, the Beautiful, 'the Siddons.'"

33. Linda Colley, *Britons: Forging the Nation, 1707–1837* (New Haven: Yale University Press, 1992), 240.

34. Judith Pascoe, *Romantic Theatricality: Gender, Poetry, and Spectatorship* (Ithaca, NY: Cornell University Press, 1997), 24.

35. *Morning Post and Daily Advertiser* (*MPDA*), London, February 3, 1785. Unless otherwise noted, all newspaper quotations can be found in Seventeenth and Eighteenth Century Burney Collection Newspapers, British Library, Gale Digital Collections. She first played the part while working in the provinces.

36. *MPDA*, London, February 3, 1785. For one of several detailed descriptions of her performance, see *Morning Chronicle and London Advertiser (MCLA)*, London, February 14, 1785.

37. Georgianna Ziegler, "Accommodating the Virago: Nineteenth Century Representations of Lady Macbeth," in *Shakespeare and Appropriation*, ed. Christy Desmet and Robert Sawyer (New York: Routledge, 1999), 119–141. Felicity Nussbaum, *Rival Queens: Actresses, Performance, and the Eighteenth-Century British Theatre* (Philadelphia: University of Pennsylvania Press, 2010), 19.

38. See Pascoe, *Romantic Theatricality*; McPherson, "Masculinity, Femininity and the Tragic Sublime"; and Engel, *Fashioning Celebrity*, 26–58.

39. *MCLA*, London, February 5, 1785.

40. *MCLA*, London, February 14, 1785.

41. Campbell, *Life of Mrs. Siddons*, 37. For more on Hannah Pritchard's significance, see Fiona Ritchie, *Women and Shakespeare in the Eighteenth Century* (Cambridge: Cambridge University Press, 2014), 112–114.

42. Charles Lamb, "On Shakespeare's Tragedies," in *The Prose Works of Charles Lamb in Three Volumes*, 3 vols (London: Edward Moxon, 1836), 1:102.

43. Engel, *Fashioning Celebrity*, 31.

44. Mary Linley Tickell was a former singer and the daughter of Drury Lane's music master and co-owner Thomas Linley. Her mother, also Mary, was the wardrobe mistress, and her sister Elizabeth married playwright and patent holder Richard Brinsley Sheridan. Her husband, Richard Tickell, was a satirist and playwright. I am indebted to Robert W. Jones for first drawing my attention to her correspondence in "Competition and Community: Mary Tickell and the Management of Sheridan's Drury Lane," *Theatre Survey*, 54, no. 2 (May 2013), 187–206, and for generously sharing thoughts on their chronology.

45. These figures are based on performances from the start of the season in September until the end of February, when benefits and oratorios begin in earnest. I have not included Siddons's first benefit night or two benefit nights for local hospitals. I have included Royal Command performances, two when Siddons did not perform, and five when she did.

46. These figures include all nonbenefit and oratorio performances for the year. Her economic impact was similar to David Garrick's, see Judith Milhous, "Reading Theatre History from Account Books," in *Players, Playwrights, Playhouses: Investigating Performance 1660–1800,* ed. Michael Cordner and Peter Holland, 101–131 (Basingstoke: Palgrave Macmillan, 2007).

47. *MCLA*, London, September 24, 1785.

48. Ibid.

49. Siddons to Miss Wynn, October 8, 1787, *Sarah Siddons [Collection of Letters 1785–1796]*, Harvard Theatre Collection, Cambridge, MA.

50. Tickell, [November 20, 1785], *Letters*, Y.d.35, 202.

51. Tickell, [October/November 1785], *Letters,* Y.d.35, 182.

52. Tickell, *Letters*, Y.d.35, 202. These three performances took in almost £730, or £242 a night, so Tickell's prediction appears to be correct.

53. For example, "being the last Time but one of her performing 'till after Christmas," *Public Advertiser*, London, November 29, 1785.

54. It is important to remember that the source of some of these notices may well be the theater, the actress, or a close associate of one of these parties. For an extended discussion of the networks of ownership and influence between theaters and the press, though of an earlier era, see Leslie Ritchie, *David Garrick and the Mediation of Celebrity* (Cambridge: Cambridge University Press, 2019), 17–43.

55. *Public Advertiser*, London, November 14, 1785.

56. *MCLA*, London, November 10, 1785.

57. *Beauties of Mrs. Siddons*, 49 and 48.

58. *MCLA*, London, November 10, 1785.

59. *MCLA*, London, November 24, 1785.

60. Ibid.

61. Boaden's comment is important, but like his version of the Henrietta Smith story, it is also something imagined after the actual event. Recounting the story in his biography of Dorothy Jordan, in fact, Boaden misremembered the role, saying Siddons was playing the lead in Robert Dodsley's *Cleone*, rather than Constance, during late pregnancy. The roles of Cleone and Constance involve similar displays of maternal grief that veers into madness. A revival of Dodsley's play was originally planned for the fall of 1785 but was delayed by a year. Boaden is correct that Cleone was not a success for Siddons, but his specific memory of the pregnant actress acting maternal grief was likely Constance. See James Boaden, *The Life of Mrs. Jordan*, 2 vols. (London: Edward Bull, 1831), 1:103.

62. An interesting reversal of Janet Adelman's reading of *Macbeth* as a fantasy of male parthenogenesis. *Suffocating Mothers: Fantasies of Maternal Origin in Shakespeare's Plays: Hamlet to The Tempest* (New York: Routledge, 1992).

63. Garrick was childless. Barry had two sons. The older, Thomas (b. 1743), acted for a time but predeceased his father in 1768. The younger's fate (Spranger Jr., b. 1748) is unknown.

64. See Phillips, "I Have Given Suck," *Shakespeare Expressed.*

65. *London Chronicle*, London, October 1–4, 1785.

66. The quotation is from Donne's *Of the Progress of the Soul: The Second Anniversary.*

67. Tickell, "Friday Morning" [October 7, 1785], *Letters*, Y.d.35, 148.

68. Tickell, "Sunday [October 30, 1785]," *Letters*, Y.d.35, 178–79.

69. Tickell, "Sunday Morning" [November 20, 1785], *Letters*, Y.d.35, 202.

70. Engel, *Fashioning Celebrity*, 45–46.

71. William Shakespeare, *Macbeth*, ed. Nicholas Brooke (Oxford: Oxford University Press, 1990), 1.3.50, 67, 86, 119. Subsequent citations in text. Where appropriate, I have noted variations in the acting versions used in 1785 and 1794.

72. Boaden, *Memoirs of Mrs. Siddons,* 2:135.

73. Ibid., 2:133.

74. Campbell, *Life of Mrs. Siddons*, 2:48.

75. Ibid., 2:18.

76. Tickell, [October/November 1785], *Letters*, Y.d.35, 182.

77. *Morning Herald and Daily Advertiser*, London, October 31, 1785.

78. The stomacher suggests a practical solution: it could be made to cover the gap in the overdress created by Siddons's belly, and either removed entirely or replaced with a narrower version once her figure returned. Similarly, the copious skirts and petticoats probably used a drawstring to create an expandable waist.

79. Garrick removed the onstage slaughter of Macduff's wife and children, drastically shortening the scene in which she appears. Kemble excised the scene entirely, so that their deaths are only reported to Macduff.

80. Knowles, *Lectures,* 167–168.

81. For more on *The Jubilee*, see Thomas King to Sarah Siddons, *Letters to Sarah and William Siddons, 1780–1796*, MS Thr 395(5). Harvard Theatre Collection, Cambridge, MA.

82. Campbell, *Life of Mrs. Siddons*, 2:6.

83. Lisa A. Freeman, "Mourning the Dignity of the Siddonian Form," *Eighteenth Century Fiction* 27, no. 3–4 (Spring-Summer 2015): 597–629, 598.

84. Ibid., 604.

85. Playing opposite her younger brother was about as close to Siddons's acting with the male version of herself as it was possible to come. They had first performed these roles together for a benefit in the spring of 1785, and he took the role permanently in the fall of 1788.

86. See Manvell, *Sarah Siddons*, 141. The role was an amalgam of Andromache in *The Distrest Mother* and Isabella in *The Fatal Marriage*; a queen resisting a tyrant who seeks her hand by threatening her son with murder, all the while believing her husband dead, only to have him return at the end.

87. *World*, London, April 18, 1788. Hygeia is the goddess of health.

88. *MCLA*, London, May 5, 1788.

89. This was not an occasion when one of Siddons's children performed with her.

90. For a detailed account of the Regency crisis, see Hedley Owen, *Queen Charlotte* (London: Butler and Tanner, 1975), 140–178.

91. Campbell, *Life of Mrs. Siddons*, 2:157.

92. Jonathan Bate, "Shakespeare and the Rival Muses" in *Notorious Muse: The Actress in British Art and Culture, 1776–1812*, ed. Robyn Aselon (New Haven: Yale University Press, 2003), 81–103, quote on 92.

93. Elizabeth Inchbald observed that the treatment of plebeians in the play was dangerous in the face of growing poverty and discontent.

94. Thomas Sheridan [and John Philip Kemble], *Coriolanus; Or, the Roman Matron. A Tragedy. Altered from the Shakespeare by Mr. T. Sheridan, Taken from the Manager's Book at the Theatre Royal in Drury Lane* (London, R. Butters, [1790?]), 7. Subsequent quotations in text.

95. Julie Kipp, *Romanticism, Maternity, and the Body Politic* (Cambridge: Cambridge University Press, 2009), 14.

96. Hedley, *Queen Charlotte*, 171.

97. *The London Stage 1660–1800*, part 5 of 5, edited by Charles Beecher Hogan (Carbondale, IL: Southern Illinois University Press, 1968), 5.2:1148.

98. West, "Siddons, Celebrity and Regality," 206.

99. Piozzi labels the illness "the P[ox!]" Siddons's miscarriages and altered appearance may be related to this complaint and the "indignant melancholy" that came with it, or perhaps to other, concurrent illnesses. See Hester Piozzi (Thrale), *Thraliana: The Diary of Hester Lynch Thrale (Later Mrs. Piozzi), 1776–1809*, 6 vols., ed. Katherine C. Balderston (Oxford: Clarendon Press, 1942), 2:769.

100. "Mrs. SIDDONS is indisposed at Exeter. Her illness, we understand, is of such a kind as precludes any *present addition* to her family," *MPDA*, London, August 24, 1789.

101. Edmund Burke, *Reflections on the Revolution in France* (London: Electric Book, 2001), 97. For more on Siddons and Burke, see Reid, "Burke's Tragic Muse."

102. *General Magazine and Impartial Review*, London: March 1791.

103. Freeman, "Mourning the Dignity of the Siddonian Form," 611. Commentary between 1789–1792 suggests that Siddons's physical appearance changed drastically between stage appearances, troubling the stable image of the actress in audiences' minds. In 1789, Fanny Burney remarked on her corpulence when she played Rosalind; two years later, Siddons was so emaciated as to make Jane Shore's death by starvation all too real.

104. See Manvell, *Sarah Siddons*, 180.

105. *World*, London, April 23, 1794.

106. Lucina is the Roman goddess of childbirth. *London Packet or New Lloyd's Evening Post*, London, February 24–26, 1794.

107. *Oracle and Public Advertiser*, London, April 16, 1794.

108. Quoted Manvell, *Sarah Siddons*, 189.

109. Siddons to Mrs. Piozzi, *Piozzi Letters*, 2:196; for 1785, see Tickell, 8 January 1786, *Letters*, (Y.d.35 [228]).

110. Sarah Siddons to Elizabeth Barrington, 5 January 1794, *Barrington Papers*.

111. Piozzi, *Thraliana*, 2:876–77. Laura Rosenthal points to a criticism of Siddons printed in 1794 that accused the actress of a lack of maternal feeling for watching a distraught mother whose baby fell out a window, studying her response for her own "ambition." See Rosenthal, "The Sublime, The Beautiful, The Siddons," 67; it is unclear if this appeared before or after Piozzi's comment, or her pregnant performances that year. I have found no digitized copy of the anonymously authored source, "The Wonderful Secrets of Stage Tricks."

112. Both quoted in Helen E. M. Brooks, *Actresses, Gender, and the Eighteenth-Century Stage: Playing Women* (New York: Palgrave Macmillan, 2015), 125.

113. Ibid., 126.

114. Piozzi, *Piozzi Letters*, 2:173.

115. See West, "Siddons, Celebrity and Regality," 196; Helen E. M. Brooks, "The Divided Heart of the Actress: Late Eighteenth Century Actresses and the 'Cult of Maternity'" in *Stage Mothers: Women, Work and the Theatre 1660–1830*, ed. Laura Engel and Elaine M. McGirr (Lewisburg, PA: Bucknell University Press, 2014), 27. Compounded by dating errors, Piozzi's comment has also been used to suggest that James Gillray's satire on Siddons, *Melpomene*, created in 1784 is proof of disapproval at her performing Lady Macbeth while pregnant ten years later. See Ellen Malenas Ledoux, "Working Mothers on the Romantic Stage: Sarah Siddons and Mary Robinson," in *Stage Mothers*, 89. Ledoux is following the interpretation provided by Lisa Plummer Crafton, *Transgressive Theatricality, Romanticism, and Mary Wollstonecraft* (Burlington: Ashgate, 2011), 130.

116. *London Packet or New Lloyd's Evening Post*, London, April 21–23, 1794.

117. Respectively, *World*, London, May 2, 1794, and *World*, London, June 7, 1794.

118. *World*, London, April 23, 1794, and *Oracle*, London, May 3, 1794.

119. West similarly claims that Siddons is spoken of and represented in progressively more fixed, sculptural terms as she ages, focus moving from her body natural to the "iconic" (celebrity) body that does not change.

120. Joseph W. Donohue, Jr., "Kemble's Production of *Macbeth* (1794), Some notes on scenic painters, scenery, special effects, and costumes," *Theatre Notebook* 21 (Winter 1966/7): 63–74.

121. See for example: David Francis Taylor, *Politics of Parody: A Literary History of Character, 1760–1830* (New Haven, CT: Yale University Press, 2018), 101–139; Mary Jacobus, "'That Great Stage Where Senators Perform': 'Macbeth' and the Politics of Romantic Theatre," *Studies in Romanticism* 22, no. 3 (Fall 1983): 353–387.

122. For an analysis of the print, see Taylor, *Politics of Parody*, 124–128. Taylor emphasizes that in the print the Queen is meant to represent Hecate, not Lady Macbeth.

123. Cleanth Brooks suggests, "It is the babe, the child, that dominates the symbolism at this piece." See Cleanth Brooks, "From *The Well-Wrought Urn*," in *Macbeth: Critical Essays*, ed. S. Schoenbaum (New York: Routledge, 2015 [first published 1991]), 209–226.

124. Colley, *Britons*, 237–281.

125. Quoted in Jacobus, "That Great Stage," 361.

126. Kemble drew attention to the consonance between *Coriolanus* and *Macbeth* when it was noted that, despite clear investment in new costumes, he insisted on wearing his Coriolanus wig for Macbeth. See Donohue, Jr., "Kemble's Production," 63.

127. Bernice Kliman emphasizes Siddons's continual study: "Splendid as Siddons was, her Lady Macbeth was not frozen but a flexible, developing work of art. . . . During the long pauses between performances of the play, she tried to develop truer, more interesting interpretations" (*Shakespeare in Performance: Macbeth*, 2nd ed. [New York: Palgrave, 2004], 35).

128. Boaden, *Memoirs of Mrs. Siddons*, 402–403.

129. Matthew S. Buckley, *Tragedy Walks the Street: The French Revolution in the Making of Modern Drama* (Baltimore: Johns Hopkins University Press, 2006), 96.

130. Cody, *Birthing the Nation*, 306.

131. Ibid.,20.

4. *Prolific Muse*

An early draft of a portion of this chapter initially appeared as "'Mrs. Pickle's Mistake': The Dating of an Eighteenth-Century Satirical Print" in *Women's History* 5 (Summer 2016): 23–25.

1. At best the result of seduction, though Daly was a known predator who used his position as manager to coerce his actresses into sexual relationships and did not take kindly to refusal. James Boaden says Elizabeth Inchbald, for example, was fired for rejecting him. See James Boaden, *The Life of Mrs. Jordan*, 2 vols. (London: William Holland, 1831), 1:11.

2. Romp: "A lively, playful girl," and hoyden: "A rude, or ill-bred girl (or woman); a boisterous noisy girl, a romp," *Oxford English Dictionary Online* (Oxford University Press, June 2015).

3. Mary Tickell to Elizabeth Ann Sheridan, 22 October 1785, *Letters from Mary Tickell to Elizabeth Ann Sheridan,* Y.d.35, 170–71, Folger Shakespeare Library, Washington, DC. Her legs were taken in plaster by the sculptor Ann Damer as the nonpareil of women's lower limbs (clipping in James Boaden, *Life of Mrs. Jordan*, 2 vols. Extra-Illustrated edition (5 vols.), Harvard Theatre Collection, TS 940.6, 3: after page 358. For a detailed analysis of Jordan's curls, see Gill Perry, "Staging Gender and 'Hairy Signs': Representing Dorothy Jordan's Curls," *Eighteenth-Century Studies*, 38, no. 1 (Fall 2004), 145–163.

4. Dorothy Jordan to William, Duke of Clarence (undated, ca. 1791), *Dorothy Jordan Papers*, MSS DJ, Box 1, item 29, Huntington Library, San Marino, CA.

5. Jordan to Clarence (undated, ca. March 1807), MSS DJ, Box 4, item 165, *Dorothy Jordan Papers*.

6. Jordan's Drury Lane compatriot Anna Maria Crouch appears as Euphrosyne, and the satyr is a self-portrait of Hoppner. Thalia and Euphrosyne are sisters, two of the Three Graces of Greek mythology.

7. William Hazlitt, *A View of the English Stage, or a Series of Dramatic Criticisms* (London: John Warren, 1821), 169.

8. M. J. Young, *Memoirs of Mrs. Crouch* (London, J. Aspern, 1806), 1:261–262.

9. I am paraphrasing Elinor Glyn and Joseph Roach. See Roach, *It* (Ann Arbor: University of Michigan Press, 2007), 4.

10. E. V. Lucas, *The Life of Charles Lamb*, 2 vols. (London: Methuen, 1905), 2:13.

11. Helen E.M. Brooks, *Actresses, Gender, and the Eighteenth-Century Stage: Playing Women* (New York: Palgrave Macmillan, 2015), 94.

12. Brooks, *Actresses*, 102.

13. Fanny Burney, January 13, 1788, *Diary and Letters of Madame D'Arblay*, 6 vols. (London: MacMillan, 1904–05), 3:385. The monikers are allegorical names that Burney used for Fulke Greville (Welbred) and Stephen Digby (Fairly).

14. The transgressions she embodied in roles like Silvia in Farquhar's *The Recruiting Officer*, Hypolita in Cibber's *She Wou'd and She Wou'd Not*, and Sir Harry Wildair in *The Constant Couple* (including pretended seductions, homoerotic innuendo, and brawling) were quite distinct from other roles, such as Viola, Rosalind, and Peggy, which focused predominantly on the failure of male disguise to transform the woman beneath. For more on her breeches roles, see Jean I. Marsden, "Modesty Unshackled: Dorothy Jordan and the Dangers of Cross-Dressing," *Studies in Eighteenth-Century Culture*, 22 (1993): 21–35 and Perry, "Staging Gender."

15. Roach, *It*, 8.

16. This is based on the pay tiers at Covent Garden that season, as we lack this information for Drury Lane. Stars like Siddons and Abington were often functionally in their own category, followed by more homogeneous clusters at different salary points (the second tier at about £8 per week, the third at about £4 per week, and so forth).

17. Tickell, 22 October 1785, *Letters*, Y.d.35, 170–71.

18. *Public Advertiser*, London, November 16, 1785. This and all subsequent citations of newspaper sources come from the British Library's Seventeenth and Eighteenth Century Burney Collection Newspapers, Gale Digital Collections, unless otherwise noted.

19. *Morning Chronicle and London Advertiser* (hereafter *MCLA*), London, December 9, 1785. In the new year, *An Essay on the Preeminence of Comic Genius* (London: T. Becket, 1786) celebrated her ascendency.

20. *MCLA*, London, December 24, 1785.

21. Brian Fothergill, *Mrs. Jordan: Portrait of an Actress* (London: Faber & Faber, 1965), 78. Siddons was making £23.7 per six-day week. The Drury Lane records do not include individual salaries for this year, but £8 per week would have made Jordan the fourth-highest paid actress on the salary list at Covent Garden.

22. *Bon Ton Magazine, or the Microscope of Fashion and Folly,* 5 vols. (London: n.p., April 1793), 3:101.

23. Fiona Ritchie's assessment largely does not concern Jordan's private life. Claire Tomalin's excellent 321-page biography, *Mrs. Jordan's Profession: The Actress and the Prince* (New York: Alfred A. Knopf, 1995) devotes a mere twenty pages of any substance to their relationship; Boaden mentions Ford only just before the relationship breaks down. Clare Jerrold provides a more comprehensive exploration of this period but offers little commentary on how the pregnancies shaped her earnings or theatrical business (*The Story of Dorothy Jordan* [New York: Brentano's, 1914]). Helen Brooks does discuss the significance of their cohabitation and children in "Negotiating Marriage and Professional Autonomy in the Careers of Eighteenth-Century Actresses," *Eighteenth-Century Life* 35, no. 2 (Spring 2011): 39–75.

24. See Drury Lane Journals for 1788–89 (W.b.291), March 14, 1789, Folger Shakespeare Library, Washington, DC.

25. In a letter to Jordan in December 1796, when she was about five months pregnant, Sheridan assured her that she "would not be called for any entertainments" for the foreseeable future (*Sheridan-Grubb papers concerning Drury Lane Theatre, 1765–1841*, MS Thr 527 [108] Harvard Theatre Collection).

26. Jordan was about three months pregnant at the end of January. The suggested dating of the letter is based on internal references ("Tuesday Morn [1787]," *Letters*, Y.d.35, f. 339–40). For more on Tickell, see chapter 3.

27. *World and Fashionable Advertiser*, London, March 29, 1787.

28. John Henry Blunt, *The Annotated Book of Common Prayer: Being a Historical, Ritual, and Theological Commentary on the Devotional System of The Church of England* (London: Longmans, Green, 1907), 231.

29. *Morning Herald*, London, May 9, 1787.

30. *World and Fashionable Advertiser*, London, August 1, 1787.

31. *Public Advertiser*, London, September 6, 1787. Lucina is the Roman goddess of childbirth.

32. *Public Advertiser*, London, November 4, 1788. In the eighteenth century, "abortion" was a general term for what we would today designate either a

miscarriage or a stillbirth (before or after the twentieth week), and therefore is unhelpful for determining precisely how far into the pregnancy Jordan was in October. Her heavy schedule, however, suggests it was early.

33. See Tomalin, *Mrs. Jordan's Profession*, 91–94.

34. *English Chronicle or Universal Evening Post*, London, November 10–12, 1789.

35. A Falstaff line from *The Merry Wives of Windsor* when he recounts the adventure of the buck basket to "Master Brooke," the alias Ford uses when urging Falstaff to seduce his wife to test her fidelity.

36. Pay book for Drury Lane Theatre 1789–1794 (W.b.347), *Records of Covent Garden and Drury Lane Theatre*, Folger Shakespeare Library, Washington, DC.

37. *Public Advertiser*, London, December 11, 1790. This pregnancy has been overlooked in every biography except that of Clare Jerrold.

38. Maria Eliza Rundell, "Manual on Pregnancy and Childcare Compiled by Maria Rundell, with Various Remedies for Pregnant Women and for Children," 17 October 1810 (MS 7106), Archives and Manuscripts, Wellcome Library, London, UK. Maria Eliza Rundell, best known for her highly successful domestic cookery books, was also an experienced mother and wife to a surgeon. She wrote this manual, which contains extensive notes on managing pregnancy and childhood illnesses drawn from her experiences and those of her deceased husband, for her daughters.

39. *Public Advertiser*, London, January 26, 1791.

40. *Oracle and Public Advertiser*, London, April 14, 1791.

41. *Jordan's Elixir of Life and Cure for the Spleen; Or, a Collection of All the Songs Sung by Mrs. Jordan, since Her First Appearance in London . . . to Which Is Prefixed Authentic Memoirs of Mrs. Jordan* (London: William Holland, 1789), 7–8.

42. *Evening Mail*, London, August 17–19, 1791 and *Morning Post and Daily Advertiser* (hereafter *MPDA*), London, September 2, 1791. Jordan played Mrs. Ford in *The Merry Wives of Windsor* in the summer of 1788, but it was not part of her London repertoire.

43. Duke of Clarence to Prince of Wales, 13 October 1791, quoted in A. Aspinall, editor, *Mrs. Jordan and Her Family, Being the Unpublished Correspondence of Mrs. Jordan and the Duke of Clarence, Later William IV* (London: A. Barker, 1951), 10. The reference to legal proofs is likely because he wanted to avoid the possibility of a public and expensive trial for criminal conversation.

44. *Dorothy Jordan Collection* (RA GEO/ADD40/27), Royal Archives, Windsor.

45. *Dorothy Jordan Collection* (RA GEO/ADD40/30), Royal Archives, Windsor.

46. Brooks, *Actresses*, 97.

47. Sharon Marcus, *The Drama of Celebrity* (Princeton: Princeton University Press, 2019), 6. Marcus argues that celebrity is created through the collaboration and competition of three interdependent constituents: the star themselves, the public, and the media.

48. A celebrity effigy is the collective image of the person in the public mind, a combination of visual depictions, stories, and feelings the figure generates. See Roach, *It,* 17 and 111–112, and Vic Gatrell, *City of Laughter: Sex and Satire in Eighteenth-Century London* (New York: Walker, 2007), 227.

49. Roach, *It,* 112.

50. *Morning Post and Daily Advertiser*, London, October 11, 1791.

51. Susanna Mountfort Verbruggen originated the role in Thomas Jevon's play *The Devil of a Wife* (1686), which became the basis for Coffey's opera.

52. Horace Walpole called Jordan "Nell of Clarence" in a letter to Miss Berry, 19 August 1795, quoted in Jerrold, *Dorothy Jordan*, 200.

53. *MPDA*, London, October 12, 1791. The "assemblage" refers to the locations Jordan conceived or birthed her children (Fanny was the daughter of Irish manager Richard Daly; Dodee was born in Scotland; and Lucy in London).

54. *Bon Ton* (London, October 1791), 1:316.

55. *Public Advertiser*, London, October 21, 1791.

56. *Dorothy Jordan Collection* (RA GEO/ADD40/30), Royal Archives, Windsor.

57. *Lloyd's Evening Post*, London, October 14–17, 1791.

58. *Morning Chronicle*, London, October 18, 1791. The terms were even used to make sly remarks in Ford's direction: "It is impossible not to admire the *greatness* of mind of MR. FORD, in *graciously* permitting MRS. JORDAN to see *his* children when she comes to pay their Annuity!" *MCLA*, London, October 20, 1791.

59. *Bon Ton* (London, November 1791), 1:324.

60. Ibid., 358.

61. *MPDA*, London, October 15, 1791.

62. "It spoke to senses that lay beyond reason too, so that, as Hogarth put it, pictures 'shadow forth what cannot be conveyed to the mind with such prevision and truth by any words whatsoever. . . . Ocular demonstration will carry more conviction to the mind of a sensible man, than all he would find in a thousand volumes.'" See Gatrell, *City of Laughter*, 214.

63. "Cracked" being a slang term for morally bankrupt, and "crack" being a lewd cant term for a sex worker. The concept of a woman as a "leaky vessel" can be traced back to Galenic medicine, and the visual symbol of a cracked jar or pot was a common way to indicate lost virginity (and sometimes, though not always, also pregnancy).

64. The cockpit (double entendre aside) was the part of the ship that housed the infirmary.

65. Mikhail Bakhtin writes that the Rabelaisian grotesque body "swallows and generates, gives and takes . . . [it] is never clearly differentiated from the world but is transferred, merged, and fused with it." See Mikhail Bakhtin, *Rabelais and His World*, trans. Hélène Iswolsky (Bloomington: Indiana University Press, 1984), 339. For more on the grotesque body, see chapter 1.

66. *Dorothy Jordan Collection* (RA GEO/ADD40/36), Royal Archives, Windsor.

67. Also absent was the role Jordan debuted for her benefit the year before, Celia in *The Greek Slave*, an adaptation of Beaumont and Fletcher's *The*

Humorous Lieutenant. The play and its epilogue were probably too topical: "The manager his want of sense evinces, / To pitch on *Hoydens* for the *love* of PRINCES! / To trick out *Chambermaids* in aukward pomp,—/ Horrid! to make a Princess of a *Romp*," quoted in *The Great Illegitimates!!! Public and Private Life of That Celebrated Actress Mrs. Bland, Otherwise Mrs. Ford or Mrs. Jordan* (London: 1830), 31. Though it is tempting to believe it references public knowledge of a relationship, it is more likely, as James Boaden asserts, to have been an unfortunate coincidence.

68. David Garrick, *The Country Girl* (London: John Bell, 1791), 74.

69. Ibid., 77.

70. *MPDA*, London, October 17, 1791.

71. *Caledonian Mercury* (Edinburgh: October 31 and November 3, 1791). Dent's cartoons "The Flattering Glass, or Nell's Mistake" and "Story of Nell's Coach" also make the cost of Jordan's sexual services to the British public clear.

72. *Saint James Chronicle*, London, November 26–29, 1791.

73. *Whitehall Evening Post*, London, November 26–29, 1791.

74. *Saint James Chronicle*, London, December 3–6, 1791. On November 18, Jordan played in *The Conspiracy* but asked Kemble to change the afterpiece as she felt incapable of performing in *Richard Coeur de Lion* the same night. Later in the year, the Duke of Clarence requested that Sheridan would restrict *Cymon*'s repetition to once a week for the sake of Jordan's health, warning that otherwise she might have to resign the part of Fatima. William, Duke of Clarence to Richard Brinsley Sheridan (ca. spring 1792), in Boaden, *Life of Mrs. Jordan*, ex. Ill., vol. 3, facing page 275.

75. Though there are mentions of the *Morning Herald* attack in other papers (see, for example, *MPDA*, London, November 29, 1791), I have been unable to find something matching the descriptions provided. Clarence took legal advice on silencing the publication and succeeded in doing so. He also attempted to suppress, and may well have bought up and destroyed, additional pamphlets and modes of attack, including satirical prints. It is striking, for example, that no cartoonist produced a satire during her absence.

76. *Oracle and Public Advertiser*, London, December 2, 1791.

77. *World*, London, November 29, 1791. The same paper later commented that, "Mrs. JORDAN has too strong interest to plead with the Public—and their own pleasure is too essentially concerned, for them wantonly to throw her aside," *World*, London, December 5, 1791.

78. All quotes from the *London Chronicle*, London, November 29–December 1, 1791.

79. *Lloyd's Evening Post*, London, December 9–12, 1791.

80. *Bon Ton* (London, June 1792), 2:153. The coincidence of the straw-colored carriage seems to be the sole reason for the joke here, though Jordan was actually about three months pregnant at the time.

81. The print shows three women whose children are dead or dying because of their dependence on gin: in the foreground, a drunken, bare-breasted mother lets her child fall from her arms into a canal; in the background, a half-naked woman is lowered into a coffin while her orphaned child cries, and another woman chases a man who has impaled her child on a sword.

82. Laura Gowing, *Common Bodies: Women, Touch, and Power in Seventeenth-Century England* (New Haven: Yale University Press, 2003), 142.

83. For evidence of the print's dating, see Chelsea Phillips, "'Mrs. Pickle's Mistake': The Dating of an Eighteenth-Century Satirical Print," *Women's History* 5 (Summer 2016): 23–25. Additional evidence is within the print itself. Ford calls to his followers, "That's your sort keep it up." "That's your sort" was a phrase popularized by Thomas Holcraft's *Road to Ruin*, which premiered at Covent Garden in February 1792.

84. M. Dorothy George, *Catalogue of Political and Personal Satires Preserved in the Department of Prints and Drawings in the British Museum*, vol. 6, no. 7835. (London: British Museum Press, 1938). In her entry for the image, M. Dorothy George defines the "charivari" as a ritual that specifically shamed "unfaithful wives." The OED entry specifies "incongruous or unpopular marriages," indicating that both partners might be targeted: "charivari, n." *OED Online*. (Oxford University Press, June 2015).

85. Physician in ordinary is analogous to a general practitioner, whereas a physician in extraordinary was more specialized (for example, an obstetrician).

86. She may have been aided by the Royal Family, who attended Drury Lane on January 4 to see the spectacular new opera *Cymon*, in which she played the role of Fatima. While there was much to attract audiences in the piece, interest in watching Jordan perform before her lover's royal parents may well have contributed to the excessive demand for access, which brought the company a box office of £580 pounds, nearly £200 more than another performance of the piece and the largest that season. When she played Peggy in *The Country Girl* for her benefit on April 16, she made £548, £200 more than either of the previous two years. Whatever else it brought, Jordan's willingness to continue performing in the wake of scandal was lucrative.

87. See Tomalin, *Mrs. Jordan's Profession*, 160, for examples.

88. Quoted in ibid., 157. Attributed to Lord Liverpool.

89. *Bon Ton* (London, April 1793), 3:103.

90. *Public Advertiser* (London, September 16, 1793).

91. *The Great Illegitimates*, 70.

92. Jordan had six more children, most given delightful nicknames: Frederick ("Freddles," December 9, 1799), Elizabeth ("Eliza," January 17, 1801), Adolphus (known as "Molpuss" and "Lolly," February 17, 1802), Augusta ("Ta," November 3, 1803), Augustus ("Stump," "Tuss," or "Tus," March 1, 1805), and Amelia ("Mely," March 21, 1807).

93. The only exception are limited appearances in 1804–05 while pregnant with Augustus. See John Genest, *Some Account of the English Stage from the Restoration In 1660 to 1830* 10 vols. (Bath: H.E. Carrington, 1832), v.7 and 8. For her comment, see Dorothy Jordan to William, Duke of Clarence. *Betty Wharton autograph collection,* Harvard Theatre Collection, MS Thr 357 (Box 1, item 51).

94. Tomalin, *Mrs. Jordan's Profession*, 166.

95. *Morning Post*, London, February 6, 1794.

96. Tomalin, *Mrs. Jordan's Profession*, 145.

97. *Telegraph*, London, February 11, 1797.

98. "Contract Between Sheridan and Dorothy Jordan to Appear at Drury Lane Theatre for 5 Years," *Richard Brinsley Sheridan additional papers*, MS Thr 5.7 Volume 1, no. 6. Harvard Theatre Collection.

99. She played it once more for a benefit in 1795 but advertised it as the absolute last time.

100. With Sophia's birth on March 4, 1795, for example, Jordan acted from October 22 to January 15, last appearing in breeches as Viola in *Twelfth Night* on November 14. Sophia was born on March 4, and Jordan was working again by April 15, when she played Peggy in *The Country Girl.*

101. Richard Brinsley Sheridan, *Pizarro*, ed. Selena Couture and Alexander Dick (Peterborough, ON: Broadview, 2017), 36–40.

102. *Evening Mail*, London, October 14–17, 1796.

103. *The Telegraph*, London, October 18, 1796. Jordan was only four months pregnant at the time, but perhaps the comment references her perceived size.

104. Fiona Ritchie, *Women and Shakespeare in the Eighteenth Century* (Cambridge: Cambridge University Press, 2014), 110–140 (129).

105. *Tomahawk and Censor General*, London, January 16, 1796.

106. *Oracle*, London, January 26, 1796.

107. *Morning Post and Fashionable World*, London, November 24, 1796.

108. Linda Colley, *Britons: Forging the Nation 1707–1839*, rev. ed. (1992, New Haven, CT: Yale University Press, 2005), 210.

109. She is therefore another example of a performer who displays Felicity Nussbaum's "exceptional virtue." See *Rival Queens: Actresses, Performance, and the Eighteenth-Century British Theatre* (Philadelphia: University of Pennsylvania Press, 2010), 27 and 93–94.

110. *The Great Illegitimates*, 70.

111. Colley, *Britons*, 272.

112. "The R—l Lover," in Boaden, *Life of Mrs. Jordan*, ex. Ill., vol. 5, facing page 269.

113. In Isaac Cruikshank's satirical print, "Cl[are]nce's Dream or Binnacle Billy Receiving an Unwelcome Visit from Ye Other World" (April 1821). British Museum.

114. William Hazlitt, *Criticisms and Dramatic Essays of the English Stage* (London: G. Routledge & Co, 1851), 50.

Conclusion

1. Wendy Williams memorably demonstrated that Beyoncé was hiding something by critiquing the way she sat down and the way her dress moved during an interview in Australia. For proof, she cited her own experiences and those of two of her staffers. Bloggers also called on personal experience—their own or witnessed behavior—to gauge the veracity of Beyoncé's pregnancy through her success or failure at performing the embodiment of pregnancy correctly. See Gabrielle Bluestone, "Did Beyoncé Fake Her Pregnancy?" March 26, 2015, BlackBag.Gawker .com, http://blackbag.gawker.com/did-beyonce-fake-her-pregnancy-1693597363.

2. Andrew Barclay, "Mary [Mary of Modena] (1658–1718)," Oxford Dictionary of National Biography, Oxford University Press, 2004; online edition, 2008.

3. Ruth Perry, "Colonizing the Breast: Sexuality and Maternity in Eighteenth-Century England," *Journal of the History of Sexuality* 2, no. 2, Special Issue, Part 1: The State, Society, and the Regulation of Sexuality in Modern Europe (October 1991): 204–234; and Felicity Nussbaum, *Torrid Zones: Maternity, Sexuality, and Empire in Eighteenth-Century English Narratives* (Baltimore: Johns Hopkins University Press, 1995).

4. Dror Wahrman, *The Making of the Modern Self: Identity and Culture in Eighteenth-Century England* (New Haven, CT: Yale University Press, 2004), 51–53.

5. In, respectively, Toni Bowers, *The Politics of Motherhood* and *Birthing the Nation: British Writing and Culture, 1680–1760* (Cambridge: Cambridge University Press, 1997), and Lisa Forman Cody, *Birthing the Nation: Sex, Sense, and Conceptions of Eighteenth-Century Britons* (Oxford: Oxford University Press, 2005).

6. Rachel Bonds, "Working Like a Mother," HowlRound Theatre Commons, September 11, 2018, https://howlround.com/working-mother.

7. Per the National Archives Currency Converter, approximately $2,300 in 2017. Siddons had resigned her post in the touring company at this point.

8. Bonds, "Working."

9. An excellent overview can be found in Robert W. Jones, "Competition and Community: Mary Tickell and the Management of Drury Lane Theatre," *Theatre Survey* 54, no. 2 (2013): 187–206.

10. Some version of each of these accommodations appears on Bonds's list of actionable steps theaters can take to become mother and parent friendly.

11. Pippa Nixon, "Breastfeeding in Rehearsals: How the West End Is Embracing New Mothers," What's On Stage, July 30, 2018, https://www.whatsonstage.com/london-theatre/news/breastfeeding-pippa-nixon-west-end-importance-earnest_47235.html.

12. Gaby Hoffman filmed an episode of the television show *GIRLS* while eight months pregnant, playing a character attempting to have a home birth. She was naked for much of the episode, the spectacle of her undeniably real body defying any dismissal that it was other than an economically viable, working body. My thanks to Sara BT Thiel for bringing this to my attention.

13. Roughly, "I cannot give birth to the same child again, but they shall be twins."

14. Joseph Roach, *It* (Ann Arbor: University of Michigan Press, 2007), 1.

15. Mike Ives, "Chrissy Teigen and John Legend Lose Baby after Pregnancy Complications," *New York Times*, October 2, 2020. https://www.nytimes.com/2020/10/01/style/chrissy-teigen-john-legend-baby.html.

16. Renee Ann Cramer, *Pregnant with the Stars: Watching and Wanting the Celebrity Baby Bump* (Palo Alto, CA: Stanford University Press, 2015).

17. Moya Sarner, "There Are Pressures to Keep Working to the End of Pregnancy—to Keep Up," *The Guardian*, September 25, 2018, https://www.theguardian

.com/lifeandstyle/2018/sep/25/women-pregnancy-generation-change-depression-anxiety.

18. Anne Helen Petersen, "Too Pregnant: Kim Kardashian," in *Too Fat Too Slutty Too Loud: The Rise and Reign of the Unruly Woman* (New York: Plume, 2017), 111–134.

19. See Cramer, *Pregnant with the Stars*, 81.

20. Miranda Bryant, "'I Was Risking My Life': Why One in Four US Women Return to Work Two Weeks after Giving Birth," *The Guardian*, January 27, 2020, https://www.theguardian.com/us-news/2020/jan/27/maternity-paid-leave-women-work-childbirth-us.

21. Kate Buck, "New Mother Becomes First Performer to Job Share in the West End," Metro, September 13, 2018, https://metro.co.uk/2018/09/13/new-mother-becomes-first-performer-to-job-share-in-the-west-end-7942585/.

BIBLIOGRAPHY

Manuscript Material

British Library, London

Barrington Papers

Bate, Henry to David Garrick. *Letters relating to the first engagement of Mrs. Siddons at Drury Lane.*

Ledger of Covent Garden Theatre, Containing Accounts Similar to Those in the Preceding Volumes; 1767–1822. Forty-seven volumes. Egerton Manuscripts.

Folger Shakespeare Library, Washington, DC

Cross, Richard, and William Hopkins. *Diaries of Drury Lane Theatre Performances Kept by Richard Cross and William Hopkins, 1747–1760, 1762–1764, 1768–1776.* 14 vols.

Drury Lane Journals for 1788–89 (W.b.291). *Records of Drury Lane Theatre, 1714–1880, undated.*

Pay book for Drury Lane Theatre 1789–1794 (W.b.347). *Records of Covent Garden and Drury Lane Theatre.*

Siddons, Sarah. *Letters from Sarah Siddons to Various Recipients [manuscript], 1783–1820.*

Tickell, Mary. *Letters from Mary Tickell to Elizabeth Ann Sheridan.*

Harvard Theatre Collection, Cambridge, MA

Jordan, Dorothy to William, Duke of Clarence (MS Thr 357). *Betty Wharton Autograph Collection.*

King, Thomas to Sarah Siddons (MS Thr 395[5]). *Letters to Sarah and William Siddons, 1780–1796.*

Richard Brinsley Sheridan Additional Papers.
Sheridan-Grubb Papers Concerning Drury Lane Theatre, 1765–1841.
Huntington Library, San Marino, CA
Dorothy Jordan Papers.
Montague, Elizabeth Robinson to Margaret Cavendish. July 6, 1747 (MSS MO 422). *Elizabeth Robinson Montague Collection.*
National Archives, Kew
"Maynwaring v. Churchill, bill and two answers (1737)." C 11/2455/26, item 1 (June 28, 1737).
Royal Archives, Windsor
Dorothy Jordan Collection.
Wellcome Library, London
Rundell, Maria Eliza. "Manual on Pregnancy and Childcare compiled by Maria Rundell, with various remedies for pregnant women and for children." 17 October 1810 (MS 7106).

Sources

An Account of the Life of that Celebrated Actress Mrs. Cibber with Interesting and Amusing Anecdotes. Also the Two Remarkable and Romantic Trials between Theophilus Cibber and William Sloper. London: n.p., 1887.

Addison, Joseph. *Cato. A Tragedy.* 7th ed. London: J. Tonson, 1713.

Adelman, Janet. *Suffocating Mothers: Fantasies of Maternal Origin in Shakespeare's Plays:* Hamlet *to* The Tempest. New York: Routledge, 1992.

Allen, Robert J. "The Kit-Cat Club and the Theatre," *Review of English Studies* 7, no. 25 (January 1931): 56–61.

Aselon, Robyn. "'She Was Tragedy Personified': Crafting the Siddons Legend in Art and Life." In *A Passion for Performance: Sarah Siddons and Her Portraitists*, edited by Robyn Aselon, 41–96. Los Angeles: J. Paul Getty Museum, 1999.

Aspinall, A., ed. *Mrs. Jordan and Her Family, Being the Unpublished Correspondence of Mrs. Jordan and the Duke of Clarence, Later William IV.* London: A. Barker, 1951.

Aston, Tony. "A Brief Supplement to Colley Cibber, Esq; His Lives of the Famous Actors and Actresses." In Watson Nicholson, *Anthony Aston, Stroller and Adventurer*, 73–98. South Haven, MI: self-pub, 1920.

Authentick Memoirs of the Life of That Celebrated Actress Mrs. Ann Oldfield. 4th ed. London: the Booksellers and Pamphlet-sellers of London and Westminster, 1730.

Bailey, Joanne. *Unquiet Lives: Marriage and Marriage Breakdown in England 1660–1800.* Cambridge: Cambridge University Press, 2009.

Bakhtin, Mikhail. *Rabelais and His World.* Translated by Hélène Iswolsky. Bloomington: Indiana University Press, 1984.

Bannet, Eve Tavor. *The Domestic Revolution: Enlightenment Feminisms and the Novel.* Baltimore: Johns Hopkins University Press, 2000.

Barclay, Andrew. "Mary [Mary of Modena] (1658–1718)." *Oxford Dictionary of National Biography.* New York: Oxford University Press, 2004; Online edition, 2008.

Barker-Benfield, G. J. *The Culture of Sensibility: Sex and Society in Eighteenth-Century Britain.* Chicago: Chicago University Press, 1992.

Bate, Jonathan. "Shakespeare and the Rival Muses." *Notorious Muse: The Actress in British Art and Culture, 1776–1812,* edited by Robyn Aselon. New Haven, CT: Yale University Press, 2003.

Baumgarten, Linda. "Dressing for Pregnancy: A Maternity Gown of 1780–1795." *Dress* 23, no. 1 (1996): 16–24.

Beaumont, Francis, and John Fletcher. *The Scornful Lady.* London: W. Freeman, 1691. Early English Books Online. ProQuest.

The Beauties of Mrs. Siddons: Or, a Review of Her Performance of the Characters of Belvidera, Zara, Isabella, Margaret of Anjou, Jane Shore, and Lady Randolph in Letters of a Lady of Distinction, to Her Friend in the Country. London: John Strahan, 1786.

Begiato, Joanne. "'Breeding' a 'Little Stranger': Managing Uncertainty in Pregnancy in Georgian England." In *Perceptions of Pregnancy from the Seventeenth to the Twentieth Centuries,* edited by Jennifer Evans and Ciara Meehan, 13–33. London: Palgrave McMillan, 2017.

Bellamy, George Anne. *An Apology for the Life of George Anne Bellamy, Late of Covent Garden Theatre.* 3rd ed. 5 vols. London: J. Bell, 1785.

Bell's British Theatre. Consisting of the Most Esteemed English Plays. 34 vols. London, 1797.

Bennett, Susan. *Theatre Audiences: A Theory of Interpretation and Reception.* 2nd ed. New York: Routledge, 1997.

———"Theatre History, Historiography, and Women's Dramatic Writing." In *Women, Theatre and Performance, New Histories, New Historiographies,* edited by Maggie B. Gale and Viv Gardner, 46–59. Manchester: Manchester University Press, 2000.

A Biographical Dictionary of Actors, Actresses, Musicians, Dancers, Managers, and Other Stage Personnel in London 1660–1800 (BDA). Edited by Philip H. Highfill, Kalman A. Burnim, and Edward A. Langhans. 16 vols. Carbondale: Southern Illinois University Press, 1973–1993.

Blunt, John Henry. *The Annotated Book of Common Prayer: Being a Historical, Ritual, and Theological Commentary on the Devotional System of The Church of England.* London: Longmans, Green, 1907.

Boaden, James. *The Life of Mrs, Jordan.* 2 vols. London: Edward Bull, Holles Street, 1831.

———. *The Life of Mrs. Jordan.* 2 vols. Extra-Illustrated Edition (5 vols). TS 940.6. Harvard Theatre Collection, Cambridge, MA.

———. *Memoirs of Mrs. Siddons, Interspersed with Anecdotes of Authors and Actors*. 2 vols. London: H. Colburn, 1827.

———, ed. *Private Correspondence of David Garrick with the Most Celebrated Persons of his Time*. 2 vols. London: Henry Colburn and Richard Bentley, 1831.

Bon Ton Magazine, or the Microscope of Fashion and Folly. 5 vols. London: n.p. [1791–1795].

Bonds, Rachel. "Working Like a Mother." Howlround Theatre Commons. September 11, 2018. https://howlround.com/working-mother.

Boose, Lynda. "The Getting of a Lawful Race": Racial Discourse and the 'Unrepresentable' Black Woman in Early Modern England." In *Women, "Race," and Writing in the Early Modern Period*, edited by Margo Hendricks and Patricia Parker, 35–54. London: Routledge, 1994.

Booth, Michael R., John Stokes, and Susan Bassnett. *Three Tragic Actresses: Siddons, Rachel, Ristori*. Cambridge: Cambridge University Press, 1996.

Borgman, Albert S. *Life and Death of William Mountfort*. Cambridge, MA: Harvard University Press, 1935.

Bowers, Toni. *The Politics of Motherhood: British Writing and Culture 1680–1760*. Cambridge: Cambridge University Press, 1996.

Bracken, Henry. *The Midwife's Companion*. London, 1737.

Bratton, Jacky. *New Readings in Theatre History*. Cambridge: Cambridge University Press, 2003.

Brooks, Cleanth. "From *The Well-Wrought Urn*." In *Macbeth: Critical Essays*, edited by S. Schoenbaum, 209–226. 1991; New York: Routledge, 2015.

Brooks, Helen E. M. *Actresses, Gender, and the Eighteenth-Century Stage: Playing Women*. London: Palgrave Macmillan, 2015.

———. "The Divided Heart of the Actress: Late Eighteenth-Century Actresses and the 'Cult of Maternity.'" In *Stage Mothers: Women, Work, and the Theatre, 1660–1830*, edited by Laura Engel and Elaine M. McGirr, 19–42. Lewisburg, PA: Bucknell University Press, 2014.

———. "Early Eighteenth-Century Performance Historiography: Problems and Possibilities." *Studies in Theatre and Performance* 31, no. 1 (2011): 33–45.

———. "Negotiating Marriage and Professional Autonomy in the Careers of Eighteenth-Century Actresses." *Eighteenth-Century Life* 35, no. 2 (Spring 2011): 39–75.

———. "Women and Theatrical Management in the Eighteenth Century." In *The Public's Open to Us All*, edited by Laura Engel, 73–95. Cambridge: Cambridge Scholars, 2009.

———. "'Your Sincere Friend and Humble Servant': Evidence of Managerial Aspirations in Susannah Cibber's Letters." *Studies in Theatre and Performance* 28, no. 2 (April 2008): 147–159.

Buchanan, Lindal. "Angels in the (Theatrical) House: Pregnancy, Rhetorical Access, and the London Stage." *Rhetorica* 30, no. 3 (Summer 2012): 277–305.

Buck, Kate. "New Mother Becomes First Performer to Job Share in the West End." Metro, September 13, 2018. https://metro.co.uk/2018/09/13/new-mother-becomes-first-performer-to-job-share-in-the-west-end-7942585/.

Buckley, Matthew S. *Tragedy Walks the Street: the French Revolution in the Making of Modern Drama*. Baltimore: Johns Hopkins University Press, 2006.

Budgell, Eustace [Philomeides, pseud.]. *The Spectator: A New Edition*. No. 341 (April 1, 1712), edited by Henry Morley. London: George Routledge and Sons, Ltd., 1891.

Burke, Edmund. *A Philosophical Enquiry into the Origins of Our Ideas of the Sublime and the Beautiful*, edited by Adam Phillips. 1990. Reprint, New York: Oxford University Press, 1998.

———. *Reflections on the Revolution in France*. London: Electric Book Co., 2001.

Burke, Peter. *Varieties of Cultural History*. Ithaca, NY: Cornell University Press, 1997.

Burney, Fanny. *Diary and Letters of Madame D'Arblay*. 6 vols. London: MacMillan Co, 1904–05.

Bush-Bailey, Gilli. *Treading the Bawds: Actresses and Playwrights on the Late-Stuart Stage*. New York: Palgrave, 2005.

Campbell, Thomas. *Life of Mrs. Siddons*. 2 vols. London: Effingham Wilson, Royal Exchange, 1834.

Carlson, Marvin. *The Haunted Stage: The Theatre as Memory Machine*. Ann Arbor: University of Michigan Press, 2001.

Centers for Disease Control and Prevention. "Syphilis during Pregnancy." In *2015 Sexually Transmitted Diseases Treatment Guidelines*. Updated June 4, 2015. https://www.cdc.gov/std/tg2015/syphilis-pregnancy.htm.

Churchill, Charles. *The Rosciad*. 3rd ed. London: 1761.

Churchill, Sarah Jennings, Duchess of Marlborough. *Letters of a Grandmother 1732–1735: Being Correspondence of Sarah, Duchess of Marlborough with Her Granddaughter Diana, Duchess of Bedford*. Edited by Gladys Scott Thomson. London: Jonathan Cape, 1943.

Cibber, Colley. *An Apology for the Life of Mr. Colley Cibber*. 2nd ed. 2 vols. London: John Watts, 1740.

———. *Cinna's Conspiracy*. London: Bernard Lintott, 1713.

Cibber, Susannah. *The Oracle. A Comedy of One Act. As It Is Acted at the Theatre-Royal in Covent-Garden*. London: R. Dodsley, 1752.

Cody, Lisa Forman. *Birthing the Nation: Sex, Science, and the Conception of Eighteenth-Century Britons*. Oxford: Oxford University Press, 2005.

Colley, Linda. *Britons: Forging the Nation, 1707–1837*. New Haven, CT: Yale University Press, 1992.

A Comparison Between the Two Stages, with an Examen of The Generous Conqueror; *and Some Critical Remarks on* The Funeral, or Grief Alamode, The False Friend, Tamerlane *and Others. In Dialogue*. London: [n.p.], 1702.

Congreve, William. *The Dramatic Works of William Congreve*. 2 vols. Glasgow: Robert Urie, 1752.

Crafton, Lisa Plummer. *Transgressive Theatricality, Romanticism, and Mary Wollstonecraft*. Burlington: Ashgate, 2011.

Cramer, Renée Ann. *Pregnant with the Stars: Watching and Wanting the Celebrity Baby Bump*. Stanford, CA: Stanford University Press, 2015.

Crouch, Kimberly. "The Public Life of Actresses: Prostitutes or Ladies?" In *Gender in Eighteenth Century: Roles, Representations, and Responsibilities*, edited by Hannah Barker and Elaine Chalus, 58–78. New York: Longman, 1997.

Curll, Edmund [William Egerton, pseud.]. *Faithful Memoirs of the Life, Amours, and Performances of That Justly Celebrated, and Most Eminent Actress of Her Time, Mrs. Anne Oldfield*. London: n.p., 1731.

Davidoff, Leonore, and Catharine Hall. *Family Fortunes: Men and Women of the English Middle Class 1780–1850*. London: Hutchinson Education, 1987.

Davies, Thomas. *Dramatic Miscellanies: Consisting of Critical Observations on Several Plays of Shakespeare: With a Review of His Principal Characters, and Those of Various Eminent Writers, as Represented by Mr. Garrick and Other Celebrated Comedians*. 3 vols. London: n.p., 1783–84.

———. *Memoirs of the Life of David Garrick, Esq*. 2 vols. Dublin: Joseph Hill, 1780.

Davis, Tracy C. "Questions for a Feminist Methodology in Theatre History." In *Interpreting the Theatrical Past: Essays in the Historiography of Performance*, edited by Thomas Postlewait and Bruce McConachie, 59–81. Iowa City: University of Iowa Press, 1989.

Donkin, Ellen. *Getting Into the Act: Women Playwrights in London, 1776–1829*. London: Routledge, 1995.

———. "Mrs. Siddons Looks Back in Anger." In *Critical Theory and Performance*, edited by Janelle G. Reinalt and Joseph R. Roach, 317–333. Rev. ed. Ann Arbor: University of Michigan Press, 2007.

Donohue, Jr., Joseph W. "Kemble's Production of *Macbeth* (1794), Some Notes on Scenic Painters, Scenery, Special Effects, and Costumes." *Theatre Notebook* 21, no. 2 (1966): 63–74.

Doran, John. *"Their Majesties Servants" or Annals of the English Stage; from Thomas Betterton to Edmund Kean, Actors—Authors—Audiences*. Edited by Robert W. Lowe. London: John C. Nimmo, 1897.

Dryden, John. *Don Sebastian: King of Portugal, A Tragedy.* London: 1710.

Duden, Barbara. *Disembodying Women: Perspectives on Pregnancy and the Unborn.* Cambridge, MA: Harvard University Press, 1993.

Dunlap, Barbara J. "The Problem of Syphilitic Children in Eighteenth-Century France and England." In *The Secret Malady: Venereal Disease in Eighteenth-Century Britain and France*, edited by Linda E. Merians, 114–127. Lexington: University of Kentucky Press, 1996.

Engel, Laura. *Fashioning Celebrity: Eighteenth-Century British Actresses and Strategies for Image-Making.* Columbus: Ohio State University Press, 2011.

———. "Stage Beauties: Actresses and Celebrity Culture in the Long Eighteenth Century." *Literature Compass* 13/12 (2016): 749–761.

Engel, Laura, and Elaine M. McGirr, eds. *Stage Mothers: Women, Work, and the Theatre, 1660–1830.* Lewisburg, PA: Bucknell University Press, 2014.

England, Select Births and Christenings, 1538–1975 [database online]. Provo, UT: Ancestry.com Operations, 2014.

Eusden, L. "Verses to the Author of the Tragedy of Cato." In Joseph Addison, *Cato. A Tragedy.* 7th ed. London: J. Tonson, 1713.

Fawcett, Julia H. *Spectacular Disappearances: Celebrity and Privacy, 1696–1801.* Ann Arbor: University of Michigan Press, 2016.

Fissell, Mary. *Vernacular Bodies: The Politics of Reproduction in Early Modern England.* Oxford: Oxford University Press, 2004.

Fitzsimmons, Linda, and Arthur W. McDonald. *The Yorkshire Stage, 1766–1803: A Calendar of Plays, Together with Cast Lists for Tate Wilkinson's Circuit of Theatres (Doncaster, Hull, Leeds, Pontefract, Wakefield, and York) and the Yorkshire Company's Engagements in Beverley, Halifax, Newcastle, Sheffield, and Edinburgh.* Metuchen, NJ: Scarecrow Press, 1989.

Fothergill, Brian, *Mrs. Jordan: Portrait of an Actress.* London: Faber & Faber, 1965.

Freeman, Lisa A. *Character's Theater: Genre and Identity on the Eighteenth-Century English Stage.* Philadelphia: University of Pennsylvania Press, 2002.

———. "Mourning the Dignity of the Siddonian Form." *Eighteenth Century Fiction* 27, no. 3–4 (Spring-Summer 2015): 597–629.

———. "What's Love Got to Do with Addison's *Cato?*" *Studies in English Literature 1500–1900* 39, no. 3 (Summer 1999): 463–482.

Gallagher, Noelle. *Itch, Pox, Clap: Venereal Disease in the Eighteenth-Century Imagination.* New Haven, CT: Yale University Press, 2018.

Garrick, David. *The Country Girl.* London: John Bell, 1791.

Gatrell, Vic. *City of Laughter: Sex and Satire in Eighteenth-Century London.* New York: Walker, 2007.

Gaylord, Karen. "Theatrical Performances: Structure and Process, Tradition and Revolt." In *Performers and Performances: The Social Organization of Artistic Work*, edited by Jack B. Kamerman and Rosanne Martorella, 135–150. New York: Praeger, 1983.

General Magazine and Impartial Review (March 1791).

Genest, John. *Some Account of the English Stage: From the Restoration in 1660 to 1830*. 10 vols. Bath: H.E. Carrington, 1832.

George, Dorothy M. *Catalogue of Political and Personal Satires Preserved in the Department of Prints and Drawings in the British Museum*. 12 vols. London: British Museum Press, 1938.

Gowing, Laura. *Common Bodies: Women, Touch, and Power in Seventeenth-Century England*. New Haven: Yale University Press, 2003.

The Great Illegitimates!!! Public and Private Life of that Celebrated Actress Mrs. Bland, Otherwise Mrs. Ford or Mrs. Jordan. London: 1830.

Greenfield, Susan C., and Carol Barash. *Inventing Maternity: Politics, Science, and Literature 1650–1850*. Lexington: University of Kentucky Press, 1999.

Hazlitt, William. *Criticisms and Dramatic Essays of the English Stage*. London: G. Routledge, 1851.

———. *A View of the English Stage, or a Series of Dramatic Criticisms*. London: John Warren, 1821.

Heddon, Deirdre E. "Verbruggen, Susanna," *Oxford Dictionary of National Biography Online* Oxford: Oxford University Press, 2004. Online edition, January 2008.

Hedley, Olwen. *Queen Charlotte*. London: Butler and Tanner, 1975.

Henderson, Christine Dunn, and Mark E. Yellin. "Those Stubborn Principles: From Stoicism to Sociability in Joseph Addison's *Cato*" *The Review of Politics* 76 (2014): 223–241.

Hill, John. *The Actor: A Treatise on the Art of Playing*. London: R. Griffiths, 1755.

———. *The Inspector*. 2 vols. London: R. Griffiths, 1753.

Holland, Peter. *The Ornament of Action: Text and Performance in Restoration Comedy*. Cambridge: Cambridge University Press, 1979.

Howe, Elizabeth. *The First English Actresses: Women and Drama 1660–1700*. Cambridge: Cambridge University Press, 1992.

Hume, David. *A Treatise of Human Nature: Being an Attempt to Introduce the Experimental Method of Reasoning into Moral Subjects*. 3 vols. London: John Noon, 1739–40.

Hume, Robert D. *The Rakish Stage: Studies in English Drama, 1660–1800*. Carbondale: Southern Illinois University Press, 1983.

———. "Theatre History 1660–1800: Aims, Materials, Methodologies." In *Players, Playwrights, Playhouses: Investigating Performance 1660–1800*, edited by Michael Cordner and Peter Holland, 9–44. Basingstoke: Palgrave Macmillan, 2007.

Jacobus, Mary. "'That Great Stage Where Senators Perform': 'Macbeth' and the Politics of Romantic Theatre." *Studies in Romanticism* 22, no. 3 (Fall 1983): 353–387.

Jerrold, Clare. *The Story of Dorothy Jordan.* New York: Brentano's, 1914.

Jones, Robert W. "Competition and Community: Mary Tickell and the Management of Sheridan's Drury Lane." *Theatre Survey*, 54, no. 2 (May 2013): 187–206.

Jordan's Elixir of Life and Cure for the Spleen. London: William Holland, 1789.

Kinservik, Matthew J. *Disciplining Satire: The Censorship of Satiric Comedy on the Eighteenth-Century London Stage.* Lewisburg, PA: Bucknell University Press, 2002.

Kipp, Julie. *Romanticism, Maternity, and the Body Politic.* Cambridge: Cambridge University Press, 2009.

Kliman, Bernice. *Shakespeare in Performance: Macbeth.* 2nd ed. New York: Palgrave, 2004.

Knowles, James Sheridan. *Lectures in Dramatic Literature.* Revised and edited by F. Harvey. London: James McHenry, 1873.

Lafler, Joanne. *The Celebrated Mrs. Oldfield: The Life and Art of an Augustan Actress.* Carbondale: Southern Illinois University Press, 1989.

Lamb, Charles. "On Shakespeare's Tragedies." In *The Prose Works of Charles Lamb in Three Volumes*, 99–132. London: Edward Moxon, 1836.

Laqueur, Thomas. *Making Sex: Body and Gender from the Greeks to Freud.* Cambridge, MA: Harvard University Press, 1990.

Ledoux, Ellen Malenas. "Working Mothers on the Romantic Stage: Sarah Siddons and Mary Robinson." In *Stage Mothers: Women, Work and the Theatre, 1660–1830*, edited by Laura Engel and Elaine M. McGirr, 79–101. Lewisburg, PA: Bucknell University Press, 2014.

Lewis, Judith Schneid. *In the Family Way: Childbearing in the British Aristocracy, 1760–1830.* New Brunswick, NJ: Rutgers University Press, 1986.

The London Stage 1660–1800. 5 parts; 11 vols. Edited by William Van Lennep, Emmet L. Avery, Arthur H. Scouten, George Winchester Stone, Jr., and Charles Beecher Hogan. Carbondale, IL: Southern Illinois University Press, 1960–1968.

Lucas, E.V. *The Life of Charles Lamb.* 2 vols. London: Methuen, 1905.

Macdonald, Joyce Green. "The Disappearing African Woman: Imoinda in 'Oroonoko' After Behn." *ELH* 66, no. 1 (Spring 1999): 71–86.

Manley, Delarivier. *The Female Tatler; by Mrs. Crackenthorpe a Lady That Knows Everything.* London: B. Baggs, 1709–10.

Manvell, Roger. *Sarah Siddons: Portrait of an Actress*. New York: G.P. Putnam & Sons, 1971.

Marcus, Sharon. *The Drama of Celebrity*. Princeton, NJ: Princeton University Press, 2019.

Marsden, Jean I. "Modesty Unshackled: Dorothy Jordan and the Dangers of Cross-Dressing." *Studies in Eighteenth-Century Culture* 22 (1993): 21–35.

———. *Theatres of Feeling: Affect, Performance, and the Eighteenth-Century Stage*. Cambridge: Cambridge University Press, 2019.

McGirr, Elaine M. "'Inimitable Sensibility': Susannah Cibber's Performance of Maternity." In *Stage Mothers: Women, Work, and the Theatre, 1660–1830*, edited by Laura Engel and Elaine M. McGirr, 63–78. Lewisburg, PA: Bucknell University Press, 2014.

McKinney, David, Melissa House, Aimin Chen, Louis Muglia, and Emily Defranco. "The Influence of Interpregnancy Interval on Infant Mortality." *American Journal of Obstetrics and Gynecology* 216, no. 3 (2017). doi:10.1016/j.ajog.2016.12.018.

McPherson, Heather. *Art and Celebrity in the Age of Garrick and Reynolds*. University Park: Penn State University Press, 2017.

———. "Masculinity, Femininity and the Tragic Sublime: Reinventing Lady Macbeth," *Studies in Eighteenth Century Culture* 29 (2000): 299–333.

Melville, Lewis [Lewis Saul Benjamin]. *Stage Favorites of the Eighteenth Century*. Garden City, NY: Doubleday Doran, 1929.

Milhous, Judith. "Reading Theatre History from Account Books." In *Players, Playwrights, Playhouses: Investigating Performance 1660–1800*, edited by Michael Cordner and Peter Holland, 101–131. Basingstoke: Palgrave Macmillan, 2007.

———. *Thomas Betterton and the Management of Lincoln's Inn Fields, 1695–1708*. Carbondale: Southern Illinois University Press, 1979.

———, and Robert D. Hume. "Dating Play Premières from Publication Data, 1660–1700." *Harvard Library Bulletin* 22, no. 4 (October 1974): 374–405.

———, and Robert D. Hume, eds. "*The London Stage, 1660–1800*: A New Version of Part 2, 1700–1729." Last updated 2001. http://www.personal.psu.edu/hb1/London%20Stage%202001/.

———, and Robert D. Hume. *Producible Interpretation: Eight English Plays, 1675–1707*. Carbondale: Southern Illinois University Press, 1985.

———, and Robert D. Hume. "The Silencing of Drury Lane in 1709." *Theatre Journal* 32, no. 4 (December 1980): 427–447.

———, and Robert D. Hume, "Theatrical Politics at Drury Lane: New Light on Letitia Cross, Jane Rogers, and Anne Oldfield," *Bulletin of Research in the Humanities* 85 (1982): 412–429.

Milling, J. "Oldfield, Anne." *Oxford Dictionary of National Biography Online*. Oxford: Oxford University Press, 2004. Online edition, January 2008.

Napier, Lady Sarah. *The Life and Letters of Lady Sarah Lennox, 1745–1826*, edited by the Countess of Ilchester and Lord Stavordale. 2 vols. London: J. Murray, 1902.

Nash, Mary. *The Provoked Wife: The Life and Times of Susannah Cibber*. Boston: Little, Brown, 1977.

Nathans, Heather. *Hideous Creatures and Beautiful Pagans: Performing Jewish Identity on the Antebellum American Stage*. Ann Arbor: University of Michigan Press, 2017.

National Archives Currency Converter, 1270–2017. https://www.nationalarchives.gov.uk/currency-converter/.

Nussbaum, Felicity. *Rival Queens: Actresses, Performance, and the Eighteenth-Century British Theatre*. Philadelphia: University of Pennsylvania Press, 2010.

———. *Torrid Zones: Maternity, Sexuality, and Empire in Eighteenth-Century English Narratives*. Baltimore: Johns Hopkins University Press, 1995.

O'Toole, Emma. "Dressing the Expectant Mother: Maternity Fashion in Eighteenth and Nineteenth-Century Ireland." *Women's History* 5 (Spring 2016): 26–33.

Oxford English Dictionary Online. Oxford University Press, June 2015.

Pascoe, Judith. *Romantic Theatricality: Gender, Poetry, and Spectatorship*. Ithaca, NY: Cornell University Press, 1997.

Paster, Gail Kern. *The Body Embarrassed: Drama and Disciplines of Shame in Early Modern England*. Ithaca, NY: Cornell University Press, 1993.

Peck, James. "Anne Oldfield's Lady Townly: Consumption, Credit, and the Whig Hegemony of the 1720s" *Theatre Journal* 49 (December 1997): 397–416.

Pepys, Samuel. *The Diary of Samuel Pepys, M.A., F.R.S.* Edited by Henry B. Wheatley. London: George Bell & Sons, 1893.

Perry, Gill. *Spectacular Flirtations: Viewing the Actress in British Art and Theatre, 1768–1820*. London: Paul Mellon Centre for Studies in British Art, 2008.

———. "Staging Gender and 'Hairy Signs': Representing Dorothy Jordan's Curls." *Eighteenth-Century Studies* 38, no. 1 (Fall 2004): 145–163.

Perry, Ruth. "Colonizing the Breast: Sexuality and Maternity in Eighteenth-Century England." *Journal of the History of Sexuality* 2, no. 2, Special Issue, Part 1: The State, Society, and the Regulation of Sexuality in Modern Europe (October 1991): 204–234.

———. *Novel Relations: The Transformation of Kinship in English Literature and Culture, 1748–1818*. Cambridge: Cambridge University Press, 2004.

Petersen, Anne Helen. *Too Fat Too Slutty Too Loud: The Rise and Reign of the Unruly Woman*. New York: Plume, 2017.

Philips, Ambrose. *The Distrest Mother*. London: S. Buckley; J. Tonson, 1712.

Phillips, Chelsea. "Bodies in Play: Maternity, Repertory, and the Rival *Romeo and Juliets*, 1748–51." *Theatre Survey* 60, no. 2 (May 2019): 205–236.

———. "'I Have Given Suck': The Maternal Body in Sarah Siddons' Lady Macbeth." In *Shakespeare Expressed: Page, Stage, and Classroom in Shakespeare and His Contemporaries*, edited by Kathryn M. Moncrief, Kathryn R. McPherson, and Sarah Enloe, 19–33. Madison, NJ: Fairleigh Dickinson Press, 2013.

———. "'Mrs. Pickle's Mistake': The Dating of an Eighteenth-Century Satirical Print." *Women's History* 5 (Summer 2016): 23–25.

———. "Pregnancy and the Restoration Stage," in *Theatrical Anecdotes*, ed. Heather Ladd and Leslie Ritchie (Newark, DE: University of Delaware Press, 2022).

Phillipson, J. D. "The Inconveniences of the Female Condition: Anne Oldfield's Pregnancies." In *Stage Mothers: Women, Work, and the Theatre 1660–1830*, edited by Laura Engel and Elaine M. McGirr, 43–62. Lewisburg, PA: Bucknell University Press, 2014.

Piozzi (Thrale), Hester. *The Piozzi Letters: The Correspondence of Hester Lynch Piozzi, 1784–1821 (formerly Mrs. Thrale)*. Edited by Edward A. Bloom and Lillian D. Bloom. Newark: University of Delaware Press, 1989.

———. *Thraliana: The Diary of Hester Lynch Thrale (Later Mrs. Piozzi), 1776–1809*. Edited by Katherine C. Balderston. 6 vols. Oxford: Clarendon Press, 1942.

Postlewait, Thomas. "The Criteria for Evidence: Anecdotes in Shakespearean Biography, 1709–2000." In *Theorizing Practice: Redefining Theatre History*, edited by W. B. Worthen with Peter Holland, 47–70. New York: Palgrave Macmillan, 2003.

Probert, Rebecca. *Marriage Law and Practice in the Long Eighteenth Century: A Reassessment*. Cambridge: Cambridge University Press, 2009.

———, ed. *Cohabitation and Non-Marital Births in England and Wales, 1600–2012*. New York: Palgrave Macmillan, 2014.

Rand, Benjamin. *Berkeley and Percival: The Correspondence of George Berkeley and Sir John Percival*. Cambridge: Cambridge University Press, 1914.

Rauser, Amelia. "Vitalist Statues and the Belly Pad of 1793." *Journal18*, no. 3 *Lifelike* (Spring 2017). doi: 10.30610/3.2017.2.

Razzell, Peter. "The Growth of Population in Eighteenth-Century England: A Critical Reappraisal." *Journal of Economic History* 53, no. 4 (December 1993): 743–771.

Reid, Christopher. "Burke's Tragic Muse: Sarah Siddons and the 'Feminization' of the Reflections." In *Burke and the French Revolution: Bicentennial Essays*, edited by Steven Blakemore, 1–27. Athens: University of Georgia Press, 1992.

Richards, Sandra. *The Rise of the English Actress*. New York: St. Martin's Press, 1993.

Ritchie, Fiona. *Women and Shakespeare in the Eighteenth Century*. Cambridge: Cambridge University Press, 2014.

Ritchie, Leslie. *David Garrick and the Mediation of Celebrity*. Cambridge: Cambridge University Press, 2019.

Roach, Joseph R. *It*. Ann Arbor: University of Michigan Press, 2007.

———. *The Player's Passion: Studies in the Science of Acting*. Newark: University of Delaware Press, 1985.

Rogers, Pat. "'Towering Beyond Her Sex': Stature and Sublimity in the Achievement of Sarah Siddons." In *Curtain Calls: British and American Women and the Theatre, 1660–1820*, edited by Mary Anne Schofield and Cecilia Macheski, 48–67. Athens: Ohio University Press, 1991.

Rosenthal, Laura J. "The Sublime, the Beautiful, 'the Siddons.'" In *The Clothes That Wear Us: Essays on Dressing and Transgressing in Eighteenth-Century Culture*, edited by Jessica Munns and Penny Richards, 56–79. Cranbury, NJ: Associated University Presses, 1999.

Russell, Gillian. *Women, Sociability, and the Theatre in Georgian England*. Cambridge: Cambridge University Press, 2007.

Rzepińska, Maria, and Krystyna Malcharek. "Tenebrism in Baroque Painting and Its Ideological Background." *Artibus et Historiae* 7, no. 13 (1986): 91–112.

Sarner, Moya. "There Are Pressures to Keep Working to the End of Pregnancy — to Keep Up." *The Guardian*, September 25, 2018. https://www.theguardian.com/lifeandstyle/2018/sep/25/women-generation-change-depression-anxiety.

Scott, Walter. *The Works of Jonathan Swift, D. D., Dean of St. Patrick's, Dublin; Containing Additional Letters, Tracts, and Poems Not Hitherto Published; with Notes and a Life of the Author*. 19 vols. Edinburgh: Archibald Constable and Co., 1814.

Seventeenth and Eighteenth Century Burney Collection Newspapers. British Library. Gale Digital Collections.

Sewell, George. *Mr. Sewell's Observations on* Cato, a tragedy. *By Mr. Addison. In a letter to *** To which is added A comparison between Cato and Caesar, by Mr. Steele*, 3rd ed. London: E. Curll, 1714.

Shakespeare, William. *Macbeth*. Edited by Nicholas Brooke. Oxford: Oxford University Press, 2008.

Sharp, Jane. *The Midwives Book, or, the Whole Art of Midwifery Discovered*. London: Simon Miller, 1671.

Sheridan, Richard Brinsley. *Pizarro*. Edited by Selena Couture and Alexander Dick. Peterborough, ON: Broadview, 2017.

Sheridan, Thomas [and John Philip Kemble]. *Coriolanus; or, the Roman Matron. A Tragedy. Altered from the Shakespeare by Mr. T. Sheridan, Taken from the Manager's Book at the Theatre Royal in Drury Lane*. London, R. Butters, 1790(?).

Siddons, Sarah. *The Reminiscences of Sarah Kemble Siddons, 1773–1785*. Edited by William Van Lennep. Cambridge: Widener Library, 1942.

Solomon, Diana. *Prologues and Epilogues of Restoration Theatre: Gender and Comedy, Performance and Print*. Newark: University of Delaware Press, 2013.

Southerne, Thomas. *The Works of Thomas Southerne*. Edited by Robert Jordan and Harold Love. 2 vols. Oxford: Oxford University Press, 1988.

Stone, Lawrence. *The Family, Sex, and Marriage in England 1500–1800*. New York: Harper & Row, 1977.

Straub, Kristina. *Sexual Suspects: Eighteenth-Century Players and Sexual Ideology*. Princeton, NJ: Princeton University Press, 1992.

Taylor, David Francis. *Politics of Parody: A Literary History of Character, 1760–1830*. New Haven, CT: Yale University Press, 2018.

Taylor, Diana. *The Archive and the Repertoire: Performing Cultural Memory in the Americas*. Durham, NC: Duke University Press, 2003.

Thompson, Anthony Todd. *The Domestic Management of the Sick-Room, Necessary, in Aid of Medical Treatment, for the Cure of Diseases*. London: Longman, Orme, Brown, Green, & Longmans, 1841.

Thompson, Edward. *The Meretriciad*. 2nd ed. London: C. Moran, 1761.

Todd, Janet. *Sensibility: An Introduction*. New York: Methuen, 1986.

Tomalin, Claire. *Mrs. Jordan's Profession: The Actress and the Prince*. New York: Alfred A. Knopf, 1995.

Trilling, Lionel. *Sincerity and Authenticity*. Oxford: Oxford University Press, 1972.

Truelove, Francis. *The Comforts of Matrimony; Exemplified in the Memorable Case and Trial Lately had Upon an Action Brought by Theo—s C—r against— S—r, Esq. for Criminal Conversation with the Plaintiff's Wife*. 6th ed. London: Sam Baker, 1739.

Tryal of a Cause for Criminal Conversation between Theophilus Cibber, Gent. Plaintiff and William Sloper, Esq., Defendant. Dublin, 1749.

Tyler, Imogen. "Skin-Tight: Celebrity, Pregnancy, and Subjectivity." In *Thinking Through the Skin*, edited by Sara Ahmed and Jackie Stacey, 69–83. London: Routledge, 2001.

Vickery, Amanda. "Golden Age to Separate Spheres? A Review of the Categories and Chronology of English Women's History." *Historical Journal* 36, no. 2 (June 1993): 383–414.

Voltaire [Aaron Hill]. *The Tragedy of Zara. As It Is Acted at the Theatre Royal in Drury-Lane*. London: J. Watts, 1736.

Wahrman, Dror. *The Making of the Modern Self: Identity and Culture in Eighteenth-Century England*. New Haven, CT: Yale University Press, 2004.

Wanko, Cheryl. *Roles of Authority: Thespian Biography and Celebrity in Eighteenth-Century Britain*. Lubbock: Texas Tech, 2003.

West, Shearer. "Beauty, Aging, and the Body Politic." In *The First Actresses: Nell Gwyn to Sarah Siddons*, edited by Gill Perry, Joseph Roach, and Shearer West, 105–120. Ann Arbor: University of Michigan Press, 2011.

———. "Siddons, Celebrity and Regality: Portraiture and the Aging Actress." In *Theatre and Celebrity in Britain 1660–2000*, edited by Mary Luckhurst and Jane Moody, 191–213. New York: Palgrave Macmillan, 2005.

Whalley, Thomas. *Journals and Correspondence of Thomas Sedgewick Whalley*. Edited by Hill Wickham. 2 vols. London: R. Bentley, 1863.

Wilkinson, Tate. *Memoirs of His Own Life*. 4 vols. York: William, Spence, and Mawman, 1790.

———. *The Wandering Patentee: Or, a History of the York Stage from 1770 to the Present Time*. 4 vols. York: Wilson, Spence and Mawman, 1795.

Wilson, Ben. *The Making of Victorian Values: Decency and Dissent in Britain 1789–1837*. New York: Penguin Press, 2007.

Wilson, John Harold. *All the King's Ladies: Actresses of the Restoration*. Chicago: Chicago University Press, 1958.

Young, M. J. *Memoirs of Mrs. Crouch*. London: J. Aspern, 1806.

Ziegler, Georgianna. "Accommodating the Virago: Nineteenth Century Representations of Lady Macbeth." In *Shakespeare and Appropriation*, edited by Christy Desmet and Robert Sawyer, 119–141. New York: Routledge, 1999.

INDEX

ABOUT THE AUTHOR

Chelsea Phillips is an associate professor of theater at Villanova University and a professional dramaturg. She has published on eighteenth-century theatre, actresses, and celebrity, as well as the performance history of and supernatural in Shakespeare's plays.